D0007712

TRANSLATING NERUDA

John Felstiner

TRANSLATING NERUDA

The Way to Macchu Picchu

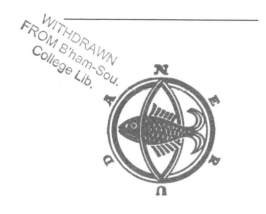

Stanford University Press

Stanford, California *1980*

Acknowledgments for the use of copyrighted material
appear on p. 275.

Stanford University Press
Stanford, California

© 1980 by the Board of Trustees of the
Leland Stanford Junior University
Printed in the United States of America
ISBN 0-8047-1079-1
LC 79-67773

To Mary

To the Chileans lost since September 11, 1973

ACKNOWLEDGMENTS

I want to thank the Chilean critic and journalist Hernán Loyola, who in 1967 first shared with me his work and bibliography on Neruda. For giving this book sensitive, thoughtful readings in manuscript, I am grateful to Fernando Alegría, Arnold Bauer, Craig Comstock, James McIntosh, David Riggs, and Marilyn Yalom. For guidance on various questions, I thank Rina Alcalay, Alexander Coleman, Donald Davie, Jean Franco, and Enrique Lihn. I am indebted to Myriam Díaz for her discerning comments on my translation of *Alturas de Macchu Picchu*.

My considerable debts to other translators and scholars are reflected in the text and notes. I also thank my students in seminars on poetry and verse translation, where many of my ideas and techniques evolved.

I was aided by Agnes Peterson of the Hoover Institution; James Breedlove and Jill Coelho of the Green Library, Stanford; the Biblioteca Nacional in Santiago, Chile; the Biblioteca Nacional in Madrid; and the Library of Congress. The National Endowment for the Humanities and the Social Science Research Council supported parts of my research. Andrea Dimino edited the book with intelligence, tact, and thoroughness. Joy Dickinson Barnes saw it skillfully through production. The manuscript was typed expertly by Jo Guttadauro.

Acknowledgments for the use of copyrighted material appear at the end of the book.

The dedication of this book, to Mary Lowenthal Felstiner, can only hint at how much she did for it and for me, while engaged in her own work in Latin American and women's history. She reviewed every aspect of the book with me. Every page of it reflects her care and thought.

J.F.

CONTENTS

TRANSLATING NERUDA

INTRODUCTION

This book recounts the genesis of a verse translation. In doing so, it identifies verse translation as an essential act and art of literary criticism. On the way to translating Pablo Neruda's *Alturas de Macchu Picchu*, I found both a need and a means for writing this book. Usually, whatever goes toward the making of a verse translation gets left behind, becomes invisible, once the new poem stands intact. The translator's own background, research, and process of composition do not appear in the finished work, any more than the scaffolding does around a finished building—or the welding torches, the lunch breaks, the labor disputes, the accidents, the delays for bad weather. Of course you can enjoy translations without knowing how they got made, yet you remain aware that they are neither perfect facsimiles nor freestanding utterances: they have their own principles and practices that set them apart from other poems.

The word "translation" itself denotes a process as well as a finished version, and I see that process, with its origin in a strange language and culture, remaining active in the finished version. To recognize a "poem in translation," as it might be called, means to connect a poem of twelve cantos that Pablo Neruda wrote in 1945 with another entitled *Heights of Macchu Picchu*. At its fullest, such a recognition would derive from historical, biographical, philological, analytic, and personal insights into the original poem as well as from explicit awareness of the translator's perspective and procedures.

The full dimensions of the translator's task, especially with a sequence as charged with purpose as *Alturas de Macchu Picchu*, have given more than one aim or aspect to this book. The book forms, in effect, an essay on the practice and theory of translation—an essay whose chief instance is a new verse rendering of Neruda's major poem. At the same time, I mean to expose in detail both the process of making this particular translation and the end product. To do so also requires explicating the original poem itself, and, since Neruda's work reached a culmination with *Alturas de Macchu Picchu*, studying the first half of his career. All of these activities belong to the process of verse translation. Sometimes they occur singly, sometimes in unison. By virtue of a full genetic process—starting from Neruda's Spanish text, retracing the life and work that built toward it, interpreting the poem itself, and finally shaping a new version line by line— verse translation emerges as a twofold activity, at once critical and creative.

Neither literary critics nor translators have committed themselves to this kind of approach. In the case of Neruda, critics in English have written articles dealing with whatever aspect of his work interested them, and in quoting they either leave the poetry untranslated or subjoin a reasonably faithful translation.[1] Those critics who do not ignore the transit between Spanish and English often deplore it instead. Reviewers (including myself) have scrutinized published translations of Neruda, but a review permits only isolated observations (or hints that the reviewer could have done better). Translators, meanwhile, generally limit themselves to a mildly hopeful preface—a few pages, followed by the book of poetry—whereas I have placed five chapters alongside a single poem. For the kind of literary venture this book attempts, there are no models I know of. As George Steiner says in his superb study *After Babel*, "Our analysis and judgement [of literature in translation] work from outside, they come after the fact. We know next to nothing of the genetic process which has gone into the translator's practice, of the prescriptive or purely empirical principles, devices, routines which have controlled his choice of this equivalent rather than that, of one stylistic level in preference to another." Steiner regrets the virtual absence of any documentation—either drafts or translators' accounts of their work—from the long history of translation, and he adds: "It is only very recently, and this *is* a revolution in the subject, that the 'anatomy' and raw materials of translation are becoming accessible to methodical scrutiny." [2] He is referring to letters, notes, a memoir, and a postscript—sources that, however illuminating, do not resemble the kind of full-scale account I believe a poem such as *Alturas de Macchu Picchu* calls for.

As a critic and translator alone, I would not have thought it so vital to embrace the whole process of translation. But as a teacher, having for some years offered workshops on verse translation, I found lively, acute, and pertinent insights into poetry emerging from our questions about translating: What options or constraints, what revealing finds or losses play a part in verse translation? It seemed at times that almost everything worth knowing about a poem must come to light naturally in examining its translation. I say "naturally" because a translator, though beginning with a fixed set of words where the poet began with none, still does in a sense begin where the poet began and follow a similar track. Having to make continuous linguistic and prosodic choices, parallel to those the poet made, brings out a kindredness between the two writers. So my workshops in verse translation have encouraged me to write not just about *Alturas de Macchu Picchu* but about translating *Alturas de Macchu Picchu*.

Essentially I mean to mesh the functions of critic and translator, because to keep them separate can make for artificial or partial views of poetry in another language. This, at least, has been my own experience: two activities, interpretation and translation, began over the course of a decade to feel more like each other, then to animate each other. A thematic concern or a line of inquiry would end up showing me how to translate some phrase in an apt way, and, conversely, an inventive rendering of some line in the original would suddenly bring out the sense of the poem at that point. I think any translator, like any reader of poetry in another language, goes through much the same process. Through a kind of symbiotic exchange—the critic and the translator living off each other—we can move toward a full sense of the poem in question. My purpose has been to make

this exchange between interpretation and translation as con-
scious a process as possible, and to devise an account of the pro-
cess. Even a reader steeped in Spanish may want to hear such
an account and to see what becomes of Neruda's poetry in En-
glish—what a verse translation reveals or obscures.

I hope the reader will imitate my own encounter with Neruda
by beginning as well as ending with the poem's lines on facing
pages, which close this book. Ordinarily the facing pages of any
bilingual edition take for granted an immense and silent leap
across the spine of the book. Here I intend to slow down and
narrate that leap. The following chapters describe my own tra-
versal from what may be the major Latin American poem of this
century to a verse translation, a North American version of the
poem.[3]

Chapter One

TRANSLATING

A cluster of related questions, usually taken for granted, hovers about the task of verse translation. Why translate at all? Why this poem? What have other translators done? Can verse come across into verse? How is translating like composing the original? How and where is a translator drawn beyond the poem? How do a poem's origins influence its translation? These questions, which clarify and deepen the enterprise of translating, bear looking into by anyone interested in poetry.

WHY TRANSLATE AT ALL?

A translation converts strangeness into likeness, and yet in doing so may bring home to us the strangeness of the original. We need translation in order to know what in us a poem is like or not like. Doing without translations, then, might confine us to a kind of solipsistic cultural prison. Now assume that we choose to dwell in our native country and our native tongue, and yet not to dwell in what George Steiner calls "arrogant parishes bordered by silence."[1] We must then become aware of a strangeness, a distance separating us from works such as *Alturas de Macchu Picchu*—a linguistic and cultural distance to be traversed.

This traversal, given Neruda's relative obscurity in the United States until the mid-1960's, implies a need to make up for near-total ignorance of his writing and the conditions of his work. As a typical reader of modern poetry in this country during the fifties, I heard of Rilke, Valéry, García Lorca, and practically nothing of the Chilean Pablo Neruda. For most people, if his name sounded at all it was like the name of some remote city whose location and precise importance remain on the fringes of consciousness. I first heard Neruda's voice in June 1966. He was speaking at an international P.E.N. conference in New York, as their principal attraction, and had not visited the United States for over twenty years. During that time he had been elected a Chilean senator, gone into five years' exile as a Communist, and published *Canto general* (1950), his 250-poem epic in which the Macchu Picchu sequence forms Book Two.[2] He had become, during the Cold War, a renowned poet nearly everywhere except in the United States. So it was with curiosity and astonishment that I listened to someone who evidently counted for a great deal among other writers. I remember him saying, in lucid, deliberate French: "I come from a country that a poet founded." He meant Alonso de Ercilla, the conquistador whose epic *La Araucana* (1569) celebrated the resistance of Chile's Indians to Spanish conquest, and I also took it that he himself was engaged in a similar task: to retell an American genesis in his poetry.

Having begun to study poetry at Harvard in 1954, I was not much encouraged to leave the mainstream that carried W. B. Yeats and T. S. Eliot along—their very initials were a guarantee of respectable authority. After all, Eliot had consummated the art in his long sequence, *Four Quartets* (1943), and had acknowledged no American masters except for his fellow expatriate Ezra Pound. Walt Whitman's resurgence after the centenary of *Leaves of Grass* (1955) was still to come, and William Carlos Williams's stubbornly indigenous poetry seemed to very few people an instructive experiment. So as a student, I cultivated affinities with British rather than American poets. What's more, the kind of openness toward South America exhibited at least nominally by Whitman, and substantially by Williams throughout his life, was quite absent from Eliot and his faithful readers. Williams (I discovered much later) translated Neruda and Octavio Paz beautifully during the fifties,[3] whereas Eliot ignored South America except for two passing touches, in which a latent disgust with sensuality combines with a distrust of alien influences.*

* Eliot's "Whispers of Immortality" associates the "rank . . . smell" of a "Brazilian jaguar" with female lubricity. "Sweeney Among the Nightingales," with its omi-

Here then came Pablo Neruda, clearly engaged in a role that Yeats in his Irish poems and Eliot in his English ones had always exemplified for me—that of voicing the genius of a place and people. Neruda had long since been recognized by readers around the world as a Latin American writer of both local and universal significance, but even in 1966, nearly fifty years after he began publishing poems, I along with most of my students, colleagues, and mentors outside of Hispanic studies knew nothing about his work. Two reasons for this ignorance come readily to mind. First, by the time Neruda became generally visible around 1950, he was identified as a Communist and therefore alien to most of the North American public. Second, the few translations of his work either were out of print by 1966 or were unconvincing as verse in English. Furthermore, no significant criticism existed to put a general or academic audience in touch with him. When a bilingual edition of *Alturas de Macchu Picchu* came out early in 1967, with Nathaniel Tarn's translation, I was only dimly oriented toward Neruda and imagined the poem to be some sort of prodigious but distant spectacle.[4]

I went to Chile in 1967 to accompany Mary Felstiner, who had a year's historical research to do there; I was to teach "American" literature at the University. On our way south, with Neruda's title in mind we flew over the Peruvian Andes to the ancient Inca capital of Cuzco. There, at 11,000 feet the night before our excursion to Macchu Picchu, with Tarn's help I first read through the poem. I am not sure how close I came to the original, with the rudimentary Spanish I had then. The next morning we took a narrow-gauge train along the Urubamba River and a small van up the steep road to Macchu Picchu. The Inca city, a complex of stone buildings, plazas, stairways, and terraces wedged between two lushly forested granite peaks, was built around 1440 and abandoned sometime after the Spanish Conquest. When an explorer from Yale, Hiram Bingham, found his way there in 1911, the site had lain overgrown and largely

---

nous sexual overtones, has a squalid setting in the tropical southern hemisphere and mentions "the River Plate."

forgotten during four centuries. For me, under the impress of Neruda's poem, a continent, a history, a culture, a language, and a poet began all at once to coalesce at Macchu Picchu.

The process of full recognition, though, began slowly, since everything about the poem was new. *Alturas de Macchu Picchu* takes its speaker and its reader line by line, canto by canto, into an unfamiliar time and place. Much of what Neruda had to confront was strange even to him—the peaks, the site, the place names, the plants and animals, the city, the builders, their oblivion—and thus how much more so to a New Yorker whose family stemmed from Eastern Europe. Nothing in a life led in the northeastern United States, and not much in California either, had prepared me for Latin America. I had a schoolchild's sand-table image of Indian civilization, had grown up singing about the Marine hymn's "halls of Montezuma" with no idea where they were or what they signified, felt a vague thrill in the word "conquistador," and sensed that life "south of the border" was seedy, somnolent, and in some way below the belt.

Venturing as far south as Chile, in fact, brought home to me a strikingly simple fact about the cultural affinities taken for granted by people living in the United States. The current of civilization that has interested and affected us most, passing as it does through dominant cultures that shaped our own, is a lateral current: Jerusalem, Athens, Rome, Paris, London, New York. Accepting this notion of a level passage of Western civilization has afforded a way of keeping one's balance, while striking south from it has to some writers felt like falling into the dark—the inexplicable slave ship off the Chilean coast in Melville's "Benito Cereno," the African river where Kurtz dies in Conrad's *Heart of Darkness*, the empty booming caves of Forster's *Passage to India*. Robert Lowell's brilliantly intuitive poem, "Dropping South: Brazil," opens with an image of his sliding down the map disastrously out of control.[5]

Given the prevalence of a laterally evolving tradition, North Americans have customarily journeyed back to the Old World, where Henry James found the essentials of high civilization that were lacking at home; where T. S. Eliot emigrated to reclaim his Anglo-European birthright; where society and nature itself seemed more firmly settled. Having devotedly if dutifully traveled in England and Europe, and later having emigrated from the Atlantic seaboard to California, I went south to the Andes and read in Canto I of *Alturas de Macchu Picchu*:

> *más abajo, en el oro de la geología,*
> *como una espada envuelta en meteoros,*
> *hundí la mano turbulenta y dulce*
> *en lo más genital de lo terrestre.*
>
> *Puse la frente entre las olas profundas,*
> *descendí como gota entre la paz sulfúrica,*
> *y, como un ciego, regresé al jazmín*
> *de la gastada primavera humana.*

I still have some dazzled notes I took that first night, pointing up these lines, so perhaps I was beginning to hear something like this in the passage:

> and deeper yet, in geologic gold,
> like a sword sheathed in meteors
> I plunged my turbulent and gentle hand
> into the genital quick of the earth.
>
> I bent my head into the deepest waves,
> dropped down through sulfurous calm
> and went back, as if blind, to the jasmine
> of the exhausted human spring.

The shock of this color and downward thrust showed me how unused I was to such behavior in a poem. Was this how the imagination worked below the equator? It felt like going beyond one's depth, with no mermaids singing as they do to Prufrock, no grail at the end of the wasteland. There are indeed myths of descent in European literature: Orpheus, Odysseus, Aeneas, Beowulf, Dante, Faust. But these journeys lead to a traditional underworld, to Hades or Hell, or in *Four Quartets* to a place of deprivation, and they are ominous occasions. Neruda plunges eagerly, potently, through sensual elements, not to some supernatural realm but to a natural source.

And we go with him. During the course of the poem, Neruda's voice and his quest intensify, so that when at the end he unites with the long-dead artisans and slaves who built Macchu Picchu, the reader feels bound to them as well:

> desde el fondo habladme toda esta larga noche
> como si yo estuviera con vosotros anclado,

> speak from the depths to me all this long night
> as if I were anchored here with you.[6]

This kind of appeal seems a far cry from Yeats imploring his "singing masters" out of holy Byzantium or Eliot invoking his "dead master" Dante in the London of *Four Quartets*. Instead they are forgotten, anonymous, voiceless Indian workers whom Neruda chooses to summon from the buried Andean city. To enter his poem I had to anchor with him at a wholly unfamiliar point in American space and time.

Alturas de Macchu Picchu first struck me as exotic in its imagery and emotion. Then later, in its deeper structure, I began to see something possibly akin to *Four Quartets*, some congruence in the two poets' patterning of history and geography, some family resemblance in the way they oriented themselves and addressed their dead. But the likenesses between these two works made their unlikeness stand out all the more critically. Since Eliot's poem and all it represented had more or less presided over my literary education, I now wanted some hold on what Pablo Neruda stood for. I could get that by taking his poem on its own terms and then translating it into my own.

WHY THIS POEM?

The best way to come at Neruda would be through the poetry that brought his development to a head. *Alturas de Macchu Picchu*, arguably his finest work and the one he valued most, was

written at the midpoint of his career after two decades of varied
and arduous evolution. Soon after the popular success of his
Veinte poemas de amor y una canción desesperada ("Twenty Poems of
Love and a Desperate Song," 1924), Neruda left Chile for five
years of minor, underpaid consular posts in the Orient.[7] Forced
into himself and his language, he registered this solitary, alien-
ated, often anguished experience in the lyrics of *Residencia en la
tierra* ("Residence on Earth," 1935), which witness or fitfully re-
sist the wasting force of time, the decay of matter and spirit.[8] On
top of that, Neruda for years had no luck in finding a European
publisher for this book. Finally, as a consul in Madrid from 1934
to 1936, he got lively recognition from the Spanish poets, which
mattered greatly to him as a Latin American, and he shared their
confidence in the rise of the Republic. But civil war and the
murder of his friend García Lorca wrenched him round decisive-
ly, from a lyric poet's prerogatives to a fellow poet's duty. "So you
ask," Neruda said to those who questioned his conversion,

> So you ask why his poems
> don't tell us of dreams, and leaves,
> and great volcanoes in his native land? . . .
> come see the blood
> in the streets![9]

For three years after the outbreak of war he worked in the Re-
publican cause, organizing and writing for Spanish refugees
and intellectuals.

The death of both parents in 1938 brought about another deci-
sive change, revealing his "endless bond with a certain life, re-
gion, and death," and he wrote his first poem about Chile.[10]
Then between 1940 and 1943, appointed by Chile's first Popular
Front government as Consul General in Mexico, he found the
muralists Rivera, Siqueiros, and Orozco "covering the city with
history and geography."[11] That example, intensified by a sympa-
thetic identification with the Soviet Union's resistance to Hitler,
strengthened Neruda's sense of the poet's public responsibility.
Just before leaving Mexico in 1943, he published *Canto general de*

Chile ("General Song of Chile") and *América, no invoco tu nombre en vano* ("America, I Do Not Invoke Your Name in Vain").[12]

On the way home from Mexico, Neruda made a kind of pilgrimage to Macchu Picchu. "There," he later said, "I felt that my own hands had worked in some distant time, digging grooves, smoothing boulders. I felt Chilean, Peruvian, American. In those rough heights, among those splendid scattered ruins, I found a profession of faith to go on with my song."[13] It was not until two years later, in 1945, that Neruda's ascent to Macchu Picchu took poetic form. Meanwhile he had campaigned hard for the Senate in Chile's northernmost mining districts, won his election, joined the Communist Party, and also received the National Prize for Literature. Europe's disastrous war had ceased and U.S. planes had just dropped atomic bombs on Japan: maybe in this critical time the ancient Andean structure offered some counterweight to momentous events outside Latin America. In August and September 1945, Neruda composed *Alturas de Macchu Picchu*. Clearly the poem arises out of deep urgency, with every mark of being a testament that would integrate personal, political, and poetic concerns.

Its first five cantos (there are twelve in all, spanning 423 lines) have nothing to do with the Inca site. Instead Neruda descends through earth and sea and retraces the anguished mood of his earlier years. Like *Residencia en la tierra*, the beginning of *Alturas de Macchu Picchu* is pervaded by loneliness, thwarted passion, disintegrative forces, and death. Then midway in the poem he climbs "through the lost jungle's tortured thicket / up to you, Macchu Picchu," naming the place for the first time (VI). "Mother of stone, spume of condors": he addresses the city as a primitive force in both the human and the natural sphere. Drawing closer, the poet calls to view clothes, hands, faces, oiled beams, scraped stones. Then despite the "transcendent measure" of this architectural monument (XI), the "permanence of stone" (VII), Neruda turns in Canto X and cries out plangently, angrily, asking the empty ruins what happened to those hands and faces:

Stone upon stone, and man, where was he? . . .
hunger, did your reef-edge climb
to these high and ruinous towers?

The inquiring force of the verse carries Neruda back in time and down to the buried worker, "as if I were anchored here with you" (XII). Then "speak to me," "tell me everything," the final canto demands. These imperatives render *Alturas de Macchu Picchu* a true *ars poetica*, demonstrating why and what he had to write: at a specifically American site, he would evoke people otherwise submerged and mute, to transfuse their suffering into his own voice.

Perhaps because this poem so integrated things for Neruda as an artist and a Latin American, nothing with its prolonged yet concentrated strength emerges in his later work, though there are many fine single poems. Publishers and readers have treated *Alturas de Macchu Picchu* distinctively—witness the dozen or more separate editions in Spanish since 1945, many deluxe and illustrated, and the amount of critical scrutiny the poem has attracted in Latin America.[14] Certainly Neruda himself set great store by this poem, recording it three times and calling it "a new stage in my style and a new direction in my concerns."[15] It is the poem at the heart of his work.

WHAT HAVE OTHER TRANSLATORS DONE?

Any estimate of a foreign writer, such as calling *Alturas de Macchu Picchu* the poem at the heart of Neruda's work, remains contingent on a set of circumstances beyond that writer's control. What has been translated, when, by whom, how well, and which versions are easily obtainable—all these questions intimately qualify the word "Neruda" in English-speaking countries. Apart from the very few ideally bilingual and bicultural persons, a literate public needs translations: like windows, they let in fresh air and they let us see out.

Though Neruda's epic *Canto general* (1950), for instance, of which *Alturas de Macchu Picchu* forms a part, was entirely translated into French, German, and Russian over twenty years ago, to get even a fraction of it now in English one has to cull a dozen anthologies. Our desultory awareness of Latin American literature until the last decade or so has depended on what a few hardy translators have made available, and any recent translator must be grateful to them. As a form of literary and cultural history, it is worth tracing how Neruda's work emerged in English. That emergence occurred roughly in three phases: before 1949– 50, he was a little-known yet representative Latin American poet of erotic love, urban alienation, Spain, and Stalingrad; next, rendered more visible by the Cold War, he became a quasi-political figure whose Whitmanesque *Let the Rail Splitter Awake!* and other militant excerpts from *Canto general* turned up regularly in the Marxist publication *Masses and Mainstream*; then from the early sixties on, Neruda was a belatedly recognized presence (honors from Yale, Oxford, the Library of Congress, and the Modern Language Association; the Nobel Prize) whose work through 1950, along with the unstinted flow of his writing since then, now became available thanks to a variety of hands.

The first real notice of Neruda in this country occurred in a semi-scholarly 1934 collection of Spanish-American modernist verse, but that contained only a few feverish lyrics Neruda had written eleven years earlier.[16] The editor, G. Dundas Craig, shows mixed attitudes. "English taste will probably be shocked by the brutal crudeness" of the poet's animal and sensual instincts—a crudeness not much alleviated by Craig's decision to render biblically the intimate Spanish *tu*, as in "thy extended flesh." Yet Craig also notices Neruda's efforts "to grasp and hold the impalpable," to express the inexpressible, likening them to Wordsworth's in the Immortality ode. Neruda's poetry did not show up again until 1942, with J. L. Grucci's perceptive selection from *Residencia en la tierra* and *Canto general de Chile*. By this time he could be introduced as "the topflight Spanish American poet," and be cited as one who eschews "the sterile and effete symbolism of T. S. Eliot and the Wastelanders. . . . There is a marvelous fusion of introspection and realism."[17] Unfortunately, the marvel of it diminishes through inert translation, with no Spanish original provided.

Also in 1942, Dudley Fitts assembled for New Directions a pioneer and resolutely bilingual anthology of ninety-five contemporary Latin American poets, a model of its kind, with three quite good versions from Neruda by Fitts and H. R. Hays and a decent one by Angel Flores.[18] Hays tries to bring Neruda forcefully onto the North American scene by noting in him a "charnel grimness" and an "interweaving of realistic material and a personal set of symbols" that make him "as much the poet of a decaying social system as is T. S. Eliot."[19] Then in 1943 Hays published his own Latin American anthology, including more translations from the love poetry, *Residencia en la tierra*, and recent political verse.[20] Terse, literal yet fairly idiomatic, they represent the poet strongly, though inevitably their terseness reduces the roll and resonance people feel in reciting or hearing Neruda recite his verse. For example, in a line from "Agua sexual" ("Sexual Water") that could serve as epigraph to all of *Residencia en la tierra*, Neruda looks out at the world *como un párpado atrozmente levantado a la fuerza*. Hays renders it well—"like an eyelid dreadfully raised by force"—but with far fewer syllables his version misses the drawn-out torture in Neruda's line.

When New Directions published a Neruda collection in 1946, with about half of *Residencia en la tierra* and selections from *Canto general de Chile*, the character and range of Neruda's work became manifest. But so did the hazard of having a non-poet as translator.[21] In Angel Flores's bilingual edition, the transit from a Spanish to an English poem tends to stall midway, failing to reactivate Neruda's palpable surprises. What results is a hybrid idiom that flattens and rationalizes Neruda's strangest creations. "Galope muerto" ("Dead Gallop"), the opening poem from *Residencia en la tierra*, begins this way:

> Como cenizas, como mares poblándose,
> en la sumergida lentitud, en lo informe.

Flores goes word by word, not taking chances though Neruda did:

> Like ashes, like seas peopling themselves
> in the submerged lentitude, in the unformed.

But "seas peopling themselves / in the submerged lentitude" does not catch the ear. Something bolder might:

Like ashes, like oceans swarming,
in the sunken slowness, in what's unformed.

Later in "Galope muerto," a crucial passage situates the poet in the alien environment typical of *Residencia en la tierra*:

Por eso, en lo inmóvil, deteniéndose, percibir,
entonces, como aleteo inmenso, encima,
como abejas muertas o números,
ay, lo que mi corazón pálido no puede abarcar.

The logic here is deliberately tentative, making these lines hard to handle. Flores writes:

For that reason, stopping in the immovable to perceive.
Then, like an immense flapping of wings, above,
like dead bees or numbers,
alas what my pale heart is not able to embrace.

Here it is the rhythm that must bring out Neruda's logic, especially in the first line, so a plain rephrasing will not quite do. Given each phrase's tentative, protracted movement in Spanish, the translator can try a similarly groping rhythm in English:

That's why, in what's immobile, holding still, to perceive
then, like great wingbeats, overhead,
like dead bees or numbers,
oh all that my spent heart can't embrace.

No English version, I'm afraid, can show why Julio Cortázar called *Residencia en la tierra* "a radical mutation of our deepest speech" and "the verbal creation of a continent."[22] In any case, I have in fact learned from studying Flores and benefited from his initiative.

With hindsight, of course, one can all too easily fault earlier practitioners or forget that one's improvements depend on their work in the first place. And possibly the early stage of translating a poet is inevitably marked by too much fealty: word-for-word or sense-for-sense renderings that stop short of exploiting the translator's own tongue. Still, the essential question is not one of stages, of early as against contemporary versions. We have always to ask if a given translation comes across in its own right, as convincing as any good poem of its day. In most cases, the idiom of translators goes stale sooner than that of other writers, so that ideally, the salient poets from any period deserve retranslating for the ear of each new generation.

Naturally, while Neruda was (or was not) getting translated, he himself went on writing. He finished *Alturas de Macchu Picchu* in September 1945, and then an odd thing happened to it. The French writer Roger Caillois, visiting Neruda in Santiago at the time, heard him read the poem and asked to translate it. In January 1946 he began publishing his version in the London-based magazine *France Libre*. By February, eleven of Neruda's twelve cantos had appeared in French translation, before the original poem was even out in Spanish—a rare event in the history of translation.[23]

Later in 1946 a Venezuelan and an Argentine magazine published the poem.[24] Then early in 1947 Neruda made his first recording of it, and the work was published separately in Chile.[25] The British poet G. S. Fraser visited Neruda around this time and heard the recording. Thanks to him the first English translations from *Alturas de Macchu Picchu* appeared in London: *Adam*, a small but hardy review, published a special Neruda number in 1948, including Canto IX and part of X along with acute commentary.[26] Later that year, H. R. Hays's version came out in a little-known, short-lived New York magazine, *The Tiger's Eye*.[27] This was the first full go at a complex, unprecedented poem, and it does a good deal of justice to what Neruda wrote. Here and there it shows signs of uncertainty: words and phrases mistaken or misunderstood, syntax misplaced, lines rendered roughly. Throughout, Hays seems unsure how much liberty he ought to take with this imposing work. Yet generally his translation does not suffer by remaining close to the original. In Canto VI, arriving at Macchu Picchu, Neruda walks where "men's feet . . . touched the soil." Hays continues:

I look upon clothing and hands,
the remains of water in the sonorous hollow,
the wall smoothed by the touch of a face,
which looked upon earthly lamps with my eyes,
which oiled the vanished beams with my hands
because everything, clothing, skin, vessels,
words, bread, wine
departed, fell to the earth.

It is an arresting passage, and Neruda's blend of elegiac speech with concrete narrative, or traditional with private symbolism, does not sound much like anything being written in the United States in 1948.

The early translator of *Alturas de Macchu Picchu* would have been hard put to find, in the strongest poets of the time, an appropriate and appropriable style. William Carlos Williams in *Paterson* was exhibiting a very different sort of historical and vernacular imagination, Hart Crane's verse was far more idiosyncratic than Neruda's, and Robert Lowell's more compacted. Some of Robinson Jeffers's rhetoric and imagery resemble Neruda's, but curiously enough I would have found myself looking to Eliot, in whom a more formal version of Neruda's characteristic historical perspective can be found. Neruda's arrival at Macchu Picchu, where he imagines feet, hands, faces, bread, and wine that "fell to the earth," recalls a moment in *Four Quartets* when Eliot journeys back to an ancestral village to conjure up his people again:

> Earth feet, loam feet, lifted in country mirth
> Mirth of those long since under earth
> Nourishing the corn. . . .
> . . . I am here
> Or there, or elsewhere.[28]

To yield a full sense of Neruda in English, however, Eliot's restrained mode would need (highly unlikely) admixtures from Whitman's *Song of Myself* and from Amerindian mythology. But why, after all, should Neruda have resembled anything heard before? As he says at the opening of *Alturas de Macchu Picchu*, "Someone expecting me among violins / met with a world like a buried tower / sinking its spiral deeper than all / the leaves the color of rough sulfur." The point is that bringing Neruda over into English was bound to challenge and expand the imaginative resources of mid-century North American poetry.

Up until 1949 Neruda had reached this country as the vibrant yet undeservedly neglected voice of Latin America. Then before he had had a decent hearing, international politics set him apart. What might be called the second phase of Neruda's emergence in the United States began in 1949—a phase to which some readers, both friendly and hostile, still relegate him. The Marxist monthly *Masses and Mainstream* began publishing him regularly, and in 1950 issued a translation of *Alturas de Macchu Picchu* by "Waldeen," a professional dancer living in Mexico City when Neruda arrived there as a Communist exiled from Chile.[29] She does not seem at home with the intensely troubled, expressionist quality of the poem's early cantos, but translated the more outspoken Macchu Picchu cantos quite firmly. As if to bring out its political drift, the text was published in company with various explicitly militant poems by Neruda and a 1949 speech. The whole collection was entitled *Let the Rail Splitter Awake and Other Poems*, thus giving *Alturas de Macchu Picchu* a partisan stamp that attracted some readers and put off others.

In 1950 Whit Burnett's widely circulated collection of "The World's Best" hundred authors included a translation of *Alturas de Macchu Picchu* by Angel Flores, with a headnote mistakenly calling it the first English version.[30] Here too the translator seems concerned to spell things out. Where Neruda implores the buried Indians, *desde el fondo habladme toda esta larga noche*, Flores says: "from out of the depths talk to me all this long night through." A tighter, more balanced line would make the biblical echo subtler and keep the urgency of Neruda's rhythm: "speak from the depths to me all this long night" (XII). Burnett's note also describes Macchu Picchu as America's oldest city, "built some 3000 years B.C." Whatever calculation produced that dating (the city was probably founded around A.D. 1440), its inaccuracy reflects the illusion of "abysmal remoteness," in George Kubler's phrase, that North Americans carry to pre-Columbian history.[31]

After the translations of *Alturas de Macchu Picchu* by Hays, Waldeen, and Flores, the fifties went by with almost nothing of Neruda in books or periodicals. For one thing, between 1948 and 1954 his Stalinist orientation affected his work, and the new poems in that vein, politically simplistic, did not much tempt the serious translator. As political insight, compare Neruda asking the dead at Macchu Picchu to

> say to me: here I was punished
> when a gem didn't shine or the earth
> give forth its stone or grain on time,   (XII)

with these lines about Stalin:

> He taught all things
> to grow, to grow,
> plants and metals,
> children and rivers
> taught he them to grow.[32]

In 1949 Neruda himself announced, in the spirit of socialist realism, that he had forbidden Hungarian translators to work on his earlier poetry from *Residencia en la tierra* because the anguish pervading that book would dishearten young readers from the struggle at hand.[33] Meanwhile in the United States, the climate of McCarthyism certainly affected publishers' choices and the public taste. For instance, while Neruda was praising Whitman, "endless as the fields of grain,"[34] the House Committee on Un-American Activities listed a "Walt Whitman Book Shop" and a "Walt Whitman School of Social Sciences" as subversive organizations.[35] Whatever they really were, for an average reader the taint was there. Probably what prejudiced Neruda's chances of reaching a wide audience was not so much his poetry as his party membership, his public role at peace congresses, and his support of Howard Fast, Charlie Chaplin, and Paul Robeson.[36]

During the fifties, another sort of criterion may slightly have worked against Neruda, though this is impossible to demonstrate. The New Criticism favored a poetry whose significance lay within an interwoven, ironic structure. Readers had the job of carefully unpacking what the poet had carefully packed, and indeed fine perceptions followed from this approach. But New Critics seldom dealt with poetry in translation, and even then they might have had trouble keeping Neruda's political motives disengaged from the angry demands his verse could make:

> Hunger, coral of humankind,
> hunger, hidden plant, root of the woodcutter,
> hunger, did your reef-edge climb
> to these high and ruinous towers? . . .
> Macchu Picchu, did you set
> stone upon stone on a base of rags?   (X)

The thing to look for during the fifties was the organizing of tensions within a limiting frame—a touchstone that does not always work for Neruda's writing. Rather than limit and frame experience, his lyrics typically impel us through it open-endedly, as in the beginning of "Galope muerto":

> Like ashes, like oceans swarming,
> in the sunken slowness, in what's unformed,
> or like high on the road hearing
> bellstrokes cross by crosswise. . . .

On its surface this poetry gives us little cohesive texture to work with, though the stanza will gather to a deeper coherence. To the cultivated eye, Neruda could seem "a great poet of disorganization," as Juan Ramón Jiménez put it, "a gleaner who finds here and there on his path a piece of coal, of glass, a shoe sole, a lost eye, a cigarette butt, and claps them together without rhyme or reason."[37] There is some truth in this, but not enough, as the astonishing reach of "Galope muerto" demonstrates. The poem was written in 1925. Not until more than thirty years later, when Galway Kinnell, James Wright, Robert Bly, and others were coming into their own, did their venturous idiom, learned partly from Neruda, create a general readiness for hearing him in this country.

During the fifties, then, Neruda's complex lyrics, his outspoken political verse, and *Alturas de Macchu Picchu*, which was both complex and outspoken, went largely untranslated. Kenneth Rexroth did publish four translations from *Veinte poemas de amor* in 1955, and Christopher Logue began making his striking "adaptations" from that book—not strictly translations, since only about half their words can be traced directly to Neruda.[38] In one delightful instance, Neruda came into the hands of William Carlos Williams, who had already done versions of Spanish Loyalist poetry and of Octavio Paz. Williams in 1958 found the kind of thing he liked in Neruda's *Odas elementales* ("Elementary Odes," 1954), choosing the "Ode to Laziness"[39] and translating quite closely while still moving to his own deft measure:

> Yesterday I felt this ode
> would not get off the floor.
> It was time, I ought
> at least
> show a green leaf. . . .
> Then,
> on the pine peaks,
> laziness
> appeared in the nude,
> she led me dazzled
> and sleepy,
> she showed me upon the sand
> small broken bits
> of ocean substance,
> wood, algae, pebbles,
> feathers of sea birds.[40]

By the late fifties, a more open poetic environment for Neruda existed in the United States. Whitman's genius was becoming fully evident, thanks partly to Allen Ginsberg, who revived a prophetic voice in English; Williams's freshness and local inspiration now mattered to a great many writers, including Lowell;[41] and Robert Bly had started his magazine *The Fifties* to counter whatever he thought academic, austere, or abstract in contemporary poetry. Bly's argument involved Neruda, for if, as he said, Eliot had mastered the unconscious too easily and other poets preferred to skirt the darker parts of the mind, the body, and the earth, Neruda's imagination ranged powerfully from blackened roots to urban fatigue, from enormous anacondas to the oppressions of Central American dictatorships.[42] Along with Williams and Rexroth, the first major poets to translate Neruda in this country were Bly, beginning in 1959, and later James Wright. In their own poems, Bly and Wright could make leaps of association like Neruda's, but though their translations are compelling, to my ear they sometimes remain caught halfway between the Spanish and a new poem in English.[43]

The first major attempt since 1946 to make Neruda widely available came from Grove Press, with Ben Belitt's bilingual *Selected Poems* (1961).[44] Readers have to let their gratitude for so plentiful a collection offset their trouble in following Belitt's verse. Evidently it can be no less hazardous to have a poet than a non-poet as translator, rebounding enthusiastically from Neruda's lines into his own creativity. Take a passage from Canto VII, which speaks elegiacally to those who once inhabited Macchu Picchu:

> Ya no sois, manos de araña, débiles
> hebras, tela enmarañada:
> cuanto fuisteis cayó: costumbres, sílabas
> raídas, máscaras de luz deslumbradora.

A close rendering could be:

> You're no more now, spidery hands, frail
> fibers, entangled web—
> whatever you were fell away: customs, frayed
> syllables, masks of dazzling light.

But Belitt wants something more:

All that spidery finger-play, the gimcrack
device of the fibers, the meshes' entanglements—
you have put them behind.
All that you were, falls away: habitudes, tatterdemalion
syllables, the blinding personae of light.[45]

Neruda has no notion of finger-play, of devices, of personae. These things, along with the idea that "you have put them behind," belong to the translator. Belitt's version resembles the wrong side of a tapestry: the design is there somewhere, only confused by extra threads.[46] He means to reincarnate the original in his own voice—a valid aim—by drawing out his lines with something sinuous and strange he heard in Neruda's. But Belitt's verbiage sounds to me empty, thus wholly violating the twofold requirement of translation: the original must come through essentially, in language that itself rings true. Unfortunately, readers in this country still get their introduction to Neruda from Belitt's paperback editions more than from any others.

Also in 1961, Carlos Lozano translated a good selection from the *Odas elementales*, and in 1962 Clayton Eshleman made vigorous translations from *Residencia en la tierra*.[47] But it was not until 1965 and 1966, when Neruda visited England and the United States, that he began to get a more general hearing in English. Tarn published *The Heights of Macchu Picchu*, and Bly and Wright issued their translations in book form; Alastair Reid began making fine versions of Neruda's later work, and W. S. Merwin of his earlier; David Ossman and Carlos Hagen published a broad, well-written selection from Neruda's early poems; and Anthony Kerrigan made lively, accurate translations from *Canto general*.[48] By now, a dozen or more titles are in print. When Neruda received the Nobel Prize in 1971, the press found it possible to provide decent illustrations of his writing. Then his death in September 1973, coming a few days after the military seizure of Chile, prompted new translations and readings for North American audiences who at that moment needed to hear Neruda's voice.

The translations of *Alturas de Macchu Picchu* by Hays, Waldeen, and Flores are out of print. Tarn's edition, to which I owe my first exposure to the poem, can usefully be examined later in this book, along with Neruda's poem itself. Having used Tarn's translation with students for ten years, I know it affords them an energetic reading. There are many memorable passages, and where now and then I take issue with his rendering, it alerts and returns me to the original, which is part of what any translation should do.

CAN VERSE COME ACROSS INTO VERSE?

Since verse translation forms both the means and the end of this book, the cherished axiom that translating poetry is a betrayal must come into account as well. Let us assume that we find the language of any fine poem in a unique, inalienable state. Does a "version" or "rendering" inevitably do just what those terms imply—turn the poem into something other than it is? Or, assuming that the translator aims to compose a new poem that speaks for itself, and yet aims to speak for the original in all its integrity: does one purpose preclude the other? These questions have a rich lineage that traces back two thousand years—a sign of vitality if also of vexatiousness. From Cicero and Horace through Saint Jerome to Ezra Pound and Walter Benjamin, the problem of verse translation has remained essentially the same. Octavio Paz phrased it in the title of a 1970 essay: "Translation: Literature and Literalism."[49]

Are there alternatives to verse translation? A trot can clarify diction, imagery, structure;[50] thorough explication can provide an intellectual grasp. Both procedures have their place. But since verse, unlike most prose, is involved bodily and specifically in its own tongue, no amount of paraphrase or interpretation can substitute for hearing a poem in one's native language. Only a verse translation, I have come to believe, can yield a vital, immediate sense of what the poet meant.

Although practitioners of the art have made major statements on its theory, and have also detailed their awareness of what gets lost in translation, the poets themselves have seldom taken the chance, except vaguely and unofficially, to convey their own sense of loss. Only the man who voiced them can really know what it feels like to have these subtly cadenced lines, *Ya no sois, manos de araña, débiles / hebras, tela enmarañada,* transmuted hypertrophically into "All that spidery finger-play, the gimcrack / device of the fibers, the meshes' entanglements—you have put them behind." But Neruda did not expect much anyway from English versions of his work.* He was once asked into what language his poems translated best:

Italian, because there's a similarity of values between the two languages. English and French . . . do not correspond to Spanish—neither in vocalization, nor in the placement, color, or weight of the words. This means that the equilibrium of a Spanish poem . . . can find no equivalent in French or English. It's not a question of interpretive equivalents, no; the sense may be correct, indeed the accuracy of the translation itself, of the meaning, may be what destroys the poem. That's why I think that Italian comes closest.[51]

Clearly Neruda laments the loss in translation of the very thing that makes him love to write: a poem's blend of sounds and rhythms, of tones and overtones, which he calls "equilibrium" because they have a physical presence for him. But this lament resembles a view of verse translation that never gets beyond the weary dualism of style and content. Bring over a poem's ideas and images, and you will lose its manner; imitate prosodic effects, and you sacrifice its matter. Get the letter and you miss the spirit, which is everything in poetry; or get the spirit and you miss the letter, which is everything in poetry. But these are false dilemmas, and the distinction they imply plays no part in Neruda's poetry. I doubt he would stand by the notion that his poems can yield a "sense," a "meaning" distinct from their form, an "interpretive equivalent." He must have known, or at least guessed from his own experience translating Shakespeare and others, that the translator of a poem whose music and meaning work indivisibly is not performing some

---

*Neruda read widely in English, and his translations from Blake and others show a solid grasp of the language. I am not sure whether he had an exact sense of idiomatic English.

stereoscopic feat, any more than the poet was in writing the poem. Let us admit that to really translate a poem is impossible—impossible yet fascinating—and start from there. Verse translation at its best generates a wholly new utterance in the second language—new, yet equivalent, of equal value. Perhaps the passage from Spanish into Italian generates nothing new. In preferring that minimal displacement, Neruda was expressing a residual uneasiness at being translated at all. Apart from the fact that translation would promote his currency abroad, the idea of new utterance, new incarnation, may not after all have appealed to him when it applied to his own poetry.

His work as a translator over the years also shows that Neruda was less interested in re-creating other writers' work through verse translation than in drawing emotional sustenance from them, or simply making them available. During his twenties he translated Baudelaire's "L'Ennemi," a fragment of Rilke's *Malte Laurids Brigge* (from Gide's translation), two pieces from Joyce's *Chamber Music*, Blake's *Visions of the Daughters of Albion* and "The Mental Traveller," and part of Whitman's *Song of Myself*.[52] All these are literal renditions that read well, and show Neruda not so much making these poets come alive in Spanish as affiliating himself with various romantic sources. Later in life, as he traveled and found himself translated everywhere, he often did versions from his friends' or his translators' work—a heartening form of literary exchange.

For Shakespeare's quadricentennial in 1964, Neruda wrote a playable and often moving version of *Romeo and Juliet*, though he made little attempt to echo Shakespeare's absolute felicities.[53] He was well aware that compared with English verse, Spanish tends toward spreading, and he found himself needing "two or more lines for each one of the original."[54] When Juliet parts with Romeo, for instance, in Act Two, scene two, she says, "This bud of love, by summer's ripening breath, / May prove a beauteous flower when next we meet." Clearly Neruda is not at home, rhythmically or verbally, in the four lines that splay out from Shakespeare's two: *Este botón de amor con el aliento / de las respiraciones del verano / tal vez dará una flor maravillosa / cuando otra vez tú y yo nos encontremos.* I do not know whether it could be done better in Spanish. Certainly Neruda knew that a loss could occur in going either way between two languages. This state of affairs did not stimulate him to be inventive as a translator, and it also left him doubtful that his own poetry might survive translation intact.

"It seems to me," he said, "that the English language, so different from Spanish and so much more direct, often expresses the meaning of my poetry but does not convey its atmosphere."[55] Again I would question this abstraction of meaning from atmosphere, seeing how palpably Neruda's verse can shape its perceptions out of sounds and rhythms. *Hambre, coral del hombre,* he says at Macchu Picchu (X), and what that means can scarcely be separated from how it sounds. Here indeed one has to wrestle with words to shape an English verse fully equal to the Spanish. "Hunger, the human coral," gets exactly the rhythmic pattern that Neruda has, but means something different. To say "Hunger, coral of man," likens hunger to coral more accurately, but less compellingly. "Hunger, coral of humankind," avoiding a specific gender, ties both "hunger" and "coral" into the sounds of "humankind"—but not nearly so closely as Neruda does, with *hambre* kept from *hombre* by only a single vowel, and with *coral* between them, its vowels modulating from one word to the other. The upshot is not so much that we get the letter in English and miss the spirit, as that translators must try for better and better verse.

Neruda's doubts about translation were shared by the Peruvian César Vallejo, often linked with Neruda though they wrote quite differently. "Everyone knows that poetry is untranslatable. Poetry is tone," Vallejo said. Poems reach out to us with the "cardiac rhythm of life," and despite translation "their tone remains, immovable, in the words of the original language."[56] Certainly Vallejo's own idiosyncratic and complex poems resist translation. But in a way, the difficulty of translating Neruda well stems from his not being difficult to translate adequately. He exhibits no struggle with language or with silence as Vallejo does. Even in the anguished mood of *Residencia en la tierra* he hardly ever doubts his element, any more than a swimmer does. However surprising or disconnected his images, words for what he has to say do not fail him, and their face value is seldom unclear, which means for the translator that a semblance of Neruda's poetry comes fairly easily.

One does not feel the poet's words struggling against their referents, because for him their source and validity came from nature. "The word was born in the blood,"[57] Neruda believed, and he said he "began to write from a vegetal impulse."[58] This prelexical source of poetic language means that a translator can often rely on the common nouns in English—"tree" for *árbol*, "dew" for *rocío*—to express what Neruda had in mind. He might be called an Orphic poet, animating the things of the world by summoning and naming them. When he says *amapola*, in translation it remains a poppy, and of course a *cóndor* stays a condor. Thus it is not usually a semantic originality in Neruda that confronts the translator. What makes his verse difficult to translate is first its sensuousness, which either may or may not find an equivalent in English, a sound and rhythm of equal value. Second, and at a deeper level, he is difficult to translate for the same reason that an average Chilean has trouble grasping some of his poetry. When Neruda has lit on an image intuitively, the translator must sometimes make an unguided choice. What does *mares poblándose* (literally, "seas peopling themselves") refer to? The face value of the phrase may not be in doubt, but is the literal translation convincing and compelling? The choice between "peopling" and some other word such as "thronging" or "swarming" has still to be made.

The question of verse translation continues to exercise translators, critics, and sometimes poets, because it goes deeper than judgments of loss or gain. Sooner or later the translator asks, Where does the nature of poetry subsist? In ideas, imagery, diction, pattern, sound, or rhythm? In all those together, of course, but perhaps most in sound and rhythm, which are specific to their own language. At one point during his last days, Neruda talked with a guest about Lithuanian translations of his poetry. They were only fair, she said, but he assured her: "Don't worry. The rhythm is all right. . . . For a poet, that's what counts."[59] To show what a difference rhythm makes, here are two of Whitman's lines that Neruda translated. In *Song of Myself*, section two, we hear:

> Urge and urge and urge,
> Always the procreant urge of the world.

We hear the dense monosyllabic "urge" copulating throughout line one; the way the word can (only in English) act as verb and noun at once; the line's taut trochaic beat released into a flow of dactyls in line two; Whitman's astonishing (and Shakespearean) "procreant" instead of "procreative"—and all of these things leave Neruda's version sounding rhythmically bulky:

> *Impulso, impulso, impulso,*
> *siempre el procreador impulso del mundo.*[60]

A friend of Neruda's remembers him working assiduously on his Whitman translation in Madrid in 1935, searching for the right words.[61] Maybe that word-for-word adherence was the trouble, since his own verse at the time, his "material songs" to wood, wine, and celery,[62] were astir with the procreant urge and the rhythm he did not confer on Whitman. Like Shakespeare, Whitman often eludes everything but mere wonder. This test points up an inalienable quality in the finest poetry, something at once meaning and music, that remains organic to the tongue it is created in. To respond to this quality, a translator moves between two extremes, neither settling for literalism nor leaping into improvisation, but somehow shaping a poem that is likewise inalienable and organic. It follows from this that the language of translation should ordinarily be the translator's native tongue and that the translator must in some sense be a poet.

What Neruda felt was getting lost in English translations of his verse might more precisely be called its physical body rather than its atmosphere. A good example occurs in "Agua sexual," the epitome of *Residencia en la tierra*. Even the English title, "Sexual Water," dissipates the surprise of the adjective by making it subordinate to the noun, whereas Spanish syntax places the adjective *sexual* in an emphatic position without losing the force of the noun *agua*. The poem's first line beautifully manifests what Neruda called the vocalization, placement, color, and weight of Spanish words: *Rodando a goterones solos / . . . cae el agua*—literally, "Rolling in large single drops / . . . the water falls." These are some options in English:

> Running in single drops (Hays, 1943)
> Rolling drop by drop (Eshleman, 1962)
> Running down in big and distinct drops (Wright, 1967)
> Rolling in big solitary raindrops (Walsh, 1973)

Hays's version makes clear why Neruda called English "so much more direct": down to six syllables, with the adjective "single" (*solos*) preemptively limiting the noun instead of climactically following it, and *solos* kept to one meaning instead of connoting "alone" as well as "single." Even with the more likely "rolling" instead of "running," Hays would lack the fullness of Neruda's sonorous back vowels, the *oh*'s and *ah*'s pulsing through *Rodando a goterones solos*. Wright transcribes Neruda faithfully at the expense of his own rhythm, and Walsh specifies raindrops, thus failing to suggest the sweat and sperm that come later in the poem. Taking off from Eshleman and Wright, another option might be "Rolling down drop upon drop." Yet that could still be improved. At least it satisfies the criterion of being exact yet idiomatic, and shows that, other things being equal, rhythm is what counts. The French version—"Roulant à grosses gouttes seules"—says just what the Spanish does but too tersely.[63] Only Italian, as Neruda said, can make a rhythmic, aural, and semantic equation with *Rodando a goterones solos*: "Rotando a gocciolones solos." It's beautiful, but is it translation?

Yes, and no. In an obvious sense, the Italian does come as close to Neruda's poem as it's possible to come—but not through any particular virtue in the translation. Only the inherited virtue of a cognate diction, grammar, and syntax stands the Italian in such good stead, so that it would actually be more accurate to speak here of transliterating from Spanish. It must in fact be a little dull to readjust Neruda into Italian; translators working in other languages need have no envy. Since English, as Neruda said, is "so different from Spanish," forging a new version in it takes the translator through a process kindred to that of the poet.

HOW IS TRANSLATING LIKE COMPOSING THE ORIGINAL?

Translating a poem often feels essentially like the primary act of writing, of carrying some preverbal sensation or emotion or thought over into words. Anyone who has slowly shaped an original sentence knows what it feels like to edge toward a word or phrase and then toward a more apt one—one that suddenly touches off a new thought. The same experience holds for poets, generating a line of verse, who find that the right rhyme or image when it comes can trigger an unlooked-for and now indispensable meaning.

So it is in the to-and-fro of verse translation, where finding how and finding why to choose a particular rendering are interdependent. In its own way the translator's activity reenacts the poet's and can form the cutting edge of comprehension. At times it even seems (to the enthusiast, at least) that only those insights feeding into or deriving from the task of translation are exactly legitimate, germane to the poem. This is not to limit or belittle the act of comprehending a poem, but to enlarge the responsibility of translating one.

The vital question about Macchu Picchu—Is the place still alive to move us now?—turns quite literally into a question of translation. In Canto IX, Neruda composes seventy-two highly figurative epithets to Macchu Picchu, telling off as many attributes of the abandoned city:

> Triangled tunic, pollen of stone. . . .
> Buried ship, wellspring of stone. . . .
> Coral of sunken time.

At one point in the sequence occurs a key image, "Gale sustained on the slope," followed by another that translators have seen in various ways:

Inmóvil catarata de turquesa.

Leaving alone the variations on "cataract of turquoise" or "turquoise waterfall," *inmóvil* raises the most interesting possibilities, since it concerns the potential of Macchu Picchu. The first English translation made it "Motionless cataract of turquoise," and semantically that will do.[64] It embodies well enough the paradox of a downflow that has no movement. Yet "motionless" renders this precious source of energy more inert than I think Neruda's poem would have it. Tarn's version also takes away energy by saying "Still turquoise cataract"—a fine image in itself, as of something shining seen from afar and arrested aesthetically.[65] The word "still," at least for me, carries echoes of those crucial moments in *Four Quartets* when perishable life is transformed by spirit, "at the still point of the turning world."[66] Such echoes heighten Neruda's image, but may do so misleadingly. Given the preceding epithet, "Gale sustained on the slope," and given Neruda's desire to reanimate the dead at Macchu Picchu, the turquoise cataract needs to be more dynamic than "still" would allow. It needs to be seen as much under the aspect of history as of art. At one stage in my own translating I tried "moveless," but that seemed precious; then "unmoving," if only to keep a potential energy in the word, but its negative prefix felt too strong; then "stilled," but this reads some outside force into the original.

Perhaps for once a better translation was waiting there all along in the exact cognate of *inmóvil*: "immobile." The English prefix "im-," counterpoised against the root word "mobile," builds up a palpable tension that expresses something we need to know about Macchu Picchu. Like an "immobile turquoise cataract," the ruined yet revisited city is being sustained, poised against whatever has stalled but not finally stopped its energy. The poet finds a word to say as much; sometimes the translator also does. Small points of tuning, like this one, can make the difference between a locked, tragic sense of Latin American history and the dynamic, prophetic sense motivating Neruda.

HOW AND WHERE IS A TRANSLATOR DRAWN BEYOND THE POEM?

In having to enact a parallel process of composition, the translator eventually imagines and returns to whatever reality the poet was after in the first place: Rilke's panther, Valéry's seaside graveyard, García Lorca's New York, Neruda's forgotten American city. This return may well occur because of, not despite, the strangeness of the original poem. It completes what I would call the full circle of translation. The circle starts with something seen or thought, but strange because unrealized in verse. A poet brings it over into words, into the idiom of a place and time. A second writer does the same again, but starting with the poet's lines, and finds a way back to what first gave rise to them.

At every stage, the task is one of translation. Neruda first had to bring himself from "the city's winter streets" to the disregarded Andean site. Then,

> Entonces en la escala de la tierra he subido
> entre la atroz maraña de las selvas perdidas
> hasta ti, Macchu Picchu.   (VI)

He went there, and as far as another and a later voice in English can take us, we come after him:

> Then on the ladder of the earth I climbed
> through the lost jungle's tortured thicket
> up to you, Macchu Picchu.

Because the community Neruda brings into reach is voiceless, he himself must translate it—literally, bear it up through the earth, and across time, to give it a new voice. Hints of this task appear toward the end of the poem. Canto XI begins with the phrase *A través* ("through"): "Through the dazing splendor, / through the night of stone let me plunge my hand." *A través*, meaning either "through" or "across," relates etymologically to *traducción,* "translation," and for Neruda the phrase bears a crucial relation to his prophetic task as well. Again in Canto XII:

> *A través de la tierra juntad todos*
> *los silenciosos labios derramados*
> *y desde el fondo habladme toda esta larga noche*
> *como si yo estuviera con vosotros anclado.*

> All through the earth join all
> the silent wasted lips
> and speak from the depths to me all this long night
> as if I were anchored here with you.

Neruda must begin, like any conscientious translator, by anchoring with his original. But ultimately he does so "as if," subjunctively, since he ends up speaking with his own voice to his own people in his own place and time. Two significantly different utterances, bracketing the last section of the poem, can actually stand for these two phases. Their difference is, in a sense, between slavish and free translation: "I come to speak through your dead mouth," the section opens, and it closes, "Speak through my words and my blood."

To speak for a voiceless people, the poet as translator must find out their real plight, the human dimension of their lives. He goes on questioning, summoning, and ultimately reaching out to a remote, silenced, enigmatic American community: "Stone upon stone, and man, where was he? / . . . Time upon time, and man, where was he?" (X). Neruda's archaeological imagination finds the Indian worker at Macchu Picchu as wretched as the poor today. He questions "buried America" about the inhabitant of such a city:

> Tell me how he slept while he lived.
> Tell me if his sleep
> was snoring, gaping like a black hole
> that weariness dug in the wall.   (X)

By the very force of its inquiry, Neruda's voice re-creates something forgotten: the mere human scale and the human cost of a great structure, a great civilization. In such a light, *Alturas de Macchu Picchu* becomes a poem that demands to be translated, especially in this country.

The ideal of translation, as George Steiner states it in *After Babel*, would be to "achieve an equilibrium . . . between two works, two languages, two communities of historical experience and contemporary feeling."[67] What might this mean in Neruda's case? Since the same wave of exploration reached North and South but left this country knowing little of the other America; and since the United States has involved itself politically and economically in Latin American nations for over a century; and since North American civilization has had its own human cost for an indigenous population, Neruda's vision of Macchu Picchu carries over in translation a likeness within its strangeness. The Spanish American's voice comes in English to sound, as we say, strangely like our own.

Yet it is not like what we have read before. Of course any poem confronts the reader with its strangeness, and this holds all the more for *Alturas de Macchu Picchu*, which discovers something new to North Americans (and to most Latin Americans too). Translation intensifies that strangeness, yoking two different languages along with their distinct cultures. Culturally, the separation between Latin America and the United States outweighs the closeness—despite the exchange of tourists and corporate executives for migrant workers and deposed dictators—and although their languages have borrowed from each other, they have not much crossbred. Translation, then, means acknowledging the other, recognizing likeness only within strangeness—surely the prime condition of joint survival between people or peoples. The challenge is to engage with a language, a poet, and a poem that land us in a foreign past and a foreign present among alien things: place names, plants, animals; people, their arts and dwellings, their hunger and death, all of which are strange to us. In translating, when two different poems envision a forgotten city, the place comes as if by parallax to take on a new depth.

As a translator of *Alturas de Macchu Picchu*, I recognize now a peculiar linguistic effect, at once an obligation and a privilege. For though I too act "as if," maintaining my own voice and place and time, I also anchor with Neruda and speak along with him in the poem's first person, saying "I." Once engaged that way, a translator can and must follow out the poet's vision, though in a different tongue.[68] Hearing *Yo vengo a hablar por vuestra boca muerta*, I am obliged to say "I come to speak through your dead mouth" (XII). The words from a "dead mouth" recur in the poet's voice, then in the translator's and the reader's voices as well, all of them sharing in the full circle of translation. Always sustaining a strangeness within each new likeness, the act of translation moves from a mute, obscured past to Neruda's Latin American cantos in 1945 to whatever prospect a contemporary North American version of the poem may have.

HOW DO A POEM'S ORIGINS INFLUENCE ITS TRANSLATION?

In continuing the process of translation begun by Neruda, I found that *Alturas de Macchu Picchu* concentrates and focuses much of his lifework, so that to arrive at a new verse translation means re-creating the larger genesis of the poem. The principle behind this book, which derives from my practice as a translator and shapes the chapters that follow, is twofold. It sees in translation both a critical and a creative task: first, to find by scholarly and analytic means how the poet came to write this work, and, second, to pursue the moment-by-moment crafting of a new version as consciously as possible.

The point of this opening chapter is to offer one person's fairly typical background with respect to Latin America and its major poet, to describe the history in English of Neruda's work, and to discuss certain questions—some familiar, some less so—that affect the translating of *Alturas de Macchu Picchu* or of any poem.

To see what shaped Neruda and thus what influences the translation of his poetry, I have to look, in Chapter Two, at the mood and ambience of his childhood, via the myths he developed about it in some hitherto untranslated autobiographical prose. A few basic experiences—the mournful rain, the damp earth, the teeming woods, the loss of his mother—gave rise to a yearning for nature and an erotic possessiveness that pervade his early love lyrics (1921–25) and will strongly color *Alturas de Macchu Picchu* as well.

The first major lyric from *Residencia en la tierra*, "Galope muerto" (1925), opens Chapter Three. Emerging at a critical moment for the poet and in a time of social unrest, Neruda's hard-earned grasp of mortal and vital forces makes for almost equally hard translating. What I call a "dynamic form" in nature and human experience later takes its most dramatic personal turn in "Entrada a la madera" ("Entrance into Wood," 1935) and becomes the principle acting within *Alturas de Macchu Picchu*.

The solitary, involuted spirit of *Residencia en la tierra* evolved slowly into the outspoken American voice of *Alturas de Macchu Picchu*. Chapter Four traces Neruda's path through the eventful decade between these works: from Spain in 1935 to García Lorca's death and the Spanish Civil War; the return home, where Neruda revived his consciousness of Chile's Araucanian Indian past; the World War years in Mexico, which broadened his American affiliations; the journey to Macchu Picchu and home again; the campaign for senator and other politically formative experiences in 1945. Almost all the pertinent material from these years has remained unearthed or untranslated. Providing it in English directly illuminates the task of translating Neruda's poem.

The heart of the book, Chapter Five, gives a close account of translating *Alturas de Macchu Picchu*. My translation was a process first, then a product, and even reporting on it has led me to better renderings and closer critical insights. This account necessarily brings out poetic, personal, and political concerns at work within Neruda's poem, and they may also have their aftermath in our own concerns, for the act of translating at its fullest remains in process for translator and reader alike.

Since a revealing study of Neruda could be written without

any attention given to the matter of translation, a book such as this one must justify its method, must come by its insights through a translator's considerations. While a critic can explain the way Neruda's voice tries to awaken dead workers at Macchu Picchu, the translator has a voice itself to find. So this book aims toward and closes with a verse translation: *Heights of Macchu Picchu*.

Chapter Two

THE EARTH OF A SON AND LOVER
(1904–1925)

MOTHER OF STONE AND SUNKEN BRIDE

Any work that answers to its author's essential concerns and shows as multifarious an imagery as *Alturas de Macchu Picchu* will bear more than one interpretation, depending on the lens a reader brings to it. From teaching the poem along with Eliot's *Four Quartets*, I know how generously both poems respond to a variety of readings. Neruda, more than Eliot, draws us in because he so clearly undertakes a quest:

> From the air to the air, like an empty net,
> I went on through streets and thin air,

his poem begins. The quest he undertakes can seem essentially personal, or poetic, or historical, or nationalist, or metaphysical, or mythic, or sexual. Each of these qualities will at one time or another color a translator's choices, and several of them may occur in any one word or image or line. In the poem as a whole, all the qualities interrelate. For the moment only, they are worth noting separately.

For Neruda personally, the hand-to-hand, voice-to-voice contact in *Alturas de Macchu Picchu* confirmed his passage out of an alienation and ineffectuality that had earlier beset him for a decade or so, particularly when he was alone in the Orient. He had been away from home during much of his twenties and thirties; this poem was his first major effort after he returned to Chile in 1943 and was elected senator. Poetically as well, a new self-confidence sounds through the voice that can say, "Give me your hand," "Tell me everything," "Speak through my words" (XII)—in effect, "Let me translate for you." By communing this way, by opening his verse to the dictates of people not heard from before, Neruda fulfills a kind of aesthetic responsibility, as he does also in refusing to let the architectural magnificence go unquestioned.

Neruda's historical imagination in *Alturas de Macchu Picchu* works to excavate a buried community, releasing from the "boundary of stone" (VI) a cluster of untold stories—stories of labor, fatigue, punishment, hunger, sleep—and carrying them across five hundred years into the Latin American present. This effort and its political overtones go along with Neruda's nationalist persuasion. Without specifying Peru, or Mexico or Chile either, the countries he knew best, his poem's very situation nonetheless insists on the value of one people living in one place over time. Neruda was not purely an Indianist; what mattered was that they were native Americans whom he had to reclaim at Macchu Picchu.

Another reading of the same imaginative effort, conditioned perhaps by *Four Quartets*, would find metaphysical and quasi-religious patterns in *Alturas de Macchu Picchu*. Within the coordinates of space and time, a speaker goes down "into the deepest waves" in order to climb "the ladder of the earth" (I, VI), and that movement creates another axis, from the past to a possible future. Though everything, "words, wine, bread, / is gone, fallen to earth" (VI), memory can redeem time's waste. The redeemer also figures in *Alturas de Macchu Picchu* as a mythic hero: he descends to fetch the dead from the earth that swallowed them, then rises up "with a branch of secret water" and with their message oracularly in his mouth (XI).

All these readings are equally germane. Another motive, more implicit perhaps, has its own kind of urgency: as a lover seeking fruition, as a son seeking maternal sustenance, and as a lover-son seeking entrance into and then birth from the native ground, the poet drives through canto after canto with an energy that seems as much sexual as anything else, an energy that animates other readings of the poem. *Alturas de Macchu Picchu* feels at times like a sexual odyssey, with one man plunging into the earth, searching vainly for some life-giving contact with humanity or nature, and then finding Macchu Picchu to be both a "mother of stone" and a "sunken bride" (VI, X). Her sons who lie imprisoned there worked until their death; so the poet must "scrape in the womb" and deliver his brothers "to be born" with him (X, XII).

If Neruda's other poetry, before and since, lacked any sexual configuration whatever, there might be less interest in construing *Alturas de Macchu Picchu* this way. The fact is, however, that his childhood in the humid, enveloping landscape of southern Chile was conditioned by forces that led him from adolescence on to compose his world and his poems as if his need for woman—the son embraced, the lover embracing—were intrinsic to all human experience. And this need for "woman" implied, as often as not, the exploiting of her, at least imaginatively.

What are the sources of Neruda's sexual imagination and how did it show up in his poetry? To perceive this inner motive of *Alturas de Macchu Picchu*, as translator or reader, means making a backward reconnaissance into Neruda's first years and then examining the early love lyrics. A sexual impulse originating in childhood persists throughout his varied and voluminous work, roughly fifty books that evolved steadily and markedly over as many years.

THE CHILDHOOD MATRIX

Neruda and his poetry came to seem bound, as if umbilically, to the rainy, forested, frontier region of Temuco, where his family moved in 1906 when he was two. During the second half of his life, he evolved his own genesis story by letting certain images and memories filter through in poems and in remarkable prose. There is no way to assess the factuality of that story, and no need to here, since his memories embody what interested Neruda most. From at least the age of sixteen he already had the habit of writing about his past, and a 1924 prose poem calls up the "Province of Childhood" with its shadowy woods, incessant rain, and mournful train whistles. To this *provincia*, which is both a place and a time, Neruda says: "Let it be you I go back to for refuge."[1]

It was not until the winter of 1938, though, when both his father and stepmother died, that he made his first extended autobiographical venture: "I belong to a piece of poor austral earth verging on Araucania," he wrote, calling Chile's southern provinces by their early Indian name,

my doings have been timed from far away, as if that wooded and perpetually rainy land held a secret of mine that I do not understand, that I ignore and must come to know, and that I search for desperately, blindly, examining long rivers, fantastic plant life, heaps of wood, the seas of the south, plunging myself into botany and the rain without ever reaching that precious spume that the waves lay down and break up, without reaching that span of special earth, without touching my true soil.[2]

This amazing sentence reveals a bent for prose composition that has gone virtually unnoticed in Neruda. Here the prose itself primes his act of memory. The wave-like rhythm of his phrases carries him back in time and space, each verb giving a further impetus: "I search . . . examining," "plunging . . . without reaching . . . without touching." Like the opening canto of *Alturas de Macchu Picchu*, this backward movement becomes a downward one into earth and sea. For Neruda, time past is a physical medium composed of *tierra, madera, vegetación, mares, olas, lluvia*, which all make up the landscape of this passage: earth, wood, plant life, seas, waves, rain.

In time as in earth and sea, life dissolves but it also regenerates; so Neruda seeks his origin by means of a verb that has strong positive connotations for him. *Hundir* can mean either "to sink" or "to plunge"; in translating *hundiéndome*, the reflexive form of the participle, I hear Neruda "plunging" himself into botany and the rain. The verb also recurs in *Alturas de Macchu Picchu*: the poet plunges his hand first into *lo más genital de lo terrestre*, "the genital quick of the earth" (I), to begin his quest, then into the wounds of people's everyday desperation (V), and finally into Macchu Picchu's "night of stone" to grasp the heart of the forgotten American (XI). All three kinds of encounter enact Neruda's basic desire to join himself to the world outside him—a desire expressed physically in the autobiographical passage. There, he says "I belong" to the southern earth and he searches it "desperately, blindly," much as a child seeks a secure embrace. Then he plunges into the rainy land to try and touch that "special earth . . . my true soil." This is Neruda's characteristic movement, and various autobiographical writings show the ways in which, as a child, he involved himself in his natural surroundings. The tone and texture of that early involvement seem to express a kind of filial sexuality, though it is important to add that the way I read—and the way Neruda wrote—his memories of childhood is influenced by the nature of his love poetry between 1921 and 1925.

At some deep, perhaps unconscious level, he assumed that a man, a poet such as himself, had to immerse in or take hold of raw, proliferating nature. The point is that long before he could identify his own impulses as sexual, or his surroundings as in any way the object of such impulses, Neruda slipped into that way of being and seeing. Behind everything else, southern Chile's long winters gave him damp, dense woods into which he often ventured, wanting to unite with them and to be embraced. Eventually the roles of child and lover fused vaguely in Neruda's early verse, possibly because the child's desire for warm parental response had spilled over into a diffuse erotic connection with the world outside his home. Given this incipient, implicit personification of the world outside, Neruda in his lyrics deals habitually with women as he deals with nature—territorially—and does so in imagery drawn from the region where he grew up.

From early on, his poetry began recurring to southern Chile as a place of origin, a physical refuge, and a source of renewal. Something of those motives made Neruda open *Alturas de Macchu Picchu* by going "back, as if blind, to the jasmine / of the exhausted human spring." The landscape where he grew up, the woods and hills and seashore only recently opened to settlement, seem actually to have been a profuse original paradise for Neruda. Not long before he died, he wrote a prose passage to open his memoirs, evoking "the tangled Chilean forest"—the giant bristling rauli trees, dripping ferns, penetrating scents of wild herbs, an enormous red spider, a golden beetle, butterflies, red copihues (a kind of bellflower), a decaying tree trunk encrusted with blue and black mushrooms.[3] The child encountered a natural world densely astir with plants and insects, especially when his father, a train conductor, took him into remote unsettled areas of Cautín province. "There, nature gave me a kind of *embriaguez*," Neruda says—*embriaguez* being intoxication, euphoria, rapture. "I was already a poet—not writing verses, but fascinated by birds, scarabs, partridge eggs. It was a miracle to find them in ravines, steely blue, dark and shining. . . . I gathered the 'snake's mothers'—a bizarre name given to the large coleopteron, black, glossy, and tough." A trainman brought him "white copihues, hairy spiders, ringdove nestlings, and once he found me the most dazzling of all, the coigüe and luma tree beetle . . . a streak of lightning dressed as a rainbow. Red and violet and green and yellow gleamed on its shell and like lightning it escaped my fingers and fled back into the forest."[4] Neruda's first world seems little removed from the South America that presented Darwin, Agassiz, Hudson, and other naturalists with countless exotic, unheard-of species. It was a pristine world, prodigal of everything a poet in the making could touch and, just as important, name. Like the gleaming beetle, though, that world sometimes threatened to remain out of reach, to evade his possession.

The environment of Neruda's childhood, rich with natural detail, was not always comfortable or benign. Life could be precarious, what with a flooding river, a nearby volcano, blowing rains, earth tremors, and frequent fires. Neruda describes one fire in an autobiographical memoir, "Childhood and Poetry" (1954), written as his fiftieth birthday approached. For twenty-two blocks "the houses burned like matchboxes," he says. "In possibly my earliest memory, I see myself sitting on some blankets opposite our house, which was burning for the second or third time."[5] The most telling memory in this talk shows the child's terrified response not to natural disaster but to nature's inherently alien and indifferent state. Neruda remembers being caught alone, at about age ten, in the pulsing envelope of the woods near his home. "Summer is scorching in Cautín," he begins, and he remembers it in the present tense:

I go out in the country in search of my poetry. I get lost around Ñielol hill. I am alone, my pocket filled with scarab beetles. In a box I have the hairy spider I just caught. Above me the sky is blocked out. The forest is always damp, I slip, suddenly a bird cries out, it is the weird cry of the chucao. It comes up from under my feet like a terrifying warning. The copihues, looking like drops of blood, are barely visible. I feel tiny as I pass under giant ferns. A ringdove flies by my mouth with a dry sound of wings. Overhead other birds are mocking me with harsh laughs. I can hardly find my way.[6]

This is memory metamorphosing into a nightmare of panic in a lonely place. In looking back to this profuse, luxuriant landscape, Neruda sees a child lost amid nature's casual excrescences. Desolate, he sees things as blocked, weird, warning, bloodlike, giant, mocking, harsh. The Ñielol hill incident continues suggestively. Returning home late, the boy finds his father absent, goes up to his room, reads a romantic travel book, and then "rain pours down like a cataract. In a moment, night and rain are covering the world. I am alone there and writing poetry in my arithmetic book."[7] The next morning he goes out early, climbs a tree and gorges on unripe plums. Neruda makes no comment on this episode, but the end makes it sound like the lost child's attempt somehow to regain physical, sensual possession of the swarming world around him.

One fact lies squarely behind this feeling of loneliness. Neruda's mother, only two months after he was born in the town of Parral, died of tuberculosis—without, as he later put it, his ever seeing her face.[8] At that time the only child, he was left for two or three years with his father's stepmother, until his father remarried and brought him south to Temuco. The sense of deprivation never left Neruda, and he regularly referred to his childhood self as *perdido*, "lost." Some verses he wrote for his sixtieth birthday, "The Austral Earth," recall how in

the gloom of the woods,
heading nowhere, and
so small, loaded with spoil,
with fruits, with feathers,
I go along lost
in the darkest
core of the green . . .
I am alone
in the natal forest.[9]

The word "core" loses a little of Neruda's *entraña*, which means "entrail" but also suggests kindheartedness. And in translating from Blake, Neruda once used *entraña* for "womb," but I am not sure he feels it just that way here.[10]

What can a child, told that his mother died after giving birth to him, make of this peculiarly invisible loss? In a poem written when he was sixteen, Neruda takes on the *tristesse* of a posthumous child:

She died. And I was born. . . .
She grafted the barren branch
of her sick life onto my new life.
The ivory of her dying hands
turned the full moon yellow in me.[11]

In a much later poem, called "Birth," the sorrow is tempered as he recalls

the cemetery where
they brought me
to see my mother
sleeping among the tombs . . .
I called across the dead to see her,
. . . she answered nothing,
and stayed there alone, without her son,
shy and elusive
in the shadows.[12]

Here he projects his own loss onto her. In his prose memoir "Childhood and Poetry," the three sentences devoted to her suggest that he identified his mother not only with his loneliness but with his early vocation as well: "There was a portrait of my mother, dead in Parral a little after I was born. She was a lady dressed in black, slender and pensive. They told me she wrote verses, but I never saw anything of her, only that handsome portrait." A few pages later he reflects, "What solitude, that of a small boy poet dressed in black, on the wide-open terrifying frontier."[13]

Much of Neruda's most compelling poetry stems from an acute sense of loss and deprivation. In the early cantos of *Alturas de Macchu Picchu,* "my outstretched hand" and "my streaming hands" find no response (II, IV), though in nature's fruitful exchanges, "flower to flower gives up the high seed" (II). The poet overcomes his solitude by climbing "through the lost jungle" up to Macchu Picchu (VI). Similarly, in the picture we get of Neruda's childhood and adolescence, he seeks his mother or his mistress in nature, projecting his state of mind onto vibrant natural scenes of decay and regeneration. In that way a poem such as "The Frontier" can take hold of deprivation and even redeem it:

> The first thing I saw was trees, ravines
> decked in wildly gorgeous flowers,
> watersoaked land, woods that took fire
> and winter pouring out behind the world.
> My childhood is damp shoes, broken tree trunks
> down in the forest, eaten away by liana
> and beetles, sweet days among the oats,
> and my father's golden beard going forth
> to the grandeur of the railways.
> In front of my house the southern water cut
> deep tracks, marshes of mourning clay
> that in summer made a yellow space
> where the carts would creak and moan,
> pregnant with nine months' wheat.[14]

From fire to winter pouring out, from broken tree trunks to beetles and oats, from mourning clay to pregnant carts, nature gave him what he felt his mother might have: an enveloping, emphatic body of sensuous experience, perishable and nutritive by turns. Neruda evolved the image of maternal nature on his own; he did not need Inca or other Amerindian mythologies to personify the fecund, changeful earth as a mother, a giver and reclaimer of life.[15] And for him, that image was more than metaphor.

From Neruda's autobiographical poems a contrasting parental image also emerges: a "hard," "brusque" father, Don José del Carmen Reyes, whom the child (who was born Ricardo Eliecer Neftalí Reyes Basoalto) regarded with ambivalence. Neruda remembers his father, at 3 A.M. after work, barging into the house with a gust of wind, leaving "frightened doors / banging like sharp / pistol shots" and "the wind fighting the rain."[16] Clearly his father's presence could violate both the home and the natural scene. Don José had already worked at farming and on the dikes, jobs that displayed some mastery over nature. Then with his "golden beard going forth / to the grandeur of the railways," opening up the "virgin forest," quarrying ballast to secure the tracks against heavy rain, he appeared now heroic, now tyrannic to a "sickly and weak" child, as the poet once described himself.[17]

Neruda's father and stepmother appear, by his own quite revealing account, to have had a traditional, provincial, turn-of-the-century marriage. He recalls his stepmother as a selfless woman, who "as soon as my father came in, just turned into a quiet shadow, like all the women of that time and place."[18] He also recalls her gentle, beneficent maternal care, but recognizes that it had its cost: "life made you bread / so we consumed you, / winter after desolate winter."[19] Evidently Neruda's feeling for his stepmother, like that for his mother, became diffused in the long, rain-filled winters of childhood.

Where the Rain Is Born, he called the first part of his 1964 autobiography.[20] The title, like many other instances throughout his writing, associates rain with the climate of infancy and with germinal nature. Given that association, one brief image of his father from *Where the Rain Is Born* says a great deal:

in the night
we recognized
his engine's
whistle
piercing the rain.[21]

Don José and his train forced their way through the matrix of rain and woods in which Neruda habitually immersed himself, and insofar as that landscape nourished the boy's poetry, his father tended to have a contrary effect. This was not in any case a man to favor his older son's making verses. "I've been asked many times," Neruda writes in his memoirs, "when my poetry came to be born." He then tells about setting down some emotional verses dedicated to the stepmother "whose soft shade protected all my childhood," and showing them timidly to his parents. His father took the paper, read it carelessly, and said "Where did you copy this?"[22] With time, as the boy continued writing, his father liked it less and less, and is said by Neruda's aunt to have whipped him for poetizing instead of heading toward a genteel, middle-class profession. The son needed a publishing pseudonym to avoid his father's notice, and at the age of sixteen he sealed his vocation as a poet by rejecting his father's name.[23] In an early notebook, a poem called "Man" appears with the signature "Pablo Neruda as of October 1920."[24]

His father's peremptory force, his stepmother's self-effacement, and the raw frontier atmosphere all bred themselves into Neruda's makeup. One particular childhood incident, which stuck in his memory, combines most of these elements: a half-savage *rite de passage* that brought some trauma to his sexual self-identification. Just after Neruda's father and stepmother died in 1938, he wrote an intense, highly suggestive piece of prose, a meditative memory called "The Cup of Blood," which opens with a long sentence about plunging toward the secret of his "true soil." He remembers as a child hearing "the night train pull in violently at timber or coal stops," and feeling "diminished and schoolboyish" with "the great damp woods of the south of the world against my heart." One winter day he is brought by some uncles into a raucous feast of roast lamb. As usual he is wearing "black, with a poet's tie" (and as a second version of the incident says, "in severe mourning, mourning for nobody, for the rain, for universal grief").[25] "My uncles are all gathered there, they are all immense," singing and drinking. "Then they cut open the throat of a trembling lamb and put a cup of searing hot blood to my mouth, amid gunshots and songs, and I feel agony like the lamb's, and I too want to become a centaur, and pale, wavering, lost in the midst of a forsaken childhood, I raise and drink the cup of blood." In this account, as compelling as any prose Neruda wrote, the coming of age seems desirable yet fearful if it is to bring him among such violent men. When he told the story a second time, Neruda added ironically, "One must learn to be a man."[26] Deeper than irony, this memory shows how steeped the grown man was in the scenes of his childhood struggle for sexual and imaginative autonomy.

THE EARLY LOVE POEMS (1921–25)

Kindred impulses moved Neruda toward nature and toward sex, and out of those encounters came his early poetry. As he said in explaining the ritual his uncles put him through, "emanations from the strong virgin earth permeated the blood" of everyone living in the south.[27] That *fuerte tierra virgen* attracted him to "go out in the country in search of my poetry"; that is, to locate both the source and the subject of his poetry in places such as the damp woods on Ñielol hill.[28]

Throughout Neruda's early work, imagery from his childhood in southern Chile enlivens and materializes every poem. That imagery has essentially—perhaps inevitably—two sources, earth and sea, the same elements into which he descends at the start of *Alturas de Macchu Picchu*. "I began to write from a vegetal impulse," he says, and at least in retrospect, Neruda takes that impulse quite literally. "My first contact with the grandeur of things was my dreams of moss, my long vigils on the humus" that "covers all the woods in my natal region" and "sprouts the forest's unique vegetative voice."[29] More than anything else, wood inspired him, as standing or fallen trees or fresh-cut timber. He even remembers writing verses on wooden walls: "They tempted me because the boards were smooth as paper, with mysterious veins."[30] Along with that material inspiration, the other inevitable presence around Temuco was the rain, and later in life he used to say he couldn't write without thinking intensely of the beat of rain on the roof.[31]

When he wrote, he said, he also remembered another sound from childhood—that of waves breaking on the sand.[32] If Neruda got his first contact with the grandeur of things from the germinal forest, his second came from the Pacific littoral, where his family spent part of its summers in a small settlement at the mouth of a river. He remembers going downriver by paddleboat and first hearing "a far-off commotion": "the wave swell was entering my life."[33] Neruda has left impressions of surf, waves, and sea all through fifty years of writing (his home from 1939 on, at Isla Negra in central Chile, overlooked the ocean). Probably the earliest impression is a prose poem written when he was eighteen:

Today at evening, high tide filling the river with its slow invasive wave, I rowed till I was exhausted. . . . This sea is clamorous and magnificent. On the beach it breaks, bursts, rises, reaches to the limit with its last waves licking the luminous sands. But in the center far away, it is pure and serene, and rounded like a mother's belly.[34]

The surf, like the woods, could show beauty but also an overwhelming wildness, and it helped to think of some central serenity, "a mother's belly," behind the clamor. Neruda closed the passage with an imperious notion of waves kissing his feet "like slave girls bearing their country's finest fruits."

Shortly after writing this prose poem he began "Beach in the South" with a threatening sexual metaphor:

> The sea's teeth tear
> at the open flesh of the coast
> where green water dashes
> against the silent land. . . .
>
> Scattered sea wind,
> keep on kissing my face.

> Drag me, sea wind,
> where no one awaits me.[35]

At the end of this poem, biting salt and spume "wipe out my last steps." Clearly the sea is not supine and inviting but immensely forceful and at times alien. His sense of the sea corroborated a feeling that Neruda when young also had about women: in embodying something deep and unknown, they might embrace and enclose but could also overwhelm him. If the inland rain gave him melancholy winters and prolific summers to immerse himself in, the ocean could seem abundant or else display a very different nature: a consuming force like night or time or death, which it would take two decades for Neruda to build into his poetry.[36]

Neruda's early lyrics are more exuberant when he likens the earth to woman than when he sees the ocean as female. Soon after arriving in Santiago in 1921, not quite seventeen years old, he took first prize for a poem to open the spring festival of the Chilean Students Federation. Some of Neruda's gallantry in "The Song of the Festival" can be suggested in English:

> This day the ripe earth sways
> with tremor, dust, and gale,
> our young souls run full-blown
> in the wind like boats under sail. . . .
>
> The night's feast trembles, bursts,
> her coach drawn through the street,
> a naked goddess bright
> with her yellow crown of wheat.[37]

From then on, what Neruda came to call his "pact" or "communication" or "unending bond" with the earth required metaphors that made woman terrestrial and the earth female.[38]

His first book, *Crepusculario* ("Twilight Book," 1923), made a clear profession: "My voice will be that of a sower singing / as into the furrow he throws seeds of ardent flesh."[39] By the age of twenty, then, in "torrents and rivers of amorous verses," Neruda was seeking his identity as an artist through his yearning for an earthbound woman.[40] A collection of some of his most fervent and florid verses bore the title *El hondero entusiasta* ("The Slingshot Enthusiast"), which indicates Neruda's disposition toward the looming world: "I throb and my slings resound. . . . / The fervent stones make night give birth."[41] He wrote these poems "on an extraordinarily quiet summer night in Temuco," gazing out his second-story window at "a river and a cataract of stars that seemed to be in motion."[42] More often than not, Neruda as lover reaches out to the universe by way of his beloved.* "Flower of my soul. Terrain of my kisses," he calls her,

> Quick water slipping its murmur through my fingers.
> Blue and winged like birds and mist.
> My nostalgia, my thirst, my desire, my fright
>   gave birth to you.
> And you burst in my arms like fruit from flowers.[43]

His tenuous control of her gives way to anxiety in the third line, leading the poet to arrogate her creative powers to himself. One of the most striking lyrics from *El hondero entusiasta* begins with a terrifying oceanic figure and then an earthy one in quick succession:

> It's like a tide, when she spikes me
> with her mourning eyes,
> when I feel her body's mobile white clay
> stretching and throbbing next to mine.[44]

Some poems from *El hondero entusiasta* were those first translated into English in 1934.[45] Neruda's metaphors, his fast and loose exchanges between the world's body and woman's body, must have seemed fairly raw and wild alongside, say, the sonnets of Edna St. Vincent Millay or E. E. Cummings.

Beneath the perfervid eroticism of Neruda's lyrics in late ado-

---

*Neruda took two lines (in Spanish translation) from Whitman's "Starting from Paumanok," 6, as an epigraph for *El hondero entusiasta*: "And I will make the poems of my body and of mortality, / For I think I shall then supply myself with the poems of my soul and of immortality." In *Claridad*, 86 (May 5, 1923), Neruda had reviewed Arturo Torres-Ríoseco's *Walt Whitman* (1922), which quotes the lines.

lescence runs the less conventional motif of a *niño perdido*, a lost or abandoned child. In one poem, written at eighteen but left unpublished, he imagines his girlfriend's death: "They will close your eyes, they will join your hands / as they joined my mother's when she died."[46] A little later, when their relationship seems to be ending, he asks in a letter whether she doesn't "grieve a little for this abandoned child who loves you?"[47] In a plaintive lyric from the same period, "With Open Arms": "I search in the dark for you like a lost child."[48] Neruda's quasi-orphanhood adds its own tinge to the familiar male transference from mother to lover. A poem called "Love," in *Crepusculario*, begins: "Woman, I should have been your son to drink / milk from your breasts as from a spring."[49]

In a number of dramatic passages from Neruda's poetry around 1923, he is still oscillating between images of a mother and a lover, still unsure what relation he has to "woman" and to the world she embodies. His sexual stance can go from forceful to recumbent, confident to fearful. The wind combs his hair "like a maternal hand," but the farm girl's breasts are "two sour and blind seeds."[50] Neruda has not staked out a fixed, one-sided role for himself: at one point in *El hondero entusiasta* he will say to his partner, "I receive you / as the furrow does the seed," and then two poems later call her "furrow for the troubled seed of my name."[51] Poem seven in the book closes with a euphonious and typically ambivalent image: *Las arañas oscuras del pubis en reposo*, "The dark spiders of the pubis at rest."[52] Considering how avidly Neruda used to collect spiders for their beauty, the notion of being caught by a spider-like pubis may not be uppermost here. Then poem eight addresses his woman more turbulently:

> Fill yourself with me.
> Desire me, drain me, pour me out, sacrifice me.
> Beg me, gather me, hold me in, hide me.[53]

Though not the finest lines from this period, they show why Neruda's love poems make him a compelling voice: he lets the mixed, conflicted nature of human passion break out with unmediated honesty. Here it is his pleading we hear, his need to be at one with life around him, even submissively—but that pleading, that submissiveness, come as imperious commands.

The *Veinte poemas de amor y una canción desesperada* ("Twenty Poems of Love and a Desperate Song," 1924), destined to go through scores of editions as a Latin American lover's breviary, are firmer than the earlier lyrics, though Neruda is no less struck by the terrestrial presence in woman.[54] *Ah, las rosas del pubis!*, he cries in poem one. The poet writes how "My rough peasant's body digs in you / and makes a son leap from under earth."[55] (This "rough peasant" was studying French in Santiago at the time; maybe the hyperbole marks his nostalgia for Temuco's vibrant natural scene.) Sometimes he yokes his girlfriend to nature by means of a simile ("your hands as soft as grapes"), but more often, with something like primitive magic, Neruda's image fuses her with nature in a metaphorical identity: she "is" the twilight, the rivers sing "in her."[56] Poem one opens by asserting an absolute identity, and then in the second line a similarity, between woman and the earth:

> *Cuerpo de mujer, blancas colinas, muslos blancos,*
> *te pareces al mundo en tu actitud de entrega.*

Here is W. S. Merwin's version:

> Body of a woman, white hills, white thighs,
> you look like a world, lying in surrender.[57]

Neruda's lines set the tone for the entire book. At such times, translation can make the difference between reporting and recreating what happens in the original: to choose the English possessive "Woman's body," as another translator does, forgoes the main chance of the poem.[58] Neruda puts the body first, then the woman. Taking him at his word means repeating the shock of that priority. I think "Body of woman," more archaic-sounding than Merwin's "Body of a woman," bears out Neruda's archetypal and unitary view of the sex.

The absoluteness, the bravado, of *Cuerpo de mujer, blancas colinas, muslos blancos*, lies precisely in the silence of its commas— in their not supplying the polite signs of simile or metaphor to justify identifying woman and nature. That effect comes through clearly in translation. Then there is another, subtler touch to the first line. Both hills and thighs can be white—that much is evident. But Neruda, by inverting the normal Spanish noun-adjective order in *blancas colinas*, intensifies his rhythm and also links hills to thighs in a way that the translator could do only by inverting the next phrase—"white hills, thighs white." But (as Merwin realized) the normal English order sounds best here:

> Body of woman, white hills, white thighs,
> you look like the world, spread out in surrender.

And it is not just "a" world, as Merwin has it, but "the" world, so as not to loosen Neruda's erotic grasp on the whole of his experience. For *Veinte poemas de amor* is as much a poet's as a lover's manual. It advances a young man's fantasies about both his imaginative and his amorous hold on life. "To outlive myself I forged you like a sword," he tells the woman, or says, "You're caught in the net of my music," realizing himself as victorious lover and poet at once.[59]

These poems can be earthy, sensual, stirring, verbally and rhythmically fascinating in ways that show why Latin American couples still recite them to each other:

> *He ido marcando con cruces de fuego*
> *el atlas blanco de tu cuerpo.*
> *Mi boca era una araña que cruzaba escondiéndose.*

> I have gone marking crosses of fire
> on the white atlas of your body.
> My mouth was a spider scuttling secretly.[60]

Julio Cortázar remembers the impact of the *Veinte poemas de amor* on Buenos Aires youth, who were "young pumas eager to bite into the heart of a deep and secret life" but were languishing under the spell of Mallarmé and the Nicaraguan Rubén Darío. "Few people knew of Pablo Neruda, that poet who suddenly gave us back what was ours, tore us away from vague notions of

European muses and mistresses to throw us into the arms of an immediate tangible woman, and teach us that a Latin American poet's love could happen *hic et nunc* and be written that way."[61] Cortázar's excitement is instructive, in its tacit equation of Latin Americans with "us" men. He also gratefully remembers "Eve speaking Spanish" in Neruda's poems, but not for a moment was she doing the speaking in *Veinte poemas de amor.* The voice is Neruda's, addressing his woman as if she were the predetermined landscape of a man's visionary quest: "In my barren land you are the last rose."[62]

In the love poems written immediately after *Veinte poemas de amor*, Neruda's view has not changed much. "The color of poppies sits on your brow," he says in "Serenata" ("Serenade," 1925), and "sweet toads rush trembling from your footsteps."[63] In "Juntos nosotros" ("Ourselves Together"), the lost child now sees himself more firmly—"my brow, thrusting like blows or roads, / my skin of a grown son ready for the plow"—and his beloved more raptly:

> light finds its bed under your eyes' full lids
> as gold as oxen, and often plump doves
> build their white nests in you.[64]

Under the conditions Neruda lays down, what is a woman to do? With poppies on her brow, toads at her feet, oxen in her eyes, and doves building nests in her, she isn't likely to do much or get anywhere at all. Or if her own erotic vision were as prescriptive as his, these poems of Neruda's would be met head-on and stymied.

A North American in the 1980's need not accept what Neruda's poems express about sexuality. The question becomes acute for translators because their selection of poems largely governs a poet's image abroad. Should they refrain from choosing poems that go against their grain in one way or another? My own situation here is peculiar. I enjoy the challenge of finding rhymes and a tone for Neruda's youthful "Song of the Festival," and the possibilities of *Cuerpo de mujer, blancas colinas, muslos blancos*, fascinate me. But at the same time, the sexual posture of Neruda's early love poems (and his later ones as well) makes me feel strange in translating them, however beautifully they may express the mores of his place and time. It must also be said that I have translated only parts of the early poems, and am aware that *Veinte poemas de amor* and *Crepusculario* have more to them than the sexual configurations highlighted here. I stress the erotic, earth-seeking impulse in Neruda's poetry because it seems so deeply rooted in his childhood, and because his image of himself as both son and lover lies at the heart of his quest in *Alturas de Macchu Picchu*.

Chapter Three

DYNAMIC FORM

(1925–1935)

THE BREAKTHROUGH OF "GALOPE MUERTO"

A year after the *Veinte poemas de amor* appeared, Neruda composed a poem reaching far beyond them, setting himself a perceptual task to which he would be answerable for decades. "Galope muerto" ("Dead Gallop") starts in blindly, as if something impelled the poet into a strange element, and then finds its way as it goes, incorporating open questions and dark hints and hard choices, edging line by line toward clarification. In its intensity the poem seems a matter of life or death: it does what any lyric has to do—render a region of experience accessible to the imagination—yet it does so more drastically than usual and more explicitly. Though Pablo Neruda wrote "Galope muerto" in 1925, his inquiring force in that poem carried through twenty years to the heart of *Alturas de Macchu Picchu* and beyond.[1]

In a way, the opening two lines of "Galope muerto" hold the seed of the later poem's basic questions and contradictions:

> *Como cenizas, como mares poblándose,*
> *en la sumergida lentitud, en lo informe.*

> Like ashes, like oceans swarming,
> in the sunken slowness, in what's unformed.

Is it ashes or swarming oceans, death or new life, to be found at Macchu Picchu? The identity of such a place will depend on how the poet goes about finding his way there. The second line of "Galope muerto" suggests an element or dimension whose strangeness can be expressed only through paradox—"sunken slowness"—and negation—"what's unformed." How can "sunken," an adjective of space, modify "slowness," which has to do with time? What's more, the space is not accessible but sunken, the time not current but slowed, like the overgrown, forgotten Inca site. Then *lo informe* ("what's unformed") negates any assurance that one is entering a familiar, structured, completed world. On the contrary, this is a space and time in which things have not quite and not yet taken final shape: an amorphous, inchoate life such as Neruda discovered at Macchu Picchu. It is not that "Galope muerto" constitutes some uncanny presentiment, twenty years before the fact. Yet I am suggesting that its five short stanzas explore the very dimension in which Neruda would eventually come upon Macchu Picchu: the *sumergida lentitud* or "sunken slowness" from which the city's builders would arise. (The word *sumergida* also occurs at two crucial moments in *Alturas de Macchu Picchu*, in Cantos IX and XI.) And I know that translating "Galope muerto" acts as training for the later, more wide-ranging poem.

Already in its urgent opening lines, "Galope muerto" has the marks of a path-breaking imaginative effort. It is the earliest piece of writing for what ultimately became the first book of *Residencia en la tierra* ("Residence on Earth," 1933), though by then the poem had awaited book publication far longer than Neruda thought proper.[2] "Galope muerto" first came out in a 1925 issue of *Claridad*, the Chilean Students Federation magazine in which his lusty, adolescent "Song of the Festival" had appeared four years earlier.[3] Soon after leaving Chile for the Orient in 1927, Neruda began putting "Galope muerto" and other poems into book form. The Spanish poet Rafael Alberti enthusiastically showed them around Madrid and Paris, but no publisher could be found.[4] Then in 1930, Ortega y Gasset printed "Galope muerto" and two other poems in Madrid's *Revista de Occidente*.[5] They were noticed, oddly enough, in T. S. Eliot's magazine, *Criterion*, thus giving English speakers their first news of Neruda. The reviewer regretted certain "problems of versification and interpretation," though these were "made more palatable by the beautiful language," and he compared "Galope muerto" to Rimbaud's "Bateau ivre"—perhaps because Neruda's exploratory lines seemed to him unruly.[6]

Neruda, however, knew he had come into his own. Just after "Galope muerto" came out in Spain, he wrote to a friend that it was "the most serious and accomplished thing I have done"—a notable admission, for since the poem's appearance in Santiago, he had been writing intensely in the same vein for five years.[7] Clearly Neruda valued this poem as the keynote of his work: when *Residencia en la tierra* was finally published in 1933, in a limited edition of a hundred copies, he placed "Galope muerto" at the head of the book. And years later he recalled this poem as one that "showed me the domain of my personality. With great clearness I found myself taking hold of ground that was unquestionably mine."[8] Or, in Neruda's words, *llegaba a poseer un territorio indiscutiblemente mío*. This notion of "possessing" his own "territory" always came naturally to him. But the love poems, appropriating an earthbound woman, do not show the hard-earned vision of things that "Galope muerto" does. As the poem's opening makes clear, Neruda cannot shape his consciousness after nature simply by summoning some metaphorical figure of woman lying ready like the earth.

"Like ashes, like oceans swarming," the poem begins abruptly, trying out two very different similes to envision something as yet obscure. But the opening lines move toward a close that never occurs. The sentence, the analogy, remain incomplete, the insights unanchored:

> Like ashes, like oceans swarming,
> in the sunken slowness, in what's unformed,
> or like high on the road hearing
> bellstrokes cross by crosswise,
> holding that sound just free of the metal,
> blurred, bearing down, reducing to dust
> in the selfsame mill of forms far out of reach,
> whether remembered or never seen,
> and the aroma of plums rolling to earth
> that rot in time, endlessly green.

Through similes and surmise the lines unfold so that we keep groping for their true subject, as we do in riddles that give the traits of a thing ("What sounds like bells but can turn to dust?") and leave us to divine the thing itself. Until the end, it feels as though an answer might come, but that final image of plums rolls off even further into the welter of a world that bears witness to something, if only we knew what.

No other poem by Neruda has elicited the fascinated uncertainty that "Galope muerto" has. For half a century its readers have sensed the crucial undertaking in it, but have not always known whether or how that undertaking succeeded. The poem's obscurity has made it less accessible than other lyrics in *Residencia en la tierra*, and its unaccountable imagery and syntax have scared off translators. Of the two previous English versions, one is to my ear too literal, the other mechanical and inaccurate.[9] As a translator I am particularly drawn to this poem. Because "Galope muerto" makes its way experimentally, the act of translating it bears a special kinship to the original poem. Of course any job of translation proceeds experimentally, trying whatever word, image, phrase, sound, or rhythm will take the new version where it needs to go. That is, the translator is moving toward, rather than departing from, a comprehension of the original poem. But when the original itself sounds as though Neruda were translating from inchoate, unworded notions into a form of verbal comprehension, then his translator will have a similar mimesis to go through. To compose the poem called "Dead Gallop" is to follow Neruda on the way to whatever reality "Galope muerto" was after. For a while, the translator can experience that "radical mutation of our deepest speech" which Julio Cortázar recognized in *Residencia en la tierra* and which enabled Neruda to enter an otherwise impenetrable world.[10]

INFLUENCES ON THE POEM

The world manifested by Neruda's "Galope muerto" is uncertain and in flux, like his inner state and like society around him at the time. Before examining the poem's text and translation, we can sketch in some of the personal, social, and literary circumstances of its writing. In all these circumstances, Neruda felt an obsolete regime being sloughed off without a new one firmly in place.

He composed these dense, dynamic verses in 1925, at a crucial stage both in his own life and in Chile's modern development. Four years earlier, as an adolescent, he had come north to the capital from the familiar, provincial atmosphere of Temuco. In Santiago he entered the university to study French, which implied a genteel career as a teacher. But he was writing for *Claridad* and other magazines, and the study of French exposed him to European symbolist and early surrealist currents.[11] Sooner or later, Santiago's bohemian milieu, mingling poetry, journalism, and politics, would show Neruda that his vocation was not to teach high school French. In 1924, at the age of twenty, he dropped out—or rather plunged into mid-current—to make it as a writer alone.

This was a critical season for him, both financially and personally. When the poet gave up his studies, his father cut off the monthly allowance, leaving him in penury. He wrote to his sister that year: "If you only knew how forsaken I am and sick of everything."[12] Though Neruda had captivated Santiago's student population with the *Veinte poemas de amor y una canción desesperada* (1924), a friend remembers him "anguished and confused" in early 1925; "his spirit was going in circles, trying to find itself."[13] Until then his poetry, in *Crepusculario, El hondero entusiasta*, and *Veinte poemas de amor*, had been either melancholy or exalted. His next work, "Galope muerto," was to take a more exploratory path.

Chile's condition was also critical when Neruda arrived in the capital in 1921.[14] The country had undergone a decade of social unrest, severe economic depression, and military reprisal against hundreds of strikes. A student leader had just been tortured to death, and seventy thousand people had marched in the funeral. University students were sharply at odds with Chile's ruling circles and were beginning to make common cause with the workers; Neruda recalls being beaten by police in the streets.[15] A charismatic new leader, Arturo Alessandri, had urged reform; with the backing of an emerging proletariat and an intellectual middle class, his supporters had just dislodged the dominant oligarchy. But the depression worsened and Alessandri's economic reforms made no headway. In September 1924 the military seized control, and Neruda joined in a student protest against the coup. Three months later Luis Emilio Recabarren committed suicide; a publicist and founder of the socialist movement, he had been a hero of Neruda's. Then in January 1925 the junta was overthrown, and Alessandri returned to power two months later. All these events are reflected in *Claridad*, a "labor-anarchist" student magazine, as Neruda called it.[16] He had experienced national upheaval at a time when his own evolving imagination was bringing him to a critical pass. Early in 1925 he wrote "Galope muerto."

Where did Neruda find the poetic means to get his state of mind into verse? To some extent he was influenced or at least unloosened by the avant-garde aesthetic tendencies of the time.[17] Beginning his career during an open season on poetic conventions, he was alert to the breakthroughs of dadaism, creationism, ultraism, and surrealism. The early twenties for him were a time when "all the isms" were "fluttering over Santiago. . . . Reverdy's influence reached Ahumada Street. I read everything as soon as I could. But I resisted it."[18] Pierre Reverdy had joined with the Chilean Vicente Huidobro in initiating Creationism, which held that poets should transform nature by creating their own realities. For Neruda, Huidobro's writing had a "dexterity" that made it an impossible model for him. He saw Huidobro's work as "playful, crystalline," in contrast with one of his own poems of 1925, *Tentativa del hombre infinito* ("Venture of the Infinite Man"), which he said came "from the darkness of one who goes step by step encountering obstacles with which he shapes his path."[19]

That poem is Neruda's closest approach to surrealist writing: an unorganized, unpunctuated sequence of striking utterances dredged from the subconscious. Critics have also called "Galope muerto" surrealist, but it does not exhibit the calculated unreality called for in the surrealist program; indeed there is nothing programmatic about the poem, as there is about much avant-garde writing of the time. Whereas *Tentativa del hombre infinito* shows Neruda using the surrealist dispensation to stake out new poetic ground, "Galope muerto" shows him working that claim according to his own instincts.

Perhaps some kinship existed with César Vallejo, although Neruda would not have seen *Trilce* by 1925.[20] Evidently Vallejo felt a kinship, for in a later series of notes on romanticism, dada-

GALOPE MUERTO

Como cenizas, como mares poblándose,
en la sumergida lentitud, en lo informe,
o como se oyen desde el alto de los caminos
cruzar las campanadas en cruz,
teniendo ese sonido ya aparte del metal,
confuso, pesando, haciéndose polvo
en el mismo molino de las formas demasiado lejos,
o recordadas o no vistas,
y el perfume de las ciruelas que rodando a tierra
se pudren en el tiempo, infinitamente verdes.

Aquello todo tan rápido, tan viviente,
inmóvil sin embargo, como la polea loca en sí misma,
esas ruedas de los motores, en fin.
Existiendo como las puntadas secas en las costuras del árbol,
callado, por alrededor, de tal modo,
mezclando todos los limbos sus colas.
Es que de dónde, por dónde, en qué orilla?
El rodeo constante, incierto, tan mudo,
como las lilas alrededor del convento,
o la llegada de la muerte a la lengua del buey
que cae a tumbos, guardabajo, y cuyos cuernos quieren
        sonar.

ism, and surrealism, he brackets himself and Neruda as the only practitioners of what he calls *Verdadismo*, "Truthism."[21] Vallejo must have felt that he and Neruda were engaged in a task for which no familiar poetic mode was adequate. At most, the avant-garde movements confirmed Neruda's sense of a new reality that included not only the world's phenomena but the mind's potential to grasp them. "Galope muerto" is Neruda's first attempt to embody—or rather, to enact—such a reality in verse.

DEAD GALLOP

Like ashes, like oceans swarming,
in the sunken slowness, in what's unformed,
or like high on the road hearing
bellstrokes cross by crosswise,
holding that sound just free of the metal,
blurred, bearing down, reducing to dust
in the selfsame mill of forms far out of reach,
whether remembered or never seen,
and the aroma of plums rolling to earth
that rot in time, endlessly green.

All of it so quick, so livening,
immobile though, like a pulley idling on itself,
those wheels that motors have, in short.
Existing like dry stitches in the seams of trees,
silenced, encircling, in such a way,
all the planets splicing their tails.
Then from where, which way, on what shore?
The ceaseless whirl, uncertain, so still,
like lilacs around the convent,
or death as it gets to the tongue of an ox
who stumbles down unguarded, and whose horns want to
    sound.

Por eso, en lo inmóvil, deteniéndose, percibir,
entonces, como aleteo inmenso, encima,
como abejas muertas o números,
ay, lo que mi corazón pálido no puede abarcar,
en multitudes, en lágrimas saliendo apenas,
y esfuerzos humanos, tormentas,
acciones negras descubiertas de repente
como hielos, desorden vasto,
oceánico, para mí que entro cantando,
como con una espada entre indefensos.

Ahora bien, de qué está hecho ese surgir de palomas
que hay entre la noche y el tiempo, como una barranca húmeda?
Ese sonido ya tan largo
que cae listando de piedras los caminos,
más bien, cuando sólo una hora
crece de improviso, extendiéndose sin tregua.

Adentro del anillo del verano
una vez los grandes zapallos escuchan,
estirando sus plantas conmovedoras,
de eso, de lo que solicitándose mucho,
de lo lleno, oscuros de pesadas gotas.[22]

That's why, in what's immobile, holding still, to perceive
then, like great wingbeats, overhead,
like dead bees or numbers,
oh all that my spent heart can't embrace,
in crowds, in half-shed tears,
and human toiling, turbulence,
black actions suddenly disclosed
like ice, immense disorder,
oceanwide, for me who goes in singing,
as with a sword among defenseless men.

Well then what is it made of—that spurt of doves
between night and time, like a damp ravine?
That sound so drawn out now
that drops down lining the roads with stones,
or better, when just one hour
buds up suddenly, extending endlessly.

Within the ring of summer,
once, the enormous calabashes listen,
stretching their poignant stems—
of that, of that which urging forth,
of what's full, dark with heavy drops.

LISTENING TO THE POEM

If translation is the last phase of assimilating a poem, then the first must be mere listening, and it has its own value. An immediate, aural sensation of "Galope muerto," prior to translation and even to understanding, catches Neruda's sonorous vowels marking the pulse of the poem: *galope, mares, poblándose, campanadas, aparte, metal, pesando, polvo, rodando.* Neruda got palpable pleasure from certain words, as much from their shape and sound as from what they denoted. *Campana, mariposa, paloma* ("bell," "butterfly," "dove") crop up throughout his early poems, and his posthumous *Book of the Questions* asks, "Is there a star more open than the word *amapola* ["poppy"]?"[23] This kind of vocal resonance had an incantatory power for Neruda, beyond what the words were saying.

In sifting for the distinctive sounds of "Galope muerto," the ear picks up two others in particular, even before we know what to make of them: *como* (the preposition "like"), twice in the first line, eleven times in the poem; and *-ando* or *-endo* (the participial "-ing"), five times in the first stanza, fourteen times in the poem. These vocal motifs become the identifying marks of "Galope muerto," especially under the impetus of the first line, which sets the norm. Neruda's recurrent similes—or, to be exact, his half-similes—draw us irresistibly toward the thing compared, which he then fails to reveal. Meanwhile his present participles insist that whatever the poem is after is in flux.

Como cenizas, como mares poblándose, we hear. There is nothing so inviting, rhetorically speaking, as a simile that opens with its figurative half. "As flies to wanton boys"—Shakespeare does it often—"are we to the gods." And there is nothing so satisfying as the simile completed: "Like as the waves make towards the pebbled shore, / So do our minutes hasten to their end."[24] But Neruda's first stanza will not or cannot give that satisfaction. "Like ashes, like oceans swarming": the opening figure engages, it practically compels our attention, since ashes and oceans are charged with various connotations. But what, then,

Neruda's emblem, a fish "that two hoops are enclosing or releasing"
(see p. 77).

are they like? Or to put it the other way around: whatever
Neruda had in mind must be essentially unlike everything from
ashes to plums, because even taken together they cannot bring
him to say what it is. The best a translation can do here is to
edge us into "Galope muerto" with as exact a movement as
possible.

The translator's primary work, even more than finding equiv-
alent diction, goes into shaping a rhythm for Neruda's abortive
sentences. Since the syntax of the first three stanzas fails to re-
solve itself in a main clause, it is tempting to call those stanzas
dislocated, inarticulate. Amado Alonso, the first critic to devote
a book to Neruda, wanted to balance the poem's opening by
prefixing a main clause to the first line: *"that which I see and feel,
that which I'm trying to poetize is* like ashes, like oceans swarm-
ing."[25] But to supply such a prefix, even silently, would vitiate
the sense of an impending resolution that these lines give us.
They develop a closely knit sequence whose linguistic detail
seems to guarantee a logical outcome. We are given alternatives

(with "or"), signs of orderly discussion ("that's why," "in such a way"), and reassuring agreements in gender and number, all of which seem to be leading somewhere. Yet no sentence in the first three stanzas comes to term. The passages are cast wholly in dependent or subordinate clauses—but dependent on what, the reader wants to know, subordinate to what order? Gradually this desire to know becomes the crux of the poem.

Alonso concedes that the incompleteness of the first stanza is only an "apparent anomaly," since it means to "express the meaninglessness of anxious life, a chaos," but still he calls the poem a "poetic failure" for not perfecting its intuitions.[26] Another prominent critic, Raúl Silva Castro, complains about Neruda's "anomalous syntax" and "incomplete propositions," calling "Galope muerto" "delirious" and "chaotic." Silva Castro, who as a young editor had presented Neruda in *Claridad*, years later faulted him for leaving this poem "in the rough, an early draft."[27] The words "anomalous" and "incomplete" do apply, and at times I wish Neruda in 1925 had had someone (a translator?) asking him if this or that detail needed to be quite so baffling. But the leaning, half-fulfilled syntax of "Galope muerto" has its purpose, not so much expressing a chaos as seeking an order and eventually finding one.

The poem's five stanzas act out a way of perceiving the physical world. That is, Neruda's writing moves tentatively because it displays a process, not a set of data. Take the three opening similes, joined by an "or" that expresses both the speaker's probing and the world's unseizability. Is what he imagines like ashes—things in space? Like oceans swarming—things acting in time? Or like hearing bellstrokes on the road—a human sensation of things acting in space and time? Probably what he imagines is like all three at once, even if unamenable to these abstract discriminations.

For Neruda to have perfected his intuitions or his syntax would have been a kind of dishonesty, as he was well aware. At work on other poems of *Residencia en la tierra* in 1928, he wrote a friend about feeling "unable to express anything or verify anything within me. . . . I'm not talking about doubt or disoriented thoughts, no, but about a hope that does not get satisfied." Then a few months later he wrote again: "Really, don't you find yourself surrounded by destructions, deaths, ruined things . . . blocked by difficulties and impossibilities? Isn't it so? Well, I have decided to shape my strength from within this danger, to take advantage of this struggle, to exploit these weaknesses."[28] The difficult sentences of "Galope muerto" had already begun this venture at making his struggle his strength.

In another letter, a year later, Neruda is still formulating what the early poem had enacted. He wants "a knowledge without antecedents . . . a physical absorption of the world, despite and against ourselves."[29] Through similes in "Galope muerto" that touch on bellstrokes, plums, pulleys, wingbeats, and dead bees but do not say what these things signify, Neruda is in effect depriving himself of unearned knowledge: he is absorbing rather than contemplating the world. As simile after simile has its referent withheld, the run of them ceases referring to some external order and builds up its own purpose. The inherent principle of things comes to reside in the poet's own attempt at grasping them.

The intuition working here and elsewhere in Neruda's poetry suggests that human perception follows one essential pattern: a trade-off, glimpsing now the form and now the flux of things. Witness the way *como* and *-ando* work together in "Galope muerto." Similes may depend on a noun alone (*como cenizas*, "like ashes") or more often add a verb (*como mares poblándose*, "like oceans swarming"). Simple nouns such as Neruda uses (*mares*) normally serve to identify things in space, and verbs (*poblándose*) to activate them in time. The nouns in his similes, then, tend to arrest or define life, to identify it, while his present participles show life's process but not any perceivable form of it.

Used this way, nouns and participles might come to be at odds, to preclude each other. Remarkably, however, "Galope muerto" interweaves nouns and participles so as to identify things and release them in the same breath. The poem's similes,

lacking any referent to fix them, keep evolving in tandem with
present participles that have no finite verb to limit them:

> *o como se oyen desde el alto de los caminos*
> *cruzar las campanadas en cruz,*
> *teniendo ese sonido ya aparte del metal,*
> *confuso, pesando, haciéndose polvo . . .*

My translation imports a participle, perhaps unjustifiably: "hear-
ing" for *se oyen* instead of "are heard." But "hearing" helps lead
toward someone or something "holding" the bell's sound:

> or like high on the road hearing
> bellstrokes cross by crosswise,
> holding that sound just free of the metal,
> blurred, bearing down, reducing to dust . . .

No sooner has "that sound" been heard and held free for a mo-
ment than we feel it "reducing to dust," though two lines later
it still may be "remembered." Then among "forms far out of
reach" Neruda thinks of "the aroma of plums rolling to earth /
that rot in time, endlessly green"—the plums that since child-
hood had embodied nature's inviting fruitfulness. A finite verb
momentarily stops the participle—"plums rolling to earth / that
rot in time"—but the very next phrase, "endlessly green," re-
gains the image's momentum and its substance alike. Here then
is the dynamic that "Galope muerto" has in mind: to bear the
brunt of things in flux and yet hold them up to be perceived.

LOOKING FOR DYNAMIC FORM

So far the question about "Galope muerto" has been how, rather
than what, Neruda perceives. With a poem of such charged
phrasings and densely accumulating rhythms, the temptation is
to keep entering and reentering them until they feel utterly fa-
miliar: one is at home in the element. Yet following the poem's
movement does not preclude focusing at the same time on its
substance. In fact its movement and its substance share the
same quality—that of arrest and release, or of stasis and flux.

Neruda in "Galope muerto" began looking for what I call dynamic form: images in which stillness and motion combine. Each quality can take on the aspect of death or life: the stillness can contain or sustain, the motion can waste or regenerate.

"Like ashes, like oceans swarming": the ashes seem a deadening way to begin, except that Neruda's free, ongoing syntax in this opening line enables the ashes as well as the oceans to be stirring with new life. "Swarming" may be too dense and agitated for *poblándose*, but "peopling themselves" lacks life. These ashes carry a spiritual sense of something consumed and reborn, as does the dust a few lines later. Like *Alturas de Macchu Picchu*, "Galope muerto" deals with death only to seek rebirth. In that light its images of ashes and dust recall a late Renaissance sonnet by Francisco de Quevedo, the poet whom Neruda cherished above all others. A talk he gave in 1939 centers on Quevedo's "Cerrar podrá mis ojos." Neruda dwells passionately on the sonnet's closing couplet, in which Quevedo foretells what our fiery veins and marrow will become after death:

> serán ceniza, mas tendrá sentido;
> polvo serán, mas polvo enamorado.

> they shall make ash, yet it shall stir with life;
> dust they shall make, yet dust that knows desire.

Neruda praised Quevedo's lines for the "cry of insurrection" in them, the "perpetual resurrection of love."[30]

Out of Quevedo's lines and Neruda's fascination with them emerges a figure of falling and rising:

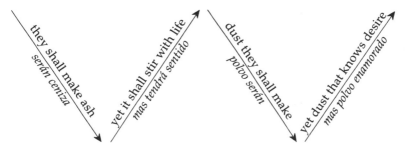

In "Galope muerto," ashes and swarming oceans move the figure from death to life, after which the plums rise and fall and rise: they release an aroma but are rolling to earth, where they rot but stay endlessly green. At the end of the second stanza this figure occurs again, when the ox stumbles down though his horns want to sound, and later "great wingbeats, overhead" fall "like dead bees." Toward the end of the poem, a sound drops down and an hour buds up. This is an elemental rhythm, familiar as a heartbeat or the inspiration and expiration of breath. Throughout the imagery that Neruda tries, a rising element often emerges from a falling one, as in nature. A year or so before "Galope muerto," he had been bringing nature's reproductive vitality into his love poems as a kind of mandate for sexual fulfillment. Now the idea of natural vigor has to contend with physical, psychic, and social breakdown as well as death itself.

At the source of the poem's twofoldness, generating its rising and falling figures, stands the title. *Galope* starts a rising, forceful movement, *muerto* kills it. And each word has its own double charge in Spanish, *galope* suggesting power but also fatal violence, *muerto* meaning "dead" but also "still," as in "still water" or "still life." All these meanings have their effect somewhere in the poem. The lilacs betoken spring but stand still around a convent; the poet enters with a sword and yet singing. Unfortunately English provides no good equivalent for *galope muerto* (the Spanish is not a technical or colloquial term). "Dead Gallop" accents the noun too much, and could even mean a flat-out run, whereas *galope muerto* takes the stress on *muerto*, conveying a real force but one that has broken or frozen. Perhaps "Still Gallop" would do. In any case, the Spanish title instigates what follows. It proposes a world of forces, breaking out and breaking up, that the poem has to work through.

Neruda was broaching a new world in "Galope muerto": the ocean where life dissolves and evolves, the mill that pulverizes to restore, the singing amid disorder. Here, in particular images, is another instance of what he was attempting with similes and their participles: somehow to catch things held fast yet flowing, contained though wasting away, consumed yet brimming with energy.* To spot this simultaneity of fatal and vital forces, Neruda had to imagine a continuous space-time in which things at once hold still and move. First he calls it by a paradox, *la sumergida lentitud*, "the sunken slowness." Then another paradox, opening the second stanza, arrests matter in motion: *Aquello todo tan rápido, tan viviente, / inmóvil sin embargo*, "All of it so quick, so livening, / immobile though." That immediate modulation from *viviente* to *inmóvil*, poising one word against the other, is worth re-creating in translation.

Wherever the poet looks he sees things spinning round yet staying put, but they are pulleys, wheels, mechanical objects that do not resolve the conflict between wasting and sustaining life. After the vision of plums *rodando a tierra*, rolling to earth yet staying green, the verbs *rodar* ("roll," "revolve") and *rodear* ("surround") both occur within the second stanza: in *ruedas* ("wheels") and *rodeo* ("whirl"). These words could have baneful associations for Neruda. He wrote a friend in 1929, "Don't you find yourself surrounded [*rodeado*] by destructions"; in "Agua sexual" the body and spirit wasting away are *rodando*—"rolling down drop upon drop"; in *Alturas de Macchu Picchu*, Canto IV, Neruda says "I roamed round [*rodé*] dying of my own death."[31] So in "Galope muerto" the pulleys, wheels, tree trunks' rings, planets' circles,[32] and lilacs around a convent all present analogies to the mortal flux encircling and enclosing Neruda: *el rodeo constante, incierto, tan mudo*, "the ceaseless whirl, uncertain, so still." To translate *rodeo . . . mudo* as a "still" whirl rather than a "mute" one brings out a version of the poem's basic paradox. And incidentally, if this rendering seems reckless, consider the French version: in *rodeo constante* it spots a Western roundup and translates it "bétail fidèle," faithful cattle![33] For the ceaseless whirl, a hapless trot—though it could happen to any translator.

What Neruda seeks is a point—a place and a moment in which

---

* On his stationery, his books, and the flag outside his home, Neruda used a personal emblem that also suggests the idea of dynamic form. He described the emblem: "My flag is blue and shows a horizontal fish that two hoops are enclosing or releasing." See "The Flag," in *Una casa en la arena* ("A House on the Sand") (Barcelona: Lumen, 1966). The emblem appears on p. 71 above.

the life around him will hold still, take form as he watches, without abating vitality. On the way to Macchu Picchu, in Canto IV, he says

> I had no place to rest my hand,
> none running like linked springwater.

Twenty years earlier, "Galope muerto" had come upon such a point. At the poem's dead center and its stillest moment, with death on the ox's tongue, the poet suddenly begins to steady himself:

> *Por eso, en lo inmóvil, deteniéndose, percibir,*
> *entonces, como aleteo inmenso, encima . . .*

> That's why, in what's immobile, holding still, to perceive
> then, like great wingbeats, overhead . . .

The rhythm feels its way, checking itself as if trying to pick up a new beat. The words *en* and *entonces*—"in" and "then"—make this a point in both space and time, a breathtaking point where and when things really can be perceived. Here it is crucial to translate *lo inmóvil* as "what's immobile," which refers to something actual and intense, rather than simply as "the stillness," which is abstract and inert.[34]

The rhythm of the third stanza's opening lines, beginning *Por eso, en lo inmóvil,* climbs slowly toward *encima* and for a moment the simile Neruda hits on signals a revelation, an epiphany, "like great wingbeats, overhead." But there is no holding still. Two more unassimilable phenomena run past, and both his rhythm and his vision collapse under "all that my spent heart can't embrace." He finds himself in the midst of crowds, unshed tears, toil, black actions, and immense disorder—a societal agony and disorder that the poet's imagination cannot seem to cure. His ways of dealing with the world around him are either impotent or violent: a "spent heart" or a "sword among defenseless men." Until this stanza the speaker, the lyric self, has not emerged except behind his question ("from where?") and behind a passive verb (bellstrokes "are heard"). Now he appears within the participle "holding still," and finally, in person, he "goes in singing."

"Well then," he says in the fourth stanza, spurred partly by exasperation and partly by the excitement of his entrance with a sword,

> *Ahora bien, de que está hecho ese surgir de palomas*
> *que hay entre la noche y el tiempo, como una barranca húmeda?*

> Well then what is it made of—that spurt of doves
> between night and time, like a damp ravine?

Now Neruda witnesses the motion not of things wasting away but of life regenerating itself. I would bring out the sexual impulse here by making the verbal noun *surgir* "spurt" instead of "surge" in the damp ravine. This burst of life has occasioned the poem's first full sentence, though still the sentence comes as a question. Amado Alonso, Neruda's early critic, asked him what the doves in his poetry signified and was obligingly answered, "The consummate expression of life, because of their perfect form."[35] But in "Galope muerto" what matters as much as their form is their dynamic, *ese surgir*, giving them a degree of freedom from "night and time." By now the poet, still seeking better ways to imagine what life is made of, can see how "just one hour / buds up suddenly, extending endlessly."

The hour *crece*, it "grows" or buds up. Though we think of time as extending horizontally, here it is also rooted in nature and rises vertically like the spurt of doves. This is Eliot's "point of intersection of the timeless with time," which both he and Neruda desired to find, and Neruda's genius makes it a natural and historical phenomenon as well as a spiritual one. Macchu Picchu is such a point of intersection. There, Neruda can climb up to the natural site while also reaching back through time to ancient America.

Having come this far, having conceived this possibility, "Galope muerto" finally yields a full and satisfying statement—no similes, questions, or exclamations, only a single image grounded in a particular place and time:

Adentro del anillo del verano
una vez los grandes zapallos escuchan,
estirando sus plantas conmovedoras.

Within the ring of summer,
once, the enormous calabashes listen,
stretching their poignant stems.

It is a vision of things held in quietude and ripeness while still brimming with life. Instead of the anxious poet closed inside a confused whirl, there are bellying gourds within a clear circle in full summer: the self need not intrude, being wholly present in what it has imagined. In *Adentro del anillo del verano*, the reader's ear can again sense what is happening. Three identically stressed and balanced words—*Adentro, anillo, verano*—make this the most rhythmically firm line of the poem, and in itself a fluent ring of *ah-* and *oh*-sounds. After the degrading fall of things, the fruitless spinning of wheels and pulleys, Neruda imagines rotund gourds within a ring: circles within a circle, perfect forms, self-contained yet still regenerative. He once said that these meaty, pumpkin-like gourds stood for *vida condensada y de plenitud*, "life packed and plentiful," and I find it hard to get that much life into the English of *grandes zapallos*.[36] Are they big, great, large, huge, enormous, fat, plump, pregnant, swelling, swollen? A verbal adjective such as "swelling" would over-translate, but it would pack the gourds with life and reinforce the stanza's other verb forms, which make the present moment fill the scene. After "once, the enormous calabashes . . . ," one expects a past tense, yet like every other verb in the poem, *escuchan* is in the present, and it releases a participle: just as one hour "buds up . . . extending," the calabashes "listen, / stretching their poignant stems."

We call this *natura naturans*, nature urging itself on.[37] The lyric could close here. It has moved from "sunken slowness" to high summer, from "what's unformed" to perfect form. But Neruda's momentum keeps even this final sentence open-ended. The daring thing about his closing lines is that, having brought us into the bright ring with his search completed, his similes fulfilled, they then take us out into mortal life again. Earlier he had asked what the animating spirit of life is made of, *de que está hecho*. Now at last he makes an answer:

> *de eso, de lo que solicitándose mucho,*
> *de lo lleno, oscuros de pesadas gotas.*

Life is made "of that," whatever the calabashes are stretching with, "of that which urging forth. . . ." Here Neruda dangles a dependent clause so that whatever "that" is, it will go on "urging forth." The poem leaves off with "what's full, dark with heavy drops"—an image of obscurely seminal or ovular potential that draws us, like Molly Bloom's "yes I will Yes" on the last page of *Ulysses*, into a rhythm of drops that are hoofbeats or churchbells or tears or ripening calabash seeds.

"GALOPE MUERTO" IN LATIN AMERICA

It is an incredible poem to come from a twenty-year-old. Where and how did he find the means to write "Galope muerto"? In translating it, proving it moment by moment against an inner ear, one can at least reenact the poem itself. Neruda's aim, which he nowhere else pursued so single-mindedly, was to catch the likeness of a land of unlikeness—to name an alien world in his own words. That precisely parallels what a translator has to do in any case; so my version is bound to "Galope muerto" in the intensest kind of kinship. And yet I can never hear this poem, the poem Neruda wrote, with the immediate ear and mind of a Spanish-American or Spanish listener.

"We were in on the verbal creation of the continent," said Julio Cortázar, describing the way his generation in Buenos Aires responded to *Residencia en la tierra*. Here was "the Demiurge determined to invert a biblical order that we Latin Americans had not established. . . . You had to enter a different dimension of the language, and from there, see in an American way [*ver americano*] as no one had ever seen till then."[38] Similarly, García Lorca prepared a 1934 Madrid audience to hear in Neruda "the stark tone of an American's great Spanish language" and "a poetry not afraid of breaking molds": "You are about to hear an authentic poet, one of those who has forged himself in a world that is not ours, and that few people perceive."[39]

The world García Lorca had in mind is geographical as well as metaphysical, for Latin Americans in the first few decades of the century were beginning to insist on their indigenous culture, their independence from Europe. Cortázar has linked *Residencia en la tierra* even more explicitly to Neruda's Americanness, saying that this "radical mutation of our deepest speech" was a means for "Latin-American man's encounter with himself, his final residence in his own land."[40] What led Cortázar and others to call this a New World poetry, and what strikes me particularly in "Galope muerto," is Neruda's struggle to identify the things of his world, as though they had lain undiscovered or had been misnamed until then.

This quality of rebellious initiative made him throughout his life a poet of human liberty. For Neruda, human activity was meant to embody the emergence, growth, and self-renewal of things in nature. "Galope muerto" keeps looking until it finds the way that natural energies can organize and fulfill themselves. This is, after all, the true potential of poetic if not also of political imagination. After 1925 Neruda tended to watch for dynamic rather than fixed or imposed forms of life. Although "Galope muerto" helped to germinate his whole outlook, he himself never exactly credited the early poetry as a source for later social attitudes. In 1954 he looked back slightly askance at his literary concerns during "those turbulent days" in Santiago between 1921 and 1925: "Without knowing it we spent every day right near the solution to our aesthetic problems. The fact is, next door to the Students Federation, where we came out each evening, was the Workers Federation" and the familiar shirt-sleeved figure of the socialist Recabarren.[41]

By "the solution to our aesthetic problems" Neruda probably meant that poetry should take on the mundane, material life of common people and their solicitings and surgings as well. If such a project is possible, "Galope muerto" begins to fulfill it, and in a profounder way than Neruda's partisan, popular poetry of the fifties. This early poem makes its way from the dead gallop to the stretching calabashes. Though both have the suspended energy that interested Neruda, the first instance in the poem is violent and terminal; the last is generous, unified, and fruitful. These two images also partake of an American historical reality. Early Indian chronicles record the dreadful trampling of horses brought from Spain, as do several poems in *Canto general*.[42] Zapallos, on the other hand (the word comes from Quechua, Peru's Incaic and modern Indian language), are purely indigenous plants with many popular uses in Chile.

In getting from the mortal force in the title of "Galope muerto" to the pulsing verses at the end, Neruda was moving through the physical world in the way his political motives would later move him: that is, away from overriding force and toward things that are "endlessly green" or "stretching their poignant stems"; away from harsh Spanish dispensations and toward the fulfillment of a native genius. He came to see Latin America's landscape, plant life, and finally its people all *solicitándose mucho*, urging themselves forth. In Macchu Picchu he saw a life that seemed frozen within the stones, a life whose beauty and potential energy called for release. Having written such a poem as "Galope muerto," he could imagine the Andean site as both still and moving, monument and motive, and could reanimate it by drawing on the image of dynamic form.

A ROMANTIC IMAGE

There is no telling where Neruda's idea of dynamic form, which is at work in his social and historical convictions as in "Galope muerto," might have come from. Whatever alerted and attracted him to the image of seemingly immobile energy, we can only trace its effect in his poetry. Before going on to look, in the light of "Galope muerto," at some other poems written for *Residencia en la tierra*, I want to cite briefly an earlier romantic poet whose perception of dynamic form may illuminate Neruda's.

During his first tour of the Lake District with Wordsworth, on October 28, 1799, Coleridge was watching the River Greta and noted this phenomenon:

Shootings of water threads down the slope of the huge green stone—
The white Eddy-rose that blossom'd up against the Stream in the scol-
lop, by fits and starts, obstinate in resurrection—It *is the life* that we
live.

It took Coleridge's rapt, staring eyes to see the shell-like hollow
in the stone catching the flow so that it "blossom'd up"—a fa-
miliar, miraculous sight. Four years later he revised this note-
book entry, drawing out the image now with his mind's eye:

The *white rose* of Eddy-foam, where the stream ran into a scooped or
scolloped hollow of the Rock in its channel—this shape, an exact white
rose, was for ever overpowered by the Stream rushing down in upon it,
and still obstinate in resurrection it spread up into the Scollop, by fits &
starts, *blossoming* in a moment into a full flower.[43]

With verbs carrying the force and nouns to give it shape, Cole-
ridge arrives at "blossoming," an instance of freedom taking
form, changeful yet exact, consumed yet new every moment.
Usually when he spoke of natural energy and growth as the
basis for the way a poem evolves, he used the term "organic
form": "it shapes, as it develops, itself from within, and the ful-
ness of its development is one and the same with the perfection
of its outward form."[44] What the rushing stream displays might
even better be called dynamic form. It is a fascinating image,
one that gave Coleridge a perception of human as well as natu-
ral identity—that is, of sameness through change, water rush-
ing against the hard rock and yet blossoming every moment.
Obstinate in resurrection, we can turn loss into flowering, expe-
rience into beauty. "It *is the life* that we live," Coleridge added in
his notebook. Neruda would have underlined it too.

Because this paradoxical image of flux generating form, of si-
multaneous movement and stillness, has so essentially to do
with the life we live and thus with the shaping effect of artistic
perception on that life, it turns up variously and crucially in any
number of poets. Wordsworth sees "the stationary blasts of wa-
terfalls" as a sign of Revelation in *The Prelude*. Keats freezes the
yearning lovers on an urn. Whitman, in "Crossing Brooklyn
Ferry," urges the primal ocean of all being to "suspend here and

everywhere." Hopkins says that he "caught" the windhover "in his riding," and much of what he meant by instress and inscape, energy and design, was manifest in the way moving water could make an exact shape: he noted one day seeing "foam-cuffs in the river of the crispiest endive spraying" and a waterfall's "fans" and "quills" and "spandrills." T. S. Eliot usually puts a spiritual cast on the image, as in the *Four Quartets*—"we must be still and still moving"—or tells us that this state of being is "neither arrest nor movement." William Carlos Williams, writing of the falls at Paterson, sees Alexander Hamilton "stopped cold / by that unmoving roar," or imagines a fish "at full speed / stationary" in the river's flood. And this figure is not confined to poetry. When Melville wants to intimate extreme beauty and terror, he calls Moby Dick "a mighty mildness of repose in swiftness." Faulkner, especially in *Absalom, Absalom!*, will often arrest some movement in order to reveal its accumulated significance, and he even coined the word "immobly."[45]

Neruda did not need to have come across this image of immobile energy in his reading, for nature abounds with it.* Such an image could also rise from memory and imagination—from the "mill of forms" either "remembered or never seen," as "Galope muerto" puts it—or it could occur in an eternal present, like calabashes heavy with seed. When midway through "Galope muerto" Neruda appeared "in what's immobile, holding still," he was beginning a search for dynamic form that took him through the next ten years of *Residencia en la tierra*, a search that his poetry never concluded.

---

*A superb example of dynamic form in Neruda's imagery of the ocean occurs in "El gran océano" ("The Great Ocean"), from *Canto general* (1950), OC, I, 654:

es el central volumen de la fuerza,	it is the central mass of force,
la potencia extendida de las aguas,	the potent reach of the water,
la inmóvil soledad llena de vidas.	immobile solitude full of lives.
Tiempo, tal vez, o copa acumulada	Time, perhaps, or all movement
de todo movimiento, unidad pura	brimming in a cup, pure unity
que no selló la muerte, verde viscera	not sealed by death, green viscera
de la totalidad abrasadora.	of the consuming whole of things.

The last five lines could express Neruda's vision of Macchu Picchu.

RESIDENCIA EN LA TIERRA (1925–35)

The imaginative reach of "Galope muerto" took Neruda so far that for a decade after 1925 he kept traversing much the same ground—a decade that the first five cantos of *Alturas de Macchu Picchu* would later depict. Inevitably his own situation conditioned the search for a personal standpoint, a way of withstanding the ruinous world. For two years he was at loose ends in Santiago, then isolated with a meager consular salary for five years in Burma, Ceylon, Java, and Singapore. There Neruda felt surrounded by rich yet alien native cultures, as well as by British colonials, and he was frustrated in getting *Residencia en la tierra* published. The poet in him suffered a kind of linguistic solitude and deprivation, and he later recalled passing through Vietnam "in my twenties waiting for death, refuged in my language." From Ceylon he wrote a friend: "I have real anguish in saying anything, even alone with myself, as if no words could speak for me. . . . I find all my phrases banal, dispossessed of my very self."[46] In 1930 Neruda began an unsatisfying marriage, and two years later he returned to Chile, his book still unpublished.

Neruda's twenties, a decade of estrangement for him, nonetheless gave rise to what many readers consider his most remarkable writing: *Residencia en la tierra*. The first part of the collection finally came out in Santiago in 1933; then both parts, fifty-six poems in all, were published two years later in Madrid. Except for a few of the later poems, *Residencia en la tierra* sustains much the same tone and material throughout, and also sustains the kind of questioning that began in "Galope muerto." Neruda spoke of his book's "solid and uniform substance, with which I persistently bring out one single force," and called the poems "very consistent, like something begun over and over, as if attempted eternally without success."[47] Reading this book, one feels him working his way unaided through an element he seems the first to have encountered. García Lorca said that Neruda "forged himself in a world that is not ours," and went

on to characterize his American friend acutely: "A poet closer to
death than philosophy, closer to pain than intellect, closer to
blood than ink." One thinks of some raw primitive conscious-
ness grasping for light, and perhaps this is the impression Ne-
ruda's *Residencia en la tierra* created among its readers in Madrid.
"He stands up to the world," García Lorca said, "full of honest
terror."[48]

What Neruda faces, and what these poems do in fact con-
sciously, carefully express, is a disintegrating world. His coping
with it may be the "single force" that Neruda felt at work in his
poems. The things he sees are broken, confused, split, flooded,
fallen, wasted, overcome, decayed, dismantled, ruined, de-
stroyed, extinguished, forgotten, abandoned, dying, dead. Ne-
ruda in 1926 had chosen some paragraphs on death to translate
from Rilke's *Notebook of Malte Laurids Brigge*,[49] and in *Residencia en
la tierra* it is death that permeates countless items and events,
forcing the poet into surreal associations to locate it under any
guise: dressed as a broom or an admiral, or sailing in coffins,
or like an endless plant "soaked by drops that fall / without
sound." The images of mortal life from "Galope muerto" recur
in many of these poems, such as "Vuelve el otoño" ("Autumn
Comes Back"):

> . . . when the solitary poet
> at the window hears the steed of autumn running
> and leaves of trampled fear crackle in his arteries,
> something hangs over the sky like a thick ox's tongue.

And behind everything in his world, Neruda hears what this
poem calls "the old gallop" of time and death.[50]

The disintegrative force at work in nature has its effect on the
human scene as well, so that Neruda sees wasted lives around
him and feels deprived of any fruitful human connection. In
leaving Chile for the Orient he had also left behind at least two
women, one in Temuco and one in Santiago. Loneliness some-
times drew into his poems whatever was sordid in the life he
felt teeming around him. Neruda read *The Waste Land*, and his

"Caballero solo" ("Gentleman [or "Cavalier"] Alone") exhibits an irredeemable urban scene of delirious widows, youthful tomcats, masturbating priests, lecherous physicians, sexually jaded professors, incestuous cousins, adulterers, and an "abject clerk," hands smelling of cigarettes, who after "the weekly tedium, the novels read in bed at night / has finally seduced his neighbor." The poet is surrounded by all this human crowd as by dense woods,

> these great tangled and breathing woods
> with enormous flowers like mouths and dentures
> and black roots shaped like fingernails and shoes.[51]

There are no plump doves or swelling calabashes or thighs like hills. In fact nature now monstrously takes after human things. The pastoral world is disrupted and with it, the erotic fulfillment the *Veinte poemas de amor* had found in that world.

Neruda's poems and later memoirs do record one passionate connection: "the torrential Josie Bliss," "a sort of Burmese panther" who wore white flowers in her black hair and was rabidly jealous.[52] In a superb poem about this affair, "Tango del viudo" ("Widower's Tango"), Neruda thinks of the torment between them but also of her legs "resting like solar waters stilled and hard, / and the swallow sleeping and flying" in her eyes. Having escaped her when he moved from Burma to Ceylon, he then wants her again, to hear her rough breath at night "cleaving to the air like a whip on horse's skin" and to hear her "urinating in the dark . . . spilling a slender, shimmering, silver, persistent honey."[53] That last notion has a welcome creaturely sympathy about it. When Neruda finally left her the second time, she kissed him frantically and fell at his feet, his memoirs tell us, only to rise with her weeping face powdered white from the chalk on his shoes.[54]

As a kind of solution to his alienated state, Neruda married a young Dutch woman, María Antonieta Hagenaar, a few months after arriving in Java in 1930. She had "a rather exotic idea of America," was "tall, slow-moving, priestly," according to Neruda's biographer, and could share neither his language nor his life.[55] Still she returned with him to Chile in 1932. It was a bad time in several ways: the marriage was crumbling, jobs and housing difficult, and Don José impatient with his son's unsettled career. After a short term as consul in Buenos Aires, Neruda took a post in Spain, where a daughter was born in 1934. She was gravely ill from the start, and three unrelievedly grim poems express Neruda's desolation: he cannot "hold up the broken steps," there is "a river falling in a wound," "girl's blood climbing to the moon's stained leaves." He cries out for "one minute when I can recognize my veins." Not long afterwards, Neruda separated from his wife. The child died at eight in Holland.[56]

Out of these troubled years—his virtual exile in the Orient from 1927 to 1932, his return to Santiago at the depth of the Depression, and his going abroad again in 1934—came some of Neruda's sharpest visions of ennui and sexual despair.[57] Surrounded (the verb *rodear* occurs frequently) by the flux of city life, he feels "like an eyelid frightfully lifted up by force," *como un párpado atrozmente levantado a la fuerza*. The image comes from "Agua sexual," which exudes an atmosphere where people and their fabrications have crowded out flora and fauna: glass, cigars, knives, blankets, hotels, and "trees of marrow bristling like rabid cats" make any human connection impossible. From beginning to end, things in the poem are "Rolling down drop upon drop," falling away "like a hurricane of gelatin, / like a cataract of sperm" with nothing to shape, sustain, and renew them.[58] We could be back in the first three stanzas of "Galope muerto," before the spurt of doves or the ripe calabashes within the ring of summer.

In the most unusual poem from this period, "Walking Around," Neruda resists the gritty attrition of urban life, the "petty fat-winged death" as he later calls it in *Alturas de Macchu Picchu* (III), with the only thing he has at the time: his verbal energies.[59] He even gave the poem an English title, as if nothing in Spanish could show how aimless he felt. In principle, the poem in translation ought to bear a title equivalently strange to the English ear, such as "Mañana" or "The Flâneur." But those fail to suggest the malaise in Neruda's title. A Depression-era Latin American might have used the phrase "walking around" with something between Charlie Chaplin and "The Hollow Men" in mind.

WALKING AROUND

It so happens I'm tired of being a man.
It so happens I walk into tailorshops and movies
all shriveled up, impervious, like a swan of felt
steering through waters of origin and ash.

The smell of barbershops makes me break out sobbing.
All I want is the quiet of stones or wool,
all I want is to see no stores or gardens,
or merchandise or eyeglasses or elevators.

It so happens I'm tired of my feet and fingernails
and my hair and my shadow.
It so happens I'm tired of being a man.

Still it would be delightful
to frighten a notary with a cut lily
or do in a nun with one smack of an ear.
It would be great
to go through the streets with a green knife
screaming until I died of cold.

I just can't go on as a root in the dark,
swaying, stretching, shivering with sleep,
downwards, in the soaking guts of the earth,
absorbing and musing, eating every day.

I don't want so much misery for me.
I can't go on being root and tomb,
isolated cellar, warehouse of frozen
stiffs, dying of grief.

That's why Monday flares up like gas
when it sees me coming with my jailhouse face,
and howls like a wounded wheel as it goes by,
and makes hot bloody tracks toward night.

And shoves me to certain corners, certain dank houses,
to hospitals with bones coming out the window,
to certain shoestores reeking of vinegar,
to streets as frightful as crevices.

There are sulfur-colored birds and hideous intestines
hanging from the doors of houses I hate,
there are false teeth forgotten in a coffeepot,
there are mirrors
that must have wept for shame and horror,
there are umbrellas everywhere, and poisons, and navels.

I'm walking around with calm, with eyes, with shoes,
with rage, with forgetfulness,
I walk along, I go past offices and orthopedic shops,
and backyards with clothing hung from a wire:
underpants, towels, and shirts that weep
slow dirty tears.

If nothing else does, Neruda's verbal exuberance gets him intact
through this world in which the ordinary horrifies the eye, and
everything that ought to be imbued with life—roots, damp
earth, birds, navels—is decaying instead. The new day shoves
him through the streets in a strongly articulated rhythm and
syntax that somehow belie the poet's sickness of spirit.

Occasionally in *Residencia en la tierra*, Neruda tries to resist
the disintegration of things by setting what is integral against
what is breaking down. "Unidad" ("Unity") begins with what
might be the calabashes again—"There is something dense,
unified, deeply seated, / repeating its number, its identical sign"
—and this image offsets the speaker "circling over myself / like a
crow over death." Neruda begins "Sabor" ("Taste") with "words
busy serving as slaves" and "dead weeks, air chained above the

cities," but ends by finding "waters deeply settled" in himself, "sleeping in sad attention." He feels a "resonant, lasting, immobile" sound within himself, "an element at rest, a live oil."[60]

With figures such as these, Neruda imagines a kind of dynamic integrity, one that at least gives him some poise against the whirl and flux, against disintegration and death. In "Sonata y destrucciones," whose very title embodies the tension between composure and disintegration, he calls himself

> *el viajero armado de estériles resistencias,*
> *detenido entre sombras que crecen y alas que tiemblan,*[61]

> the journeyer armed with sterile resistances,
> held between shadows that grow and wings that tremble.

To translate *detenido* as "prisoner," as Donald Walsh does, chooses a different kind of arrest than Neruda means, I think.[62] He is *deteniéndose*, as in "Galope muerto," trying to hold still between contrary forces. Later in the poem Neruda confirms this difficult position, describing it as "the strange witness I uphold," *el testimonio extraño que sostengo* (with another form of the key verb *tener*). Another poem, "Significa sombras" ("It Means Shadows"), takes its stand at the core of the mortal world, where conflicting forces seem regenerative instead:

> Let the tremor of deaths and of births not disturb
> the deep site I want to keep for myself forever.

> Let this then be what I am, in some place and any time,
> a settled and sure and ardent witness,
> carefully destroying and preserving himself ceaselessly,
> clearly engaged in his original duty.[63]

This deep site corresponds to Neruda's *residencia en la tierra*. The title, chosen while he was far away from Chile, is usually translated "residence on earth" but could as well imply someone dwelling *in* the earth, committed to its fundamental dynamic of destroying and preserving.

Time and change are the trouble in *Residencia en la tierra*, and words such as "perpetual," "permanent," "continual," "lasting," and "ceaseless" turn up regularly. They are symptoms of Neruda's wanting to make change his spur and ally, not to stop or avoid it. He knew, as García Lorca said, "that the reed and the swallow are more permanent than the hard cheek on a statue."[64] That is, he did not look for any more formal integrity, in life or in verse, than was consistent with movement and momentum. Thus "Galope muerto" closes with the calabashes listening, then stretching, and then urging forth. A more explicit credo occurs in one of the last poems from *Residencia en la tierra*:

> If you ask where I've been
> I've got to say "It happens."
> I've got to say how the ground goes dark with stones,
> how the river enduring breaks itself down.[65]

That last line, *del río que durando se destruye*, needs if possible to retain its order in translation, though I can see why Tarn shifted the emphasis to "the river ruined in its own duration." And the line needs to keep its own present participle, rather than Belitt's "the river's duration, destroying itself."[66] Neruda never avoided the destructiveness he saw, but responded with his own sense of permanence, stressing *durando* against *destruye*.

"ENTRANCE INTO WOOD" (1935)

It was the precariousness of Neruda's posture, and the risks this New World imagination took in coping with raw existence, that led García Lorca in 1934 to think of "stone blocks about to sink, poems suspended over the abyss by a spider's filament."[67] The welcoming, intuitive grasp of Neruda's work by García Lorca and other Madrid writers helped bring him out of the alienated years between 1925 and 1934. He flourished in the pre-Civil War days of the Republic, composing among other things an unprecedented set of *cantos materiales*, "material songs" that put him deeply in touch with the rhythm of decay and growth in things.[68] The three poems, "Entrada a la madera" ("Entrance into Wood"), "Apogeo del apio" ("Apogee of Celery"), and "Estatuto del vino" ("Ordinance of Wine"), were printed separately in 1935 as a homage from Neruda's Spanish friends. They form the culmination—Gabriela Mistral called them the "complete recompense"—of *Residencia en la tierra*.[69]

In the most daring of them, "Entrada a la madera," Neruda imagines himself penetrating the utterly perishable substance of wood, whose "mysterious veins" he had loved as a child, and then inspiriting that substance with his own voice.[70] Coming halfway between "Galope muerto" and *Alturas de Macchu Pic-*

ENTRADA A LA MADERA

Con mi razón apenas, con mis dedos,
con lentas aguas lentas inundadas,
caigo al imperio de los nomeolvides,
a una tenaz atmósfera de luto,
a una olvidada sala decaída,
a un racimo de tréboles amargos.

Caigo en la sombra, en medio
de destruidas cosas,
y miro arañas, y apaciento bosques
de secretas maderas inconclusas,
y ando entre húmedas fibras arrancadas
al vivo ser de substancia y silencio.

Dulce materia, oh rosa de alas secas,
en mi hundimiento tus pétalos subo
con pies pesados de roja fatiga,
y en tu catedral dura me arrodillo
golpeándome los labios con un ángel.

Es que soy yo ante tu color de mundo,
ante tus pálidas espadas muertas,
ante tus corazones reunidos,
ante tu silenciosa multitud.

chu, this extraordinary poem has affinities with both, particularly in its dynamic of motion and stillness, and of loss and renewal. Neruda falls into "the midst of things broken down" but can feel green matter gathering in the wood's "desolate stillness," and at the end he can implore the wood: "clasp me to your life, to your death." This poem could be a dream prefiguring Neruda's entrance into Macchu Picchu.

ENTRANCE INTO WOOD

With scarce my reason, with my fingers,
with slow waters slow flooded,
I fall to the realm of forget-me-nots,
to a mourning air that clings,
to a forgotten room in ruins,
to a cluster of bitter clover.

I fall into shadow, the midst
of things broken down,
and I look at spiders, and graze forests
of secret inconclusive wood,
and I pass among damp uprooted fibers
to the live heart of matter and silence.

Smooth substance, oh drywinged rose,
in my sinking I climb your petals,
my feet weighed down with a red fatigue,
and I kneel in your hard cathedral
bruising my lips on an angel.

Here am I faced with your color of the world,
with your pale dead swords,
with your gathered hearts,
with your silent horde.

Soy yo ante tu ola de olores muriendo,
envueltos en otoño y resistencia:
soy yo emprendiendo un viaje funerario
entre tus cicatrices amarillas:
soy yo con mis lamentos sin origen,
sin alimentos, desvelado, solo,
entrando oscurecidos corredores,
llegando a tu materia misteriosa.

Veo moverse tus corrientes secas,
veo crecer manos interrumpidas,
oigo tus vegetales oceánicos
crujir de noche y furia sacudidos,
y siento morir hojas hacia adentro,
incorporando materiales verdes
a tu inmovilidad desamparada.

Poros, vetas, círculos de dulzura,
peso, temperatura silenciosa,
flechas pegadas a tu alma caída,
seres dormidos en tu boca espesa,
polvo de dulce pulpa consumida,
ceniza llena de apagadas almas,
venid a mí, a mi sueño sin medida,
caed en mi alcoba en que la noche cae
y cae sin cesar como agua rota,
y a vuestra vida, a vuestra muerte asidme,
a vuestros materiales sometidos,
a vuestras muertas palomas neutrales,
y hagamos fuego, y silencio, y sonido,
y ardamos, y callemos, y campanas.[71]

Here am I with your wave of dying fragrances
wrapped in autumn and resistance:
it is I embarking on a funeral journey
among your yellow scars:
it is I with my sourceless laments,
unnourished, wakeful, alone,
entering darkened corridors,
reaching your mysterious matter.

I see your dry currents moving,
broken-off hands I see growing,
I hear your oceanic plants
creaking, by night and fury shaken,
and I feel leaves dying inwards,
amassing green materials
to your desolate stillness.

Pores, veins, circles of smoothness,
weight, silent temperature,
arrows cleaving to your fallen soul,
beings asleep in your thick mouth,
dust of sweet pulp consumed,
ash full of snuffed-out souls,
come to me, to my measureless dream,
fall into my room where night falls
and incessantly falls like broken water,
and clasp me to your life, to your death,
to your crushed materials,
to your dead neutral doves,
and let us make fire, and silence, and sound,
and let us burn and be silent and bells.

97

How can a poem, or dream, or nightmare vision so pervaded by negative experience still create a sense of replenishment and renewed energy? In the opening stanza we hear of scarceness, slow flooding, falling, mourning, forgotten ruins, bitterness. Yet the speaker moves through these elements in a deliberate way—"With . . . with . . . with . . . I fall to . . . to . . . to . . ."— and the stanza ends up accumulating a kind of potential energy. That energy derives partly from small rhythmic effects that can also occur in translation. Neruda's opening, *Con mi razón apenas* (literally, "With my reason scarcely"), by delaying and thus emphasizing the adverb *apenas*, disqualifies reason in a startling way. What kind of rendering will catch that? Tarn coins a phrase, "By the skin of my reason," and Walsh stays close, "Scarcely with my reason."[72] I prefer something between the two to begin Neruda's descent: "With scarce my reason, with my fingers, / with slow waters slow flooded." Into an element very much like the "sunken slowness" of "Galope muerto" or the "deepest waves" of *Alturas de Macchu Picchu*'s opening canto, this speaker falls unseeing, unconscious, but with a measured rhythm that changes his fall into a half-willed descent.

The descent takes on added force in light of a sentence from Neruda's memoirs, recalling his early train rides north from Temuco: "I always felt myself drowning when I came out of the great forests, out of the maternal wood."[73] "Entrada a la madera" carries Neruda down and thus back in time to "a mourning air" and "a forgotten room." He often used the word "mourning" about his childhood, and the second stanza strongly evokes the southern forest. Again Neruda's verse rhythm matters, for its accenting marks his fall. Translating *Caigo en la sombra, en medio / de destruidas cosas*, Walsh says "I fall into the shadow, amid / destroyed things," but a more stressful English rhythm would give pace and shape to the descent:

> I fall into shadow, the midst
> of things broken down . . .
> and I pass among damp uprooted fibers
> to the live heart of matter and silence.

With this entrance into the bole to reclaim a germinal source, "Entrada a la madera" feels like a regression to what Neruda's memoirs call the "maternal wood."

The poem moves formally, ritually. By the third stanza Neruda can speak to the wood directly: *Dulce materia . . . en mi hundimiento tus pétalos subo* ("Smooth substance . . . in my sinking I climb your petals"). He aligns the motions of sinking and climbing, fixing the kind of axis along which he will also move at Macchu Picchu. There, and here in the wood, this difficult venture of sinking through space and time creates a potential energy for climbing. Having reached the dark core of the wood, in the fourth and fifth stanzas, the speaker says *soy yo . . . soy yo*, "It is I." By exposing himself to matter at this depth, he can join in its essential dialectic of death and life. Three successive images yoke these contrary forces: "dying fragrances," "autumn and resistance," "yellow scars." To this wood he again says *soy yo*, as if crying for recognition, and then homes in on the source like an utterly needful child,

> unnourished, wakeful, alone,
> entering darkened corridors,
> reaching your mysterious matter,

your *materia misteriosa*. The last phrase enfolds a profane pun on *mater misteriosa*—the silent, compacted matter, the wood metamorphosed into a mother. Both *materia* and *madera*, the poem's key words, are cognate with *madre* ("mother"), the word that need not appear because the poem's whole configuration is maternal.[74] "Entrada a la madera" discovers the mystery that moved Neruda: matter and spirit joined in the maternal wood.

Many times over he has called the wood *tu*, the intimate singular for "you." Now three more times in the sixth stanza he addresses it that way, bringing himself even closer than before. He sees, hears, and feels things as if his own physical processes were interfused with the wood's:

> I see your dry currents moving,
> broken-off hands I see growing,

> I hear your oceanic plants
> creaking, by night and fury shaken,
> and I feel leaves dying inwards,
> amassing green materials
> to your desolate stillness.

What Neruda now senses is more than simple noun phrases such as "your petals" and "your gathered hearts" had been able to express in earlier stanzas. "I see your dry currents moving," he says, *Veo moverse tus corrientes secas.* Unlike Romance languages, English cannot follow a transitive verb ("I see") with an infinitive ("to move"), which means a subtle loss. Nor do we have the slight push of the Spanish reflexive, *moverse,* for we see the dry currents either "move" or "moving." My participle does point up a new phase in the poem: this *materia misteriosa* is not inert in space but moves in time. Neruda can now perceive a dynamic of currents dry yet moving, hands broken off yet growing, leaves dying yet massing. In each figure a generative element works against something contrary, so that in effect the wood feels green yet still. And desolate—why? Because it lies out of sight and time, deeper in the ground of existence than people normally want to probe. Or is it that the child's mother died and he abandoned the wooden houses and proliferating woods of his frontier childhood?

The final stanza opens in passionate supplication to a vaguely maternal sphere of being: "Pores, veins, circles of smoothness, / weight, silent temperature." For circles of *dulzura,* as for *dulce materia,* translators regularly say "sweetness," but "smoothness" fits both the woody and the maternal figures in the poem. These heavy, deep-set rings have more appeal than the "silenced, encircling" ones in "Galope muerto," which are simply "existing like dry stitches in the seams of trees." In fact the wood Neruda speaks to here resembles the listening calabashes. Its pulp, "thick mouth," and "silent temperature" are quiescent but alive, its "beings" are only "asleep." In other words, what Neruda invokes has the potential of organic, even animate being.[75]

The stanza virtually makes up a poem in itself:

> Pores, veins, circles of smoothness,
> weight, silent temperature,
> arrows cleaving to your fallen soul,
> beings asleep in your thick mouth,
> dust of sweet pulp consumed,
> ash full of snuffed-out souls,
> come to me, to my measureless dream,
> fall into my room where night falls
> and incessantly falls like broken water,
> and clasp me to your life, to your death,
> to your crushed materials,
> to your dead neutral doves,
> and let us make fire, and silence, and sound,
> and let us burn and be silent and bells.

This fourteen-line sentence delivers a sort of sonnet whose movement tells as much as its matter. In the first six lines Neruda goes out toward the compacted wood, then in the next three he calls the wood to him, then again in the next three he turns and binds himself over to the wood. This alternating movement, something like the lungs breathing, builds up to a closing couplet where Neruda, now in the first-person plural, can ask the wood to act together with him. Linking its "fallen soul" to his own night falling like broken water, he makes the wood's life and death his own. Or rather it is he who activates life against death in the wood, by bringing his own spirit to its otherwise "crushed materials."

The closing stanza, like the whole poem, is highly rhetorical yet never for a moment empty or bloated. One effect, however, vanishes in translation. Through the first six lines, Neruda addresses the wood singly as *tu*. Then, as if recognizing its dust and ash and sleeping beings as a collective force, he summons them with the familiar plural: *venid a mí*, "come to me." Even in Spanish one hardly notices this new form, but the same shift occurs significantly at the end of *Alturas de Macchu Picchu*, where

Neruda convokes the dead artisans, asking them to clasp him to their life and death.

In the closing couplet of "Entrada a la madera," Neruda goes beyond rhetoric into pure inspiration. Perhaps it can be voiced in English, though I am not sure. "Clasp me," he has just said, and the last two lines have as much sexual as metaphysical urgency:

> and let us make fire, and silence, and sound,
> and let us burn and be silent and bells.

The poet and the wood, human interfused with non-human being, make a fire that is pure passion; it consumes to silence as it releases the sound of bells. That is a plausible reading of these lines, but their impetus leaves interpretation behind:

> *y hagamos fuego, y silencio, y sonido,*
> *y ardamos, y callemos, y campanas.*

The strongly accented parallelism, the alliterations, the assonance between *hagamos* and *ardamos*, give these lines a thrust that surprises us even after so forceful a stanza. At the poem's climax—no other term will do—Neruda cries to this *madera-madre*, "let us burn and be silent and *campanas*." I leave the word untranslated here because it shocks just about as much in its Spanish context. Neruda's rhythm and sound and grammar (*y ardamos, y callemos, y* . . .) call for a final hortatory subjunctive, perhaps *sonemos* ("let us sound," "let us ring"). *Campanas* ("bells") is not such a verb, yet it acts like one. The English line can begin a rising rhythm, but then what? When the sound and movement of *ardamos* and *callemos* echo in *campanas*, the immobile bells resonate. It is a wild touch on the poet's part (though not the translator's) and a beautiful instance of dynamic form, the noun vibrating with verbal energy—*campanas*!

Chapter Four

TOWARD MACCHU PICCHU
(1935–1945)

SPAIN BEFORE THE WAR (1935–36)

How did Neruda, his twenties ridden with emotional and literary frustration, develop in his next decade the leading prophetic voice of Latin America? How did the poet of "Galope muerto" with its "ceaseless whirl," of "Walking Around" with its "offices and orthopedic shops," of "Entrada a la madera" with its "dying fragrances"—how did this poet of solitary perceptions and involuted verse come to write *Alturas de Macchu Picchu*? These questions point to a sequence of events that engaged Neruda between 1935 and 1945. Political and cultural activities took him from Spain to France, then home to Chile, to France again and back to Chile, to Mexico and then home again, with brief journeys to the United States and throughout Latin America. During this turbulent period, certain decisive experiences went into the broadening of his poetic imagination: the trauma of civil war in Spain, his repossession of his native land, three years in Mexico during the Second World War, the journey to Macchu Picchu, a new regard for Chile's Araucanian ancestry, election to the Chilean Senate. After "Entrada a la madera" (1935), no other poem for ten years had such imaginative penetration or focused so closely on the image of dynamic form, but it took those years before Neruda could write *Alturas de Macchu Picchu* the way he did.

"Life led me through the world's farthest regions," he once said, "before I reached what should have been my point of de-

parture: Spain."[1] His discovery of the mother country gave Ne-
ruda what he had lacked in Chile and even more so in the Ori-
ent: a deeply rooted sense of his language and its classics, along
with a community of poets who, under the Republic, felt in
touch with their people. Despite increasing conflicts across the
political spectrum, Spain in 1935 was for Neruda the high point
of his life until then. For a young Chilean, recognition in Spain
counted greatly. Rafael Alberti was circulating poems from *Resi-
dencia en la tierra* even before Neruda's arrival as Chilean consul,[2]
and in December 1934, García Lorca introduced Neruda with
acute sympathy to a Madrid University audience.[3] Then early in
1935, as a "Homage to Pablo Neruda from the Spanish Poets,"
his *Tres cantos materiales* (including "Entrada a la madera") were
published with a eulogy of "the young and noteworthy Amer-
ican writer" whose work "does honor to the Castilian lan-
guage."[4] Shortly after that, the first full edition of *Residencia en la
tierra* I and II appeared in Madrid, and also a Spanish edition of
Veinte poemas de amor.[5] At the same time, Neruda tightened his
Iberian affiliation by presenting, in the Madrid monthly *Cruz y
Raya,* selections from two Baroque poets of Spain's Golden Age,
the Conde de Villamediana (1580–1622) and Francisco de Que-
vedo (1580–1645).[6]

Neruda was finding new bearings in other ways as well. In
1933 he had published translations from James Joyce's *Chamber
Music*—the heavily cadenced, image-laden, melancholy lyrics
beginning "All day I hear the noise of waters / making moan"
and "I hear an army charging upon the land."[7] These lyrics in
Spanish recall Neruda's own earlier work. Then late in 1934 he
made some better translations, choosing William Blake's *Visions
of the Daughters of Albion* and "The Mental Traveller."[8] Here he
could try out a more declaratory voice along with Blake's vision
of erotic and imaginative freedom. A few months later he also
translated, for *Cruz y Raya,* three sections from Walt Whitman's
Song of Myself.[9] Generally quite faithful, they catch Whitman's
drift of mind, though his rhythmic swell does not survive a con-
version into wholly Latinate diction:

Neruda (*right*) and García Lorca, Buenos Aires, 1933 or 1934.

Out of the dimness opposite equals advance, always
   substance and increase, always sex,
Always a knit of identity, always distinction, always
   a breed of life.

Desde la oscuridad, opuestos iguales avanzan,
siempre la substancia y la multiplicación,
siempre el deseo,
siempre un tejido de identidad, siempre la diferenciación,
siempre la procreación de la vida.

Somehow without Whitman's rolling dactyls the Spanish is not altogether convincing, though his doctrine of regeneration certainly suited Neruda. Perhaps what matters more than style or even substance is that in translating Blake and Whitman, Neruda was aligning himself with an authoritative literary tradition, much as he was in editing Quevedo. He already had something of Blake's and Whitman's erotic inspiration and their faith in the individual imagination; now he was feeling his way toward their visionary, prophetic assurance.

Another means of orienting himself came to Neruda just after *Residencia en la tierra* appeared in 1935. He was asked to edit a new review, *Caballo Verde para la Poesía* ("Green Horse for Poetry"), and for each of the first four numbers he wrote a prose prologue.[10] At the time, the Spanish poet Juan Ramón Jiménez "was publishing tortuous commentaries against me every week," according to Neruda.[11] Probably they resembled what Jiménez later wrote, likening the Chilean's imagination to a sewer and a dungheap, calling him a gleaner of coal hunks and shoe soles who fails to understand the essence of things.[12] Neruda says he did not respond to those weekly attacks, but his first prologue for *Caballo Verde*, "On a Poetry Without Purity," defends with a new firmness the residence on earth he had been creating over the last decade. "It is well," the piece begins, "at certain times of day or night to look deeply at objects in repose: wheels that have run long dusty distances bearing great loads of vegetables or minerals, coal sacks, barrels, baskets, carpentry hafts and handles. They give off the feel [*el contacto*] of man and earth as a lesson for the anguished lyric poet."[13] There is a trace of Whitman here, in Neruda's sensuous attachment to life's used and humble objects. "All truths wait in all things," Whitman says in a passage Neruda had recently translated, "The insignificant is as big to me as any, / (What is less or more than a touch?)"—*un contacto*, as Neruda translated it.[14]

The prose for *Caballo Verde* continues with the most explicit profession he had yet made: "Let this be the poetry we are looking for, worn down as if with acid by the hand's obligations, permeated by sweat and smoke, smelling of urine and lilies splattered by the various trades practiced inside or outside the law." Then he names the poet's guiding principles: "The sacred law of the madrigal and the decrees of touch, smell, taste, sight, hearing, the desire for justice, sexual desire, the sound of the ocean, without deliberately excluding anything, without deliberately accepting anything, entrance into the depth of things in a headlong act of love."[15] Again the prose (in English) sounds like Whitman, with its democratic embrace of common life—a quality that would mark Neruda's writing more and more in the coming years.

"On a Poetry Without Purity" closes with a gibe in the direction of Jiménez: "Whoever shuns bad taste will fall on the ice."[16] Then in December 1935 another prose note, "Behavior and Poetry," deplored poets who cling to "the artistic" instead of "the briny song that must leap from the deepest waves." Neruda asks what will remain of the "nasty little chills of hostility" among poets, and ends by answering his own question in a trenchant, ominous sentence: *Nada, y en la casa de la poesía no permanece nada sino lo que fue escrito con sangre para ser escuchado por la sangre*, "Nothing, and in the house of poetry nothing lasts but what was written with blood to be heard by blood."[17] It is hard not to sense in Neruda's words the tragic change that was coming over Spain and his own poetry.

Four numbers of *Caballo Verde para la Poesía* were published.[18] Besides writing his own brief manifestos for them, Neruda had the pleasure of printing the poets who had welcomed his own work: García Lorca, Vicente Aleixandre, Jorge Guillén, Luis Cer-

cabezas cortadas de Federico García Lorca y Pablo Neruda autores de este libro de poemas!

Este Patético dibujo fue realizado la tarde del Martes 13 de 1934 en la ciudad de Santa María de los Buenos Aires así como todos los demás dibujos —

Drawing by García Lorca. The caption reads: "Severed heads of Federico García Lorca and Pablo Neruda authors of this book of poems. This pitiful drawing was executed on the evening of Tuesday the 13th in 1934 in the city of Santa Maria de los Buenos Aires as were all the other drawings" (see p. 109).

nuda, Miguel Hernández. For the fifth number, he asked his Spanish friends to contribute to a special issue on the Uruguayan poet Julio Herrera y Reissig, who had influenced him and other Latin Americans of his generation. This number, ready to be collated and sewn in July 1936, never had the chance to be published.[19]

"All that time before the war holds a memory for me as of grapes whose sweetness is almost gone," Neruda wrote years later.[20] These two prewar years in Madrid had been, apart from his marital misfortune, like bright daylight after years of darkness. He had thrived among the writers and artists, particularly Rafael Alberti, who "was already a poet of the people and of revolution," Neruda said, and whose "courageous attitude deeply influenced my political ideas."[21] Late in 1934, Neruda had also met Delia del Carril, who shared his life for the next fifteen years. Older and more radical, she is said to have guided him politically.[22] Above all, though, it was the unpolitical Federico García Lorca, "popular as a guitar," "candid and comical . . . shy and superstitious, radiant and graceful," who typified Spain for Neruda.[23] For them both, the friendship also seems to have meant recovering a bond between the mother country and Hispanic America.

Neruda and García Lorca had known each other since 1933, when the Spanish poet came to Buenos Aires to present his play *Blood Wedding*.[24] A sympathy must have sprung up between the two men there, to judge from a lively dialogue they put together on the Nicaraguan poet Rubén Darío for the Buenos Aires P.E.N. club.[25] And from García Lorca's hand a more remarkable document of that period has survived. He had seen Neruda's most recent poems, and they inspired him one March evening in 1934 to do a series of bizarre designs very much in the manner of Miró and Dali: surreal, grotesque, spidery line drawings of eyes, lips, hands, hair, genitals, and blood, done as a kind of illustration to "Agua sexual," "Sólo la muerte," "Materia nupcial," and "Walking Around."[26] These are astonishing and astonished responses to the surrealist tendency in *Residencia en la tierra*. They also show what prompted García Lorca's revealing

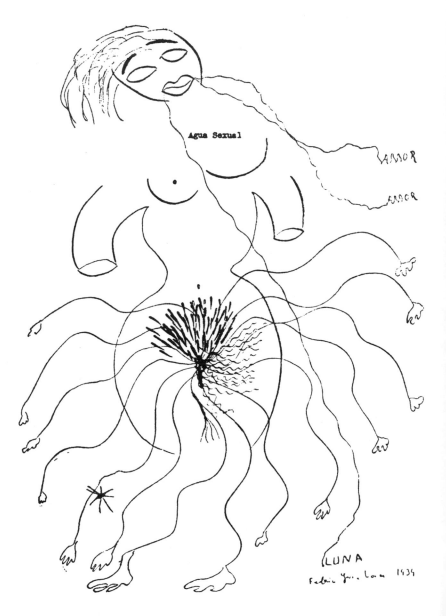

Drawing for Neruda's "Agua sexual," by García Lorca, Buenos Aires, 1934 (see p. 109).

words, some months later in Madrid, about Neruda inhabiting
"a world that is not ours," under the "broad, romantic, cruel,
extravagant light of America."[27]

At about that time in Madrid, over a year before the war,
Neruda also composed a lengthy "Ode to Federico García Lor-
ca."[28] As much an imaginative flight as an appreciation of his
friend, the ode scatters fantastic images among loose, often cas-
ual verses:

> Cities with a smell of wet onions
> wait for you to come by singing raucously,
> and silent sperm boats pursue you,
> and green swallows nest in your hair,
> and even snails and weeks,
> coiled masts and cherries
> plainly move about when your pale
> fifteen-eyed head looms up
> and your mouth suffused with blood.

Clearly the thought of García Lorca released a buoyant, halluci-
natory energy in Neruda, yet this poem repeatedly veers toward
disaster:

> Come and I'll crown you, youth of health
> and the butterfly, pure youth
> like a black flash forever free,
> and just between you and me,
> now that no one's left among the rocks,
> let's talk simply since you are you and I'm me:
> what good are verses if not for the dew?
>
> What good are verses if not for that night
> when a bitter dagger finds us, for that day,
> for that dusk, for that broken corner
> where man's beaten heart prepares to die?

The poem ends with an obscure premonition: "On your own al-
ready you know many things. / Others you'll slowly be getting
to know." Later Neruda told how one day in July 1936 he had
arranged with García Lorca to go watch some wrestling in a

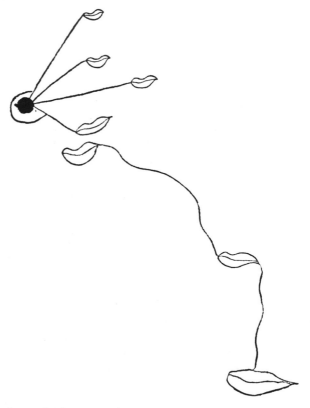

Walking around

Drawing for Neruda's "Walking Around," by García Lorca, Buenos Aires, 1934 (see p. 109).

Madrid circus. "Federico never showed up. He was already on the way to his death."[29]

CIVIL WAR (1936–38)

A month after the outbreak of civil war, Falangists murdered García Lorca in Granada, and the whole tragedy of the war hit Neruda. Some months later in Paris he spoke about his friend and epitomized Spain's losses in the poet whose name is "so weighted and so pierced with meanings that in uttering it one utters the names of all who fell defending the very substance of his songs." This grave and angry elegy also stressed García Lorca's popularity in an "America separated by centuries of ocean from the classic masters of the language," and then Neruda closed by declaring his own newly forged loyalty: "Having just come from Spain, I, a Latin American, Spanish by race and by language, could not have spoken of anything but her afflictions. I am not political and have never taken part in political debate, and my words, which many would have preferred neutral, have been stained with passion."[30]

Not many outsiders, especially among the writers, had originally been as close to Republican Spain or then worked as hard for its survival as Neruda. His partisan activity, for which he lost his consular position in 1936, took the form of starting a magazine with the English expatriate Nancy Cunard, organizing propaganda, and helping to found support groups in Paris and Santiago. Along with W. H. Auden, Stephen Spender, Louis Aragon, Heinrich Mann, and others in 1937, he signed a fierce letter published in England against the Spanish Fascists,[31] and at that time, he began to be known politically in the United States.[32] Amidst all this, Neruda was reorienting his own writing. Earlier, his manifesto "On a Poetry Without Purity" had asked for "the feel of man and earth" in poetry, and for "vigilance, prophecies, declarations of love and hate, beasts, quakes, idylls, political beliefs, denials, doubts, assertions, taxes."[33] As a statement of principle, this anticipates remarkably well his poetic subjects in the years to come. However, under the actual impress of García Lorca's death and of the violence in Spain,

Neruda's growing poetic militancy took form chiefly in a more outspoken, outreaching voice than he had needed before, a voice beginning to be heard in "Entrance into Wood" and the García Lorca ode but not yet galvanized by the emergency of war.

That voice sounds most clearly in "Explico algunas cosas" ("I Explain Some Things"), his strongest Civil War poem, which first appeared in Madrid on July 1, 1937.[34] The shock and outrage at what is happening register on the speaker, on his friends, and on his house, which was in fact shelled while he was in Paris.[35] But the poet of "Galope muerto" is not now baffled by the turbulence around him, nor can he go on writing, in the vein of that poem, about "lilacs around the convent." He will speak out, as the title itself insists, knowing which people he speaks against, and those he speaks for and to:

I EXPLAIN SOME THINGS

You'll ask: And where are the lilacs?
And the metaphysics matted with poppies?
And the rain that kept drumming
his words filling them
with pits and birds?

I'll tell you everything that's happening to me.

I lived in the outskirts
of Madrid, with bells,
with clocks, with trees.

From there we looked out
on Castile's lean face
like an ocean of leather.
                    My house was called
house of the flowers because everywhere
geraniums were bursting out: it was
a fine house
with dogs and children.

                    Raúl, remember?
You remember, Rafael?
                    Federico, do you remember
under the ground,
remember my house with balconies
where June light drowned flowers in your mouth?
                                        Brother, my brother!

Everything was
loud voices, salted goods,
piles of palpitating bread,
market-stalls of my Argüelles quarter with its statue
like a whitish inkstand amid the hake:
oil rose up in the spoons,
a deep pulsing
of feet and hands filled the streets,
meters, liters, keen
essence of life,
                    fish stacked up,
rooftops woven under a cold sun
that wears down the weathervanes,
fine ivory delirium of potatoes,
tomatoes in waves out to the sea.

And one morning all this was blazing
and one morning bonfires
shot from the earth
burning up lives,
and since then fire,
gunpowder since then,
and since then blood.
Bandits with planes and with Moors,
bandits with finger-rings and duchesses,
bandits with black friars blessing
came out of the sky to kill children,
and in the streets the blood of the children
flowed easily, like children's blood.

Jackals the jackal would deny,
stones the dry thistle would bite and spit,
vipers the vipers would despise!

I have seen the blood of Spain
rise up against you
to flood you in a single wave
of pride and knives!

Traitor
generals:
look at my dead house,
look at broken Spain:
but from every dead house burning metal flows
instead of flowers,
from every crater in Spain
emerges Spain,
from every dead child a gun with eyes,
from every crime bullets are born
that will someday track down
your heart.

So you ask why his poems
don't tell us of dreams, and leaves,
and great volcanoes in his native land?

Come see the blood in the streets,
come see
the blood in the streets,
come see the blood
in the streets!

Neruda's closing lines have burned into the minds of two generations of people who care for Spain:

Venid a ver la sangre por las calles,
venid a ver
la sangre por las calles,
venid a ver la sangre
por las calles!

García Lorca had called his friend a poet "closer to blood than ink."[36] True as it may be to the bloodshot vision of "Agua sexual" or "Walking Around," that telling phrase becomes tragically inadequate to describe the horror behind Neruda's imperatives in this poem of 1937. And if *Residencia en la tierra* revealed "a world that is not ours," as García Lorca said, then in "Explico algunas cosas" Neruda witnesses yet another sort of world and tells us we must come and make it ours. In translation, the poem's voice and thus our sense of its audience lose part of their complexity because English imperatives and pronouns have no singular or plural "you." Actually Neruda has a threefold or fourfold audience and as many moods in this poem. *Preguntaréis*, he begins, "You'll ask," and *Os voy a contar*, "I'll tell you," he says to those acquainted with his poetry who may want their soulful lyric poet back or disapprove of his partisanship. Then he turns gently to particular friends, Raúl, Federico, Rafael: *te acuerdas?*, "do you remember?" Then in his anger it is jackals, vipers, and traitors he addresses, *Frente a vosotros* ("against you"), saying to them *mirad*, "look at broken Spain." By the end of the poem his *Preguntaréis* ("So you ask") and *Venid a ver la sangre* ("Come see the blood") are speaking out not just to former readers but to everyone capable of responding.* And perhaps he has all along been arguing with himself as well—with whatever in him might have preferred dreams, leaves, and volcanoes to political struggle.

"The world has changed and my poetry has changed."[37] Neruda's remark, made in 1939, has gotten more quotation than scrutiny. He knew what he was saying, and there are poetic maneuvers in "Explico algunas cosas" that could not have occurred before. A stark parallelism—"look at my dead house, / look at broken Spain"—aligns the poet ineluctably with the history of a

---

* *Preguntaréis* is second-person plural future, *Os* is the second-person plural pronoun: in Latin American Spanish they might imply a special relationship with the speaker, but in Spain they are used regularly to address a "you." *Acuerdas* is second-person singular present; *vosotros* is the second-person plural pronoun, *mirad* and *venid* are second-person plural imperatives. "Raúl," "Federico," and "Rafael" are the Spanish poets, Raúl González Tuñón, Federico García Lorca, and Rafael Alberti.

place and time, as does the sequence of tenses in his poem, from past to present to future. At the end, Neruda shapes his imperatives with line breaks that show a stronger, simpler touch with both his subject and his audience than anything he had written before:

> Come see the blood in the streets,
> come see
> the blood in the streets,
> come see the blood
> in the streets!

All these points of technique manifest a new purpose, a sense of what to speak for and whom to speak to, without which *Alturas de Macchu Picchu* is inconceivable.

It is hard to imagine what Neruda's poetry would have become if the war in Spain had not intervened. But this does not mean that he could leave everything behind in 1936 and begin with a totally clean slate. His first Civil War poem, which Rafael Alberti printed anonymously in the anti-Fascist weekly *El Mono Azul*, takes up Neruda's habitual theme of life against death. In this "Song to the Mothers of the Dead Militia," those who fell "are standing in the wheat," "smiling from the earth," "their poor ruined bones work in the earth," "their raised fists contradict death."[38] Neruda's militant purpose here is fed by images of the natural vigor he had sought throughout *Residencia en la tierra*, and by Quevedo's resurrective spirit (he admired Quevedo's phrase, "the agriculture of death").[39] What he had not conceived of before was the need to call together and exhort his audience as he does the mothers in this poem: *Dejad/ vuestros mantos de luto, juntad todos / vuestras lágrimas,* "Let go / your mourning cloaks, join all / your tears." At Macchu Picchu it would be workers, not mothers—"All through the earth join all / the silent wasted lips"—but the formal phrasing is the same. The next Civil War poem Neruda wrote, "Song on Some Ruins," laments the ruin of bells, watches, tools, glass, wool, the "deep materials / gathered and pure . . . all fallen / never to be born." Then his imagery intensifies:

> Heavenly thirst, doves
> with floured waist: ages
> of pollen and grapes, see how
> the wood breaks
> down into grief: there are no roots
> for man: everything barely rests
> on a tremor of rain.[40]

Neruda's familiar pastoral tokens, his images of natural whole-
ness and fecundity, are breaking now under the pressure of
what he had to witness. These two poems from 1936 are not
among his finest, but they do show that his response to a histor-
ical emergency involved earlier premises as well as new real-
izations.

The change in Neruda's writing, usually called by his less
sympathetic critics a conversion and by others a development,
consisted of a twofold realization, as he himself saw it: that he
should give up his subjective, irrational, melancholy investiga-
tions and that he should join his fellows in the common strug-
gle.[41] From the 1940's on he made this point quite explicitly.[42] Its
earliest expression comes in a poem that refers to the beginning
of the Spanish Civil War, "Meeting Under New Flags." Until
then, he says, he had

> . . . listened to all
> the dismal salt: by night
> I went planting my roots:
> I examined what's bitter in the earth:
> it was all night or lightning for me.

But that life-denying process ended when

> . . . a day
> throbbing with human
> dreams, a wild
> grain reached
> my consuming night
> so I might join my alien steps
> to the steps of man.[43]

One can understand Neruda's wanting to go beyond the self-enclosed desperation of much of *Residencia en la tierra*, yet not every poem in that book is "saturated with pessimism," as he said in 1949 and 1950.[44] Both "Galope muerto" and "Entrada a la madera" end up springing with energy, and even "Walking Around" derives a kind of humor and energy from its excessive frightfulness. It is also true that Neruda's subjective concerns did not wither away in 1936. In writing *Alturas de Macchu Picchu*, he was again preoccupied with his own psychic temper and with death. The change that did occur, with García Lorca's death and the damage to Spain's land and people, meant in effect that Neruda entered history. Having been troubled by time's impersonal force, which acts on nature and humanity alike, he now felt the drastic pull of historical time and the need to reach ordinary people caught within it.

The Civil War poems show in various ways Neruda's altered sense of vocation. For his first two poems he began using the term *canto*, implying the role of a bard, and in several others his outspokenness turns against the enemy in the traditional form of high-pitched invective. He continued writing about Spain while sailing home from Europe in 1937, and within a few weeks of arriving in Santiago he had published the collection entitled *España en el corazón* ("Spain in My Heart").[45] One of the newer poems, "What Spain Was Like," shows him aware of how a nation and a landscape could be transformed by history. It also brings off a poetic feat that must have impressed both Spanish and American readers. Part way through the poem he begins incanting the names of Spanish towns and villages, two or three per line with no other words, quatrain after quatrain for fifty-six lines:

> *Miñogalindo, Ossa de Montiel,*
> *Méntrida, Valdepeñas, Titaguas,*
> *Almodóvar, Gestaldar, Valdemoro,*
> *Almoradiel, Orgaz.*[46]

It is a translator's holiday, in a way, and yet perfectly untranslatable, for compared to the poem's earlier lines these names guard every bit of their strangeness and genius. By gathering them into his own quatrains from all over Spain—Castile, Catalonia, Andalusia, Estremadura, the Basque provinces—Neruda is affirming the Hispanic side of his heritage and doing it the way he liked, territorially.

This gesture of allegiance was dramatically sealed by the first publication in Spain of *España en el corazón*.[47] In November 1938, with the war still going on, Republican Army soldiers printed the book on the Catalan front, setting the type and working the press themselves. Being short of paper, they made a pulp not only from rags but from bandages, a Fascist flag, and a Moroccan prisoner's shirt.[48] The Spanish editor, Manuel Altolaguirre, prefaced the text by saying that Pablo Neruda had "lived through the war's first months with us. Then while at sea, as from an exile, he wrote the poems for this book." Evidently Neruda could now be called an exile, *un destierro*—from Spain!

CHILE (1938–40)

In closing "Explico algunas cosas," Neruda had turned toward his listeners:

> So you ask why his poems
> don't tell us of dreams, and leaves,
> and great volcanoes in his native land?

Yet six months after the poem appeared in Santiago, he was writing about the rock and soil and snow of his native land, the *país natal*. What accounts for this kind of return? Somehow Spain's trauma affected Neruda unexpectedly: in teaching him a form of patriotism, an identification through time with a land and people, the war on Spanish soil tightened his bond to Chile. One affiliation prepared the next. While still gripped by Spain, Neruda more and more felt the need, as he said in 1938, to reach and touch "my true soil." *

---

* An article on Ercilla's *La Araucana* and the "heroic constancy of the Araucanian Indians" had appeared in the same issue of Madrid's Loyalist weekly *El Mono Azul*, 2, no. 22 (July 1, 1937), that first published Neruda's "Explico algunas cosas."

In May of 1938 another death, quite unlike García Lorca's, precipitated his emotional resettlement in Chile. From Temuco he got news that his father was gravely ill, and going there, found him semiconscious. Neruda remembers him "reproaching me: 'Why are you so twisted?' he murmured. 'Straighten yourself out.'"[49] The death of Don José, who years before had so harshly crossed his son's poetic sensibility, moved Neruda to a deeply appropriate act. The night his father died, he shut himself in the study and composed his first poem about Chile, "Almagro," which was the germ of *Canto general de Chile* ("General Song of Chile," 1943) and later appeared in *Canto general* (1950) as "Discoverers of Chile."[50] What he wrote shows the first clear stirring of an allegiance that for the rest of Neruda's life would never be far from his poetry. Evidently his father's death released in him the desire to testify for Chilean nationhood.

The conquistador Diego de Almagro, outmaneuvered by Pizarro in Peru, left Cuzco in 1535 to conquer Chile, and on the way saw thousands of his Indians and soldiers freeze to death in the Andes. Chile's native tribes turned him back, and he was later executed by Pizarro.[51] Neruda's poem does not retell that story but embodies the affront the Spaniards posed, the shadow they cast over his country's physical body. It begins:

> From the north Almagro brought his crumpled spark.
> And over the land, between sunburst and sunset,
> day and night he bent as over a map.
> Shadow of thorns, shadow of thistle and wax,
> the Spaniard at one with his dry form,
> observing the dark strategies of the soil.
> Night, snow, and sand give shape
> to my slender homeland.

Noche, nieve y arena hacen la forma / de mi delgada patria. For the first time in his verse Neruda refers to Chile as *patria.* "Fatherland," the word's inner sense, works uncomfortably in translation, but something more than "land" is needed to distinguish *patria* from *territorio* ("region," "land," as in Almagro bending "over the land") and from *tierra* ("earth," "land").

The death of his father drew Neruda painfully back through a biological link to the *patria*. It also led him to speak of his native land, as he had begun to speak of Spain, with a close physical affection. In "Almagro," Chile's "coal fills it with mysterious kisses. / Like an ember the gold burns in its fingers." The poem closes by insisting on the country's original integrity, and does so without the animus against Spain's conquistadors that would later emerge in *Canto general*:

> The Spaniard seated near the rose one day,
> near the oil, near the wine, near the ancient sky,
> could not conceive of this point of fierce stone
> coming to birth under the seabird's dung.[52]

What Almagro could not imagine was the dynamic of Chile's national emergence—the point of stone born from formless yet fertile nature. This poem reflects Neruda's political state of mind in 1938. While still working and writing for the Spanish Republican cause, the poet who at García Lorca's death had called himself "Spanish by race and by language" was discovering a *patria* that had imperial Spain as its foil. In "Almagro," Neruda's American genesis began to take a clear shape, though it had far to go before culminating in *Alturas de Macchu Picchu*.

Only three months after his father died, Neruda's stepmother also died, toward the end of winter in 1938. Soon afterwards, in "La copa de sangre," he wrote a strange account of their deaths, which accompanies the narrative about searching for his rainy land and swallowing his manhood in a cup of lamb's blood. Neruda's text is worth translating in full. He had an intense dramatic gift, and this incident seized his imagination:

> Not long ago my father died—a strictly secular occurrence and yet something funereally sacred happened in his tomb, and now is the time to reveal it. Several weeks later my mother also expired, as the dreadful newspaper jargon has it, and to let them rest together we removed the dead gentleman from his niche. My brother and I went at noon with some railroad friends of the deceased, we opened the sealed and cemented niche and took out the urn though now it was full of fungus and had on it a palm leaf with black wilted flowers. The dampness of the region had parted the coffin and in taking it down from its

place, unable to believe our eyes we saw quantities of water fall from it, endless liters were falling from inside, from its essence.

But all became clear: this tragic water was rain, rain perhaps of a single day, perhaps a single hour of our southern winter, and this rain had penetrated roofs and balustrades, tiles and other materials and other bodies to reach my parent's tomb. So then this terrible water, this water issuing from an impossible, unfathomable, extraordinary hiding place to tell me its torrential secret, this original and fearful water with its mysterious overflow was revealing to me again my endless bond with a certain life, region, and death.[53]

The long winter rains that pervaded his forsaken childhood now come back as if in a breaking of amniotic waters, bringing Neruda home to a second birth midway through his life.

If his parents' death dramatically revealed this bond, Neruda's own activity was also engaging him more deeply with Chile. By August 1938 he was leading the Alliance of Chilean Intellectuals for the Defense of Culture; he saw new Chilean editions of *España en el corazón*, *Veinte poemas de amor*, and *Residencia en la tierra* come out;[54] and he was directing a new magazine, *Aurora de Chile* ("Dawn of Chile").[55] To its first issue he contributed an elegy and a poem that show his thoughts still divided, though not in conflict, between Spain and Chile. César Vallejo had died recently in Paris. The Peruvian's passionate sequence on the Civil War, *España, aparta de mí este cáliz* ("Spain, Let This Cup Pass from Me"), had like Neruda's been printed by Republican soldiers, but of that edition all the copies were lost.[56] With Neruda and others he had helped establish a committee for the defense of Spain, and legend has it that he died with the words "I'm going to Spain" on his lips.[57] In a prose elegy for his fellow Latin American, Neruda dwells on the inner struggle that made Vallejo so very different from him: "Spain was gnawing at your soul. That soul so fretted away by your own spirit, so stripped, so wounded by your own ascetic need. Spain was the daily drill into your immense virtue."[58]

Perhaps these remarks about Vallejo's ascetic need gave Neruda a way of musing on his own rather different condition. After the anguish reflected in *Residencia en la tierra*, he had embraced the struggle in Spain with a fierceness that made his writing more forthright, as in "Explico algunas cosas." Some critics value him less than Vallejo for being less demanding of the language, of himself, of his reader.[59] The contrast, however one feels about it, does apply to their poetry during the Civil War. Spain's political and social crisis clarified Neruda's voice and turned it directly toward the people who were to take heart or comfort from it. Then back in Chile, a similar imperative turned him toward his own people and the landscape he saw marked by their hard lives. His "Winter Ode to the Mapocho River," published in the same issue of *Aurora de Chile* as his elegy to Vallejo, shows for the first time in Neruda's work an acute consciousness of the poor in *mi patria desnuda*, "my naked homeland." He asks the river: "who dragged you from the eagle's peak / down to where your pure waters touch / the terrible rags of my native land? / . . . Bitter river go back, go back to your snow-filled cup."[60]

That same winter of 1938, in July or August, one event in particular brought Neruda dramatically in touch with the Chilean people. During the year he had given readings for Spain and for the Popular Front presidential candidate in Chile. One reading, at Santiago's huge Central Market, he later remembered as a "revelation." He had gone to the market before but had never noticed the men and women working there. Now he found himself nervously facing a group of porters who wore rough sandals and sacks as aprons. He read from *España en el corazón*, almost the whole book, sensing "a terrible emptiness" as the porters "listened to me in strict silence." He wondered if they could grasp this poetry in which "the knot of obscurity is only beginning to open." Then he ended, and experienced "the most important event of my literary career. Some applauded. Others lowered their heads." One man stood up and said to him, "We are forgotten people, I can tell you, we've never felt such great emotion"; then the man broke into tears. After this face-to-face, voice-to-voice communion, Neruda says, "I felt I was in debt to my country, to my people."[61]

Soon afterwards, still as preoccupied with Spain as with Chile, Neruda undertook a humanitarian task that sealed the connection between the two countries for him. Early in 1939, while the Republic was crumbling, Chile's Popular Front government sent Neruda to France to bring back Spanish refugees. On the way he gave fervent speeches in Uruguay about Quevedo, García Lorca, and "my mother, mother Spain . . . the bleeding mother of our blood," who "brought forth our marvelous language."[62] Just before Hitler took over Europe, Neruda spent difficult months in Paris managing the exodus of over two thousand refugees to Chile—a job that greatly moved him.[63] While sailing home in December 1939 he wrote "Hymn and Return," rounding out his mission to the refugees: *Patria, mi patria, vuelvo hacia ti la sangre. . . .*

> Land, my native land, I bring this blood back to you.
> But I entreat you, like a child full of tears
> to its mother.
>   Accept
> this blind guitar
> and this fallen front. . . .
> I want now to sleep at your heart.[64]

The guitar and the fallen front are Spain's, but now the true mother, as in his childhood rambles and early love poems, is again Chile.

Once home, and having acquired a house on the seacoast at Isla Negra, Neruda continued writing in the vein of "Almagro," "Winter Ode to the Mapocho River," and "Hymn and Return." Three new poems, addressed to Chile's southern ocean, its northern desert, and its plant life, display the topographical instinct of a son and a lover that was quickly becoming second nature to him.[65] In the first, a highly figurative lyric, he calls the ocean "mother salt, bloodstained salt, mother curve of the water," and somehow his momentum also leads him in the second poem to call the Atacama desert "mother of the ocean." Both ocean and desert appear familiarly as *tu*. The most remarkable of the three poems, "Botánica," breaks into a kind of animated field guide:

Mugwort and grama-grass surround
the oregano's eyes
and radiant frontier laurel
perfumes outlying provinces.

What's remarkable is Neruda's avidity for naming, for confer-
ring surprising poetic figures on some two dozen different
plants. His childhood in the south gave him a love for the
names and the feel of flora and fauna, and since then he had
become a knowledgeable naturalist and collector. Some of the
things in "Botánica" allow of translation into English: hazelnut,
mugwort, saltwort, oregano, laurel, fuchsia, poppy, cinnamon,
oak. But most of the names have to be transported intact: *litre,
boldo, quila, quelenquelén, ulmo, copihue, doca,* and others. They
are indigenous to Chile, most being Araucanian Indian words,
and their untranslatability acts as proof of the "endless bond
with a certain life, region, and death" that Neruda was re-
newing.[66]

MEXICO (1940–43)

"I want now to sleep at your heart," Neruda said to Chile after
bringing Spanish refugees there in 1939.[67] There was not to be
much time, for early in 1940 the Popular Front government ap-
pointed him Consul General to Mexico. At the farewell ceremo-
ny he recited "Almagro" along with the other Chilean poems.[68]
In Mexico he persisted in the project of a *Canto general de Chile,* a
contemporary national epic, saying to an interviewer: "I want to
counterbalance the effect of the great poetry of the classics, such
as Ercilla and Pedro de Oña"—Alonso de Ercilla being the con-
quistador who, according to Neruda, had "founded" his coun-
try by writing *La Araucana* (1569), and Oña the Chilean-born au-
thor of a sequel, *Arauco domado* (1596).[69] The poems Neruda
wrote in Mexico touch yearningly on features of Chilean land-
scape and life. One of them, "I Want to Go Back to the South,"
begins: "Sick in Veracruz, I remember a day in the South, my
land." Later the poem says, "I want to go / behind the wood
along the fragrant / Toltén River . . . stretch out near cow dung,

/ die and revive chewing grain."[70] Other poems, not ground-
ed in this physical nostalgia for the south, sound at times as
though Neruda were somewhat mechanically practicing the so-
cial conscience awakened in Spain:

> My people, what are you saying? Sailor,
> laborer, mayor, nitrate miner, are you listening to me?
> I hear you, dead brother, live brother, I hear you.[71]

In an otherwise densely written poem, these simplistic lines
show Neruda cultivating a voice that at Macchu Picchu would
dramatically question both the city and its builders.

Historical circumstances continued to bring out the public,
partisan poet in Neruda. Shortly after arriving in Mexico he was
asked to read at the funeral of the country's leading composer,
Silvestre Revueltas,[72] and during his 1941 visit to a Guatemala
still under Jorge Ubico's dictatorship, he recited his poems be-
fore a student audience while four machine guns, he says, were
trained on him.[73] That same year in Mexico, before an emotional
university audience, he read "Un canto para Bolívar"; amid the
applause a Fascist group started demonstrating wildly and
fighting broke out.[74] At another gathering, as Roosevelt was
being toasted, some Nazis physically attacked and injured the
poet.[75] These experiences could only intensify his abhorrence of
Fascism, so that when the Russians defended Stalingrad, his
sympathies were immediately crystallized. In September 1942
he wrote and read aloud his "Canto to Stalingrad," which linked
Russia, the violated mother of heroic sons, to Republican Spain.
These verses were put up on posters around Mexico City.[76] Un-
aware, evidently, that since 1937 Stalin had been purging many
Communists who fought in Spain,[77] Neruda began looking
more to the Soviet Union than the United States for democratic
resistance to Fascism. In February 1943 he visited New York,
where he said that the war "was being won almost exclusively
by Russia," and criticized the United States government's atti-
tude toward Spanish Republicans. He also questioned the abil-
ity of United States consular officials in Latin America to get a

"real sense of our people" or of "social and cultural move-
ments," since they dealt only with "Creole oligarchies."[78] On
such an issue, less commonplace in 1943 than today, Neruda
was gradually defining his own Americanness apart from the
powerful neighbor to the north.

There were other inflences, more germane to his literary
imagination, during Neruda's stay in Mexico. Soon after arriv-
ing he came to know the muralists and their work—Diego
Rivera, José Clemente Orozco, David Alfaro Siqueiros. "These
Mexican painters," he wrote in his memoirs, "were covering the
city with history and geography, with civil uprisings, with iron-
hard polemics."[79] Their example of an epic style and subject fur-
thered the aim he had set himself. When a fragmentary version
of Canto general de Chile came out in Mexico in 1943, it carried
(along with epigraphs from Ercilla and Oña) a note saying that
the author hoped to embrace "all of Chile's geography and his-
tory and their repercussions for man."[80] Later, in 1950, the first
edition of Neruda's Canto general carried illustrations by Rivera
and Siqueiros. Several things must have impressed him in their
work besides its manifestation of history and geography. Like
Neruda in Canto general, the muralists worked on a large scale
with the whole of their history. They crowded the canvas with
people and events and vivid images, drew their bias boldly, en-
nobled the Indian and the revolutionary, and perhaps most im-
portant were "covering the city" with their vision, making it ac-
cessible to the people (and at the government's behest!).

As it happened, Neruda was able to make the muralists' art
directly accessible to the Chilean people. Four days after Neruda
arrived as Consul in Mexico in 1940, Leon Trotsky's assassina-
tion occurred. Siqueiros, a Stalinist, was in prison at the time for
having led an earlier attack on Trotsky and his family. Appar-
ently at the request of the Mexican government, Neruda gave
the painter a visa to Chile on the condition that he do a mural
there, which Siqueiros did paint in the library of a school in
Chillán.[81] Soon after Siqueiros, another Mexican artist, Xavier
Guerrero, painted a mural in the same school, and Neruda

imagined that "the peasants of my country will stop their horses near the decorated school and pause for a long time in front of Guerrero's figures, divining in them the hidden roots, the hidden waters that unite us beneath our great continent." [82]

Neruda's intimacy with the hidden roots and waters of America was unexpectedly attested to in 1942 by the Spaniard Juan Ramón Jiménez. An exile in Coral Gables, Florida, Jiménez reconsidered his earlier estimate of Neruda. In an open letter, he set some deep truths alongside his unrelenting view that this representative American lacked the order and clarity of a civilized poet:

Now evident to me is your exuberant attempt at a general and authentic Hispanic American poetry, with all this continent's natural revolution and metamorphoses of life and death. I regret that a considerable part of Hispanic American poetry should be like this to such a degree.
. . . Chaotic accumulation comes before definitive grace, the prehistoric before the posthistoric, the turbulent and confined shadow before the preferable and open light. You come before, prehistoric and turbulent, dark and confined. [83]

Knowing the way Neruda had held his own against Jiménez in his 1935 manifesto "On a Poetry Without Purity," one can guess that this open letter only prodded him further toward "a general and authentic Hispanic American poetry."

The years in Mexico and his trips to Guatemala, Cuba, and the United States opened up Neruda's perspective beyond the *Canto general de Chile*. A month before leaving Mexico and wending his way back home, he published his first group of poems embracing Latin America as a whole. By its title, *América, no invoco tu nombre en vano* ("America, I Do Not Invoke Your Name in Vain"), Neruda probably meant that it was not heedless or useless of him to call forth a specifically American genius in July 1943. [84] Though war was distant from these poems, the landscape within which he imagines himself is struggling for its life. Neruda seems to have sensed that the conflict in Europe would leave Latin Americans out of focus and at a loss unless they conceived some sort of autonomy for themselves. Besides, there was poverty and oppression at home to contend with; he had seen them in Central America. The most impressive poem in this collection, "The Dictators," denounces tyranny in the way Neruda was best equipped to do it—as a perversion of the natural order:

> A stench has stayed on among the cane fields:
> a mixture of blood and bodies, a sharp
> sickening petal.

The poem satirizes a "delicate satrap" in his palace and then presents a natural index of the damage a dictatorship causes:

> Weeping lies hidden like a plant
> whose seed falls ceaselessly on the soil
> and lightlessly pushes up great blind leaves.
> Hatred has grown scale upon scale,
> blow upon blow in the frightful water of the swamp,
> with a snoutful of slime and silence.[85]

Because Neruda kept a taproot open to the organic natural world of his childhood, he felt that political affronts to humanity perverted all of nature.

In the last three poems of *América, no invoco tu nombre en vano*, he inhabits a landscape that attracts him like the fecund natural scene of his early years. The brief lyric "A River" appeared in this 1943 collection but was inexplicably dropped from *Canto general* and from the *Obras completas*.[86] It deserves translating, particularly because Neruda imagines approaching this Mexican river with some of the same figures that would later take him to Macchu Picchu:

> I want to go along the Papaloápan
> as on the earthy mirror so many times,
> touching my fingers to the potent water:
> I want to go to the matrix, to the original
> frame of its crystal branchwork:
> to go, to wet my face, to plunge in the secret
> tumult of the dew
> my skin my thirst my dream.

The shad shooting from the water
like a silver fiddle,
and redolent flowers on the bank,
and immobile wings
in a zone of heat defended
by blades of blue.

I do not know why Neruda dropped this poem. It has the quiet ecstasy of the end of "Galope muerto," the centeredness of "Entrada a la madera," and its "immobile wings" and shad "like a silver fiddle" envision forms of dynamic energy within a specifically American setting. After "A River," the last two poems of *América, no invoco tu nombre en vano* find Neruda totally at home in the "belly" of the continent, "in the womb of your births." Utterly at one with his origins, he is "soaked in sperm from your species," he tells America, and "suckled on blood from your legacy." [87]

During these years, Neruda felt another part of his lineage tugging on him, and by 1943 he had fully brought to mind the story of Chile's Araucanian past. The story remained active in him for the rest of his career, linking him to native America and to Chile as well.[88] In Mexico "I felt myself intertwined," he said, "because every Chilean's roots extend under the earth and come out in other regions. . . . Lautaro was related to Cuahtemoc." [89] Here Neruda links a young Araucanian chief with the Aztec prince who defied Cortés. Lautaro had raised his people in revolt when Pedro de Valdivia came south to establish Spanish settlements. In 1553 he killed Valdivia in a crucial battle, and after that the Spaniards never crossed below the Bío Bío River.[90] Throughout four centuries the Araucanians maintained their independence of Inca, Spanish, and then Chilean hegemony despite periodic, often harsh, campaigns of pacification and segregation. Finally in 1881 Chile's government sent troops down to subdue the Indians. A treaty was signed at Ñielol hill, the Araucanians ceded land for the founding of a frontier town called Temuco, and pioneers flooded in to clear the forests and extend the railroad.

Neruda grew up there scarcely a generation later, taking his rambles on Ñielol hill. But between the boy and the actual Mapuche Indians of his childhood, a sadly dispossessed remnant of Araucania, there was no intercourse: "They lived totally apart." He saw them only when they came into town—"the man on horseback, the woman on foot"—to sell wool and lamb, or when he rode his father's train and they waited at stops with their goods. The Araucanian place names were "redolent of wild plants," Neruda later said, "their syllables captivated me," but as for the Indians themselves "we had absolutely no communication with them. We didn't know their language, except a few words, nor did they speak Spanish."[91] And Neruda did not have the Indian blood of his Guatemalan friend Miguel Ángel Asturias, whose mother was Mayan, or the Peruvian César Vallejo, whose grandmothers were Chimú and who thus "belonged to an older race than mine" in America.[92]

His lack of direct attachment did not prevent Neruda from retelling the Araucanian story for himself. Probably the Indianism of Mexico's muralists helped to send him back to his own native origins, and there was precedent as well in Chile's Creole patriots, seeking independence in 1810, who viewed Araucanian resistance to Spain as the nation's heroic infancy.[93] Neruda's first hint of the theme comes in 1938: "I belong to a piece of poor austral earth verging on Araucania."[94] Then at Silvestre Revueltas's funeral in 1940, a line from Neruda's elegy assures his listeners that "Araucania's unconquerable rivers" will pick up the lament.[95] The theme was taking hold in him: when he started a magazine later that year as Consul General in Mexico, he called it *Araucanía*.[96]

Neruda's first extended account of the Araucanians occurs in "Journey to the Shores of the World" (1943), a rambling, reminiscential talk he gave in Mexico. Their story exemplified for him the integrity of Chile as a nation and of America. Like the Indians at Macchu Picchu, these original tribes had a contemporary political force for Neruda: "Their terrific struggle . . . becomes clearer to us in these recent years of clamorous blood. While the Aztec and Inca oligarchies were giving in to the invader after a brief struggle," he says, with a suggestion of class analysis, Araucania's tribes "united in the first national front against an invader. They came victorious through a bloody campaign that lasted three hundred years and was borne into history and poetry by . . . don Alonso de Ercilla."* Then, having named Chile's epic forebear, Neruda turns to the pacification of Araucania in the late nineteenth century:

> The warriors' death agony, the end of a race that seemed immortal, made it possible for my parents . . . to come with the first pioneers in an old hackney, crossing stretches of hitherto unknown land, to the new frontier capital settled by Chileans. It was called Temuco and that is the history of my family and my poetry. . . . I was born in 1904 and by 1914 began writing my first poems there.[97]

The stream of history itself seems to move straight from Araucania's demise into the very genesis of Neruda's poetry.

In aligning himself with Ercilla and Araucania during these "recent years of clamorous blood," Neruda was continuing a brilliant example: an epic singer linked with a popular resistance to invasion. With that inspiration, he let himself in for large tasks in 1943, such as invoking "America" like a very palpable mother and rallying Latin Americans to her. Since nothing so drastic was going on in Latin America as in Europe, Neruda's posture may now seem somewhat excessive. But his experience in Spain and his sympathy for Russia carried over

---

*The suggestion of a class difference between Araucanians and Incas or Aztecs is borne out by Neruda's poem "Se unen la tierra y el hombre" ("Earth and Man Unite"), in *Canto general* (1950), OC, I, 364:

> My Araucanian fathers had no
> plumy luminous headdress,
> did not recline on nuptial flowers
> or spin gold for the priest:
> they were stone and tree, roots
> in the shaken shrubbery,
> leaves shaped like lances.

Neruda also held a theory that Chile's mestizo population, unlike that of other invaded regions, descends not from conquistadors and native concubines or wives but from Araucanian warriors and captive Spanish women. Historians do not bear out this theory. See Rita Guibert, *Seven Voices*, p. 51, and Magnus Mörner, *El mestizaje en la historia de Ibero-América* (Mexico City: Instituto Panamericano de Geografía e Historia, 1961), p. 18.

into Latin America, where in any case the shock waves of war and Fascism were felt.[98] At the time, Neruda was welcomed by many as a kind of prophet of Latin American unity. Some two thousand people came to hear him read at a farewell banquet in Mexico City's jai alai stadium, when he was about to leave for home. The next day a newspaper called him "interpreter of the mystery of our lineage and our destiny. . . . Historical man rooted in the earth, he shares the toil of humanity."[99]

TO MACCHU PICCHU (1943)

On September 1, 1943, Neruda left Mexico for Chile, stopping in several countries en route. He made the journey to Macchu Picchu on October 31. Some of the things said by him and to him during those two months can indicate the fairly complex state of mind Neruda brought to the pre-Columbian city—a state of mind that joined Golden Age Spain, the Republic, a hatred of Fascism, Latin America's integrity, and his own poetic aims. Stopping first in Panama, he spoke fervently about Spanish America's discovery of Republican Spain, "the mother's womb unknown until then," and he stressed at the same time America's continued independence from the Old World. Neruda valued sixteenth-century Spain, the founder of Spanish America, mainly for its link with the courageous Republic, its poets, and the Castilian language itself. He hoped that Spanish-American intellectuals would struggle alongside the people and that the fight against Fascism, which was far from won, would echo *a través de mi pequeña voz de poeta*, "through my small voice as a poet."[100]

In Colombia, Neruda read three of his *Viajes* ("Journeys"), including one that blended his experience in the Orient, his distrust of the Gandhi cult that "rests the future on a single human head," his enthusiasms for Spain's Golden Age poets, his shell collecting in Mexico and dismay at pre-Columbian human sacrifice, and his consciousness of Chile's Araucanian Indians, whose resistance to conquest created "a lesson inchoate then but alive today more than ever." In its most passionate mo-

ments, this *viaje* looks toward the country whose "long south-
ern winters infused the marrow of my soul and have accompa-
nied me around the globe." Neruda declares himself "a poet of
war and cities" but also of "those somber woods I remember
now with pervasive force," and this combination of history and
nature suggests how he came to envisage Macchu Picchu.[101]
Some verses he spoke in Colombia also suggest, in quite general
terms, ideas and language that the Inca site in particular would
evoke. He spoke of "obscure fallen lives" that he was born to
make known, of "ruins and fragments / from which life rises
anew," and of "the deep carpet that poets weave / across cen-
turies and water, in the depth, deeper than navigations"—*a
través de los siglos y del agua, en el fondo, más abajo de las navega-
ciones.*[102] This last line sounds much like Neruda's traversal of
time and space to regain the lost Andean city. The wonder is
that such vague notions soon found a subject that rendered
them necessary and exact.

In late October 1943 Neruda reached Lima. "For me Peru has
been the womb of America, an arena encircled by high and mys-
terious stones," he told a gathering of intellectuals, and he made
no reference to the rigors of Inca rule or the organizational con-
trol that must have been exerted to build the empire and its
monuments. Instead he allowed himself a wild surmise:

There is something cosmic in your Peruvian earth, something so strong
and brilliant that no fashion or style has been able to conceal it, as if
underneath your land an immense statue, mineral and phosphoric,
monolithic and organic, were still lying there covered by fabrics and
sanctuaries, by centuries and sand, and could show its vigorous form
in the height of the abandoned stones, in the unpeopled soil that we
have a duty to discover.[103]

Something like Macchu Picchu must have been in Neruda's
mind, along with a redemptive aim that his poem would em-
body two years later.

The talk he gave in Lima also dwelt on *fértiles conquistadores
incaicos,* but out of deference to his hosts he did not emphasize
the fact that before the Spanish Conquest, the Araucanians had
to stop the Incas at the Bío Bío River: "When my land felt waves

Macchu Picchu (1934). Photograph by Martín Chambi (1891–1973), courtesy of Edward Ranney and the Chambi family. Chambi, a Peruvian mestizo and Quechua-speaker whose studio was in Cuzco, first went to Macchu Picchu in the 1920's; this photograph was made shortly after the Peruvian government began clearing the ruins.

of fertile Inca conquerors who brought the woven touch of gar-
ments and liturgy to Arauco's grating shadows; when the ani-
mistic throbbing of watchful southern forests touched the sa-
cred turquoise and the vessel brimming with spirit, there is no
telling how far the vital waters of Peru invaded my country in its
awakening, immersing it in an earthly ripeness whose natural
expression is my own poetry." [104] Within the orotund language
and fanciful logic, Neruda means to derive his poetry from
Araucanian natural genius blended with Inca spiritual genius,
from the earth's grating shadows blended with Macchu Picchu's
vessel of spirit. Such may have been his frame of mind on going
to the site a few days later.

After speaking in Lima he traveled over the Andean cordillera
to Cuzco, the Incas' ancient capital standing at eleven thousand
feet. [105] There the mayor, the head of the Provincial Council, em-
inent citizens, and writers paved Neruda's way with eulogies
welcoming this "militant heart of America." [106] Someone from
the University of Cuzco opened his address: "There has reached
these high sierras of Irredentist America one of its most out-
standing sentinels." Neruda then read his own work, and local
poets also addressed their verses to him:

> You have sunk to the root of our collective tragedy
> and are the hurricane dwelling in a belfry of crystal and steel
> that proclaims the Gospel of the exaltation of the lowly.

The only really interesting document preserved from this visit
to Cuzco is a poem to Neruda in Quechua by Kilko Warak'a. It
appeared in the daily *El Sol*, and its translator into Spanish apol-
ogized for missing all the original's "grandeur, onomatopoeic
vigor, and singular novelty of image." Here is a stanza, now
doubly removed in English, in which the Quechua poet tells
Neruda of some Inca remains near Cuzco:

> The very stones of Sacsahuamán
> Awoke from their centuries' sleep
> And opened their frozen breasts
> When they knew you had arrived.

With that warrant, as it were, Neruda the next day (October 31, 1943) traveled north along the Urubamba River and climbed on horseback up to Macchu Picchu.

His journey was a good deal more arduous than what now happens when Braniff's passengers go to visit Peru. Probably the seventy-mile trip from Cuzco down the gorge of the Urubamba took him six or seven hours by train, and in 1943 there was no road for buses to make the steep climb up to Macchu Picchu (before long, tourists may be scooted up in a few minutes by aerial tramway).[107] The city had been discovered in 1911 by Hiram Bingham, an enterprising explorer from Yale and later Connecticut's governor and senator. Bingham describes being led by an Indian boy into "an untouched forest" and suddenly confronting the finest-grained Inca stonework he had ever seen, "partly covered with trees and moss, the growth of centuries, but in the dense shadow, hiding in bamboo thickets and tangled vines, appeared here and there walls of white granite ashlars carefully cut and exquisitely fitted together."[108] Bingham thought that he had found the legendary pre-Inca site of Tampu-tocco, and that the site corresponded to Vilcabamba, the last Inca's refuge after the Conquest. In fact the city was neither (Vilcabamba has since been found), but was probably begun around 1440 by the conqueror and builder Pachacutec. The period between the founding of Macchu Picchu and the arrival of the Spaniards in 1532 saw an incredible expansion of the Inca empire, until it encompassed six million subjects from what is now Ecuador through Peru and Bolivia to Argentina and central Chile. Inca rule, embodied in an emperor descended from the sun, was absolutely firm but seldom destructive. A kind of theocratic socialism under the direction of governing and priestly castes, it levied tribute in goods and labor but seems to have supported its people efficiently. The Incas mastered agricultural terracing and irrigation, set up a vast network of granaries and storehouses to provide against times of need, and built thousands of miles of roads and bridges to help organize the empire. Perhaps the Indians did not know hunger, as Neruda imagines, so much as an inescapable systemic oppression.[109]

Macchu Picchu (1977), Torreón complex. Photograph by Edward Ranney.

One fact in particular about the Inca site must have made a great difference to Neruda, though he does not say as much. Because of its inaccessibility, the conquistadors never got to Macchu Picchu and may not have known about it. Unlike Sacsahuamán or Cuzco itself, the place stayed free of Spain's colonial, Catholic settlement. In Cuzco, for instance, you can still walk around the slow, smooth, curving, yellowish grey stone perimeter of the Temple of the Sun, the center of Inca religion. But you remain only partially aware of the temple, because for centuries these stones have formed the foundation of a Dominican monastery. Macchu Picchu never underwent the Conquest. It seems arrested in time with a native people latent in it.

Neruda's sense that Macchu Picchu still spoke to the contemporary human condition, his intuition of the city's human cost, apparently came to him later, in writing the poem. At first he felt only astonishment that such a staggering American achievement could have lain so long unnoticed. A month after his visit he gave an interview to *El Siglo*, Chile's Communist newspaper. Even after speaking about Mexico's social revolution and Diego Rivera's art, he put more pride than politics into his remarks about Macchu Picchu. He spoke of structures

whose existence is unknown to so many of us—they constitute the most important archaeological unit in the entire world. It's something stupendous to sit on those stone benches surrounded by an amphitheater of immense structures at the peak of America's highest mountains. Right there, among the soaring condors who make their home in that site, in the solitude of the ruins—some archaeologists have set the age of Macchu Picchu at 12,000 years.[110]

His dating, which would put Macchu Picchu in the Pleistocene epoch, shows Neruda awe-struck at what seemed to him the origin of American culture. Two years later, when he wrote his poem, those "soaring condors" had turned ominous—"like a black ship / the ravening shadow of the condor cruises" (VIII)—but in 1943 Neruda above all felt a profound sense of discovery at Macchu Picchu.

The city itself gives you a feeling of physical improbability. Perched on a saddle between two pinnacles two thousand feet

Macchu Picchu (1975), Crypt of Torreón. Photograph by Edward Ranney.

above the Urubamba, its walls, towers, stairways, and roofless houses seem to be clinging organically onto the grassy ridge. The architectural historian George Kubler describes "terraced contours falling away abruptly on the east and west into blue-green abysses. . . . The rush of the river waters rises to the ear on all sides" along with "Chinese washes of fog and mist."[111] Wherever you go in the city you are moving up or down. Its precipitous site and massive, intricate stonework lead the mind back to Macchu Picchu's construction, which, as Kubler casually remarks, may not have "endured more than a generation or two." Polygonal monoliths or rectangular blocks were fitted precisely by a process of slow abrasion one against the other to form straight, sloped, or circular walls. Many of the structures arise integrally from rock or earth, and the masonry courses, lintels, stairs, stepped water conduits, and overlapping plazas all continue the scaled terracing beneath them. Clearly the Incas brought a sophisticated, harmonious architectural spirit to this wild site. As for the builders, no trace remains of their dwellings or those of the various artisans and farmers who supported such a community.

The purpose of this settlement remains tantalizingly obscure. Historians and archaeologists have called it a sanctuary for the Virgins of the Sun, a citadel (though it is not fortified), an outpost for surveying frontier tribes, even a resort.[112] Another kind of view, suggested in 1930 by the Peruvian socialist and historian José Uriel García, is appealing but hard to prove. In the "ensemble expression and intimate feeling," in the fact that no two buildings are alike, and in the "vertical triumph" of Macchu Picchu, he sees an early Inca spirit that preceded the rational, utilitarian, purely political genius for which they are renowned.[113] Kubler in 1960 carried this idea further, calling Macchu Picchu an architectural "escape" whose "extreme rhythmic and plastic variety" within a mysterious natural setting "transcends any idea of mere utility."[114]

In Canto XI of *Alturas de Macchu Picchu*, Neruda acknowledges the city's dazzling design but weighs against it the "heart of forgotten man." Here also Uriel García's ideas may well have affected the way Neruda perceived Macchu Picchu. They were friends, and in 1943 it was the Peruvian, then a senator for Cuzco, who guided Neruda around the site. Uriel García a few years before had published the second edition of his book on "the new Indian," and he was later to make a study of Macchu Picchu.[115] These writings stress the human role in choosing such a site and the "Quechua artificers" who shaped the city. In general he follows the lead of a radical Peruvian political thinker whom Neruda also admired, José Carlos Mariátegui (1895–1930). Mariátegui believed that the true Peru lay in the mountains, that its development had been arrested by the Conquest, and that a modern Peruvian socialism would need to regenerate the Indians' communal and corporate economy.[116] On two occasions in 1943, before visiting Macchu Picchu, Neruda had mentioned Mariátegui enthusiastically.[117] What he later said about that visit shows an affinity with Mariátegui's ideas:

I could no longer segregate myself from those structures. I understood that if we walked on the same hereditary earth, we had something to do with those high endeavors of the American community, that we could not ignore them, that our neglect or silence was not only a crime but the prolonging of a defeat. . . . I thought many things after my visit to Cuzco. I thought about ancient American man. I saw his ancient struggles linked with present struggles.*

What were those links, as Neruda saw them? He had come away from the years in Spain, Chile, and Mexico, and from the trip to Macchu Picchu, with his own mixture of ideas about ancient and present struggles—ideas that drew from Latin American Indianism, nationalism, and Communism of the thirties and forties. He prized the Araucanian Indians both as native

---

*"Algo sobre mi poesía," p. 12. This talk, which is not in OC, contained other remarks about Macchu Picchu: "When I traveled to Upper Peru I went to Cuzco and ascended Macchu Picchu. Some time before, I'd come back from India and China, but Macchu Picchu is even more grandiose. History books tell us about the civilizations of Assyria, the Aryans and Persians and their colossal constructions. After seeing the ruins of Macchu Picchu, the fabulous cultures of antiquity seemed to me papier-mâché. India itself seemed to me minuscule, sketchy, banal, a popular bazaar for the gods, next to the lofty solemnity of the abandoned Inca towers. . . . Aristocratic cosmopolitanism had brought us to worship the past of the most distant peoples and had kept us ignorant, so that we did not discover our own treasures."

Americans and as a first manifestation of Chilean nationhood. Although a poem on Macchu Picchu could not reflect Spanish exploitation of the New World, Neruda used the Inca regime, with its forced labor, to prefigure later exploitations.* As for Spain, his anger at the rape of America could be tempered by love of Spain's Golden Age and the Republic. In *Canto general*, he exposed the brutality of the Spanish Conquest but could at the same time include common Spanish soldiers among "the countless and punished / family of the poor of the world" ("They Reach the Gulf of Mexico, 1493").[118] Two of the writers he cherished most emerged from the Spanish Conquest with double affinities: Ercilla, the Spaniard who spoke for the Indians, and Garcilaso de la Vega, offspring of a conquistador and an Inca princess, who settled in Spain but chronicled Inca history. At bottom, it was the Americanness in each of these writers that drew Neruda to them. He too wanted to tell the story of America, and Macchu Picchu gave him a vantage point to do so. In this city that was "eaten and corroded by the passage of centuries," he recalls, "I felt Chilean, Peruvian, American."[119]

CHILE (1943–45)

Neruda's return from Mexico to Chile in 1943 ended a period of sixteen years during which only three had been spent at home. *Yo no puedo vivir sino en mi propia tierra*, he said of this return, "I cannot live except in my own land." The word *tierra* here does not mean fatherland or nation; like "land" it connotes both homeland and earth. "I can't live without putting my feet, my hands, and my ear on her, without feeling the circulation of her waters and shadows, without feeling my roots reach into her clay for maternal nourishment."[120] Admittedly the choice of "her waters" for *sus aguas* and "her clay" for *su légamo* takes liberties with what Neruda may have heard as neuter pronouns, yet his writing and imagery provide a continual warrant for this particular liberty. He really seems to have felt the dead metaphors

---

*It is worth remembering that Chile and Peru were old enemies, from the Inca incursions through the Independence period to the War of the Pacific (1879–83) and after.

of "roots" and "mother earth" as live ones. They infused his patriotism with a primitive kind of attachment to Chile, so that his return there held out the possibility of renewing a physical and historical bond.

"A long time later I wrote the poem on Macchu Picchu," Neruda said.[121] The two years between visiting the site and composing the poem seemed a long time because his intervening experiences affected him decisively, taking him from an astonishing ruin to *Alturas de Macchu Picchu*. In 1943 he was welcomed back, according to the Communist press, as a Chilean who "for perhaps the first time in American history" had revealed "the fabulous flamethrower of poetry" to the common people.[122] Neruda himself, on coming home, found not only "my country's loveliness" but "terrible poverty in the mining regions and elegant gentry crowding into their country clubs. I had to make a decision."[123] He entered politics. In 1944 Neruda began campaigning for the Senate to represent Chile's northernmost provinces of Tarapacá and Antofagasta. This tough, solitary desert area with its rich deposits of nitrate and copper had been taken from Peru and Bolivia in the War of the Pacific (1879–83), at the same time that Chilean troops went south to subdue Araucania. During Neruda's lifetime the region saw unbridled capitalist exploitation with periods of severe unemployment, and a labor movement was organized there by Luis Emilio Recabarren, who later founded the Communist Party in Chile. From 1900 on there were many strikes, including ones just before and after Neruda's election. The miners' existence was always hard. As Neruda put it: "Few places in the world show a life so difficult and deprived of anything to sweeten it. It takes unspeakable sacrifices to transport water, keep a plant that will yield even the feeblest flower, raise a dog, a rabbit, a pig."[124]

To know what Neruda's campaign meant to him depends on knowing how struck he was by the *Norte grande*, as it is called, the "Great North." Chile extends over twenty-six hundred miles along the west coast of South America, from absolute desert, the driest in the world, to Antarctic ice. The south, where Neruda grew up, has a rainy climate and lush vegetation, whereas the north is barren. "I come from the other extreme of the republic," he said about campaigning in the north. "The mere fact of confronting that lunar desert overturned my existence."[125] He describes his long tours through the harsh terrain, the strikes in progress, the rallies, the poor shacks where he was put up, the miners' scorched, forsaken faces, the rasping handshakes, the grievances of men and women. Yet people always asked him to read from his work, and despite their mute response "my poetry opened the way for communication and I could go among them and be received as a brother." It impressed Neruda deeply that this should happen, and in such austere settings—"I who am a southern aboriginal used to fields and woods, copihues and ferns drenched by heavy dew."[126]

The key to this experience can be found in a passage Neruda wrote while revising his memoirs, not long before his death. He says that for years he had explored all kinds of worlds, including the anguished human heart, yet never the fundamental plight of humankind in cities and in the countryside. But when war broke out in Spain, "my poetry paused like a ghost in the streets of human anguish and up through it a current of roots and blood began to rise." Then he says: *Y de pronto veo que desde el sur de la soledad he ido hacia el norte que es el pueblo,* "And suddenly I see that from the south of solitude I have gone toward the north which is the people."[127] From the south to the north, childhood to adulthood, melancholy to responsibility, solitude to solidarity: the image of roots and rising blood took an actual form in Neruda's months of campaigning. These months were also taking him from the heroic Indian past to the Chilean people's actual needs. The point here is not that Neruda suddenly forgot the south and Arauco. In fact, from *Canto general* on, they turn up steadily when he wants to evoke a national genius and occasionally when he deplores the Indians' present condition.[128] Nor did he cut himself off from the dark, sunken, unconscious element his poetry had frequented. *Alturas de Macchu Picchu* came to be grounded in that element. But early in 1945, Neruda mainly felt himself moving "toward the north which is the people."

He could not help but carry that feeling into his political cam-
paign. To open a typical meeting, Neruda would read the richly
rhyming stanzas of his "Salute to the North":

> Norte, to your fierce silent zone
> of minerals I come at last,
> seeking your voice and thus my own.

The poem then points up his southern origin with an image
of copihues, the forest flower that is Chile's national emblem.
Neruda's second stanza (allowing for the oddness in English of
close rhyming) sounds like this:

> The country's waist may be overspread
> with a branch of the copihue's red
> but above its splendid face is set
> shining upon the darkened head
> a coronet of sweat.[129]

Though the verse itself runs to facile effects, the underlying
logic of this poem prefigures that of *Alturas de Macchu Picchu*: in
"Salute to the North" Neruda prizes the spare beauty of the
"puma-colored" desert, just as he would prize the stunning An-
dean site, but draws into his poem the privation of those who
work there, and every few stanzas he asks that his voice be the
voice of this place and people. Whatever role his poetry played
in the campaign, the northern provinces elected him in March
1945. It was the greatest satisfaction of his life.[130]

Two months later Neruda also won his country's National
Prize for Literature, which provoked political objections but
bound him closer to his *pueblo* and *patria*, as he said, his people
and his native land.[131] Then on July 8, 1945, he formally joined
the Communist Party. A week later he was invited to São Paolo
to welcome back the Brazilian revolutionary Luis Carlos Prestes
from ten years in prison. Prestes, a legendary figure, had in
1924 led a revolt and a six-thousand-mile march through the
Brazilian hinterland. Later on, according to Neruda, the Bra-
zilian government handed his German-born wife over to Nazis,
who murdered her. She had just given birth and Prestes's moth-

er rescued the baby.[132] When the mother died in Mexico in 1943, with Prestes in prison, Neruda read an emotional elegy at her grave, calling on Latin America's dead heroes to fill in for her son.[133] His 1945 mission to São Paolo was thus a dramatic one. In an immense stadium thousands of Brazilians cheered him and Prestes; Neruda slowly enunciated a poem he had written a few hours earlier, and to his relief the Brazilian crowd understood it.[134] The poem alternates between anecdote and declamation, bringing word "from the Andean snows, from the Pacific," from Chile's workers and children to "their captain silenced for so many hard years of solitude and shadow." In context, Neruda's rhetoric must have been impressive. He ended, "I ask America for silence from snow to pampas," and introduced Prestes with an idea that in recent years had also become associated with himself: "Silence: Let Brazil speak through his mouth." [135] About his reception in São Paolo, Neruda later said, "Those cheers resonated deeply in my poetry. A poet who reads his verses to 130,000 people does not go on as before." [136] After more recitals in Río de Janeiro, Buenos Aires, and Montevideo, he returned home and began *Alturas de Macchu Picchu*. The achievement of it is that Neruda could distill his public experience and rhetorical habit, those of an American poet through whom the people speak, into so personal and intense a work as *Alturas de Macchu Picchu*.

He wrote the poem "at Isla Negra, facing the sea," during August and September 1945.[137] The bombs that had just dropped on Hiroshima and Nagasaki must have confirmed what he knew already—that the war had created a superpower to the north, and that in a hemisphere under United States dominance, a radical Latin American voice would have to call on deep resources to be heard. There is a news report from this period with some particularly appropriate words of Neruda's. The poet Gabriela Mistral, who taught him in Temuco when he was young and whom he later came to know as a friend, received the Nobel Prize just after he finished writing *Alturas de Macchu Picchu*. In the Chilean Senate he spoke of her as though he were also musing on himself: "Gabriela's entire work has in it something subterranean . . . as if the anguish of many people spoke through her mouth and told us of painful and nameless lives." [138]

About the poem's moment of composition we have a brief report from the French writer Roger Caillois, for whom Neruda recited his just-completed cantos: "Neruda read them in a voice that went from tremulous to sonorous, monotone to brilliant, as litany followed upon invective and grief upon anger." [139]

Chapter Five

TRANSLATING *ALTURAS DE MACCHU PICCHU*

FROM VOICE TO VOICE

Perhaps the real "original" behind any translation occurs not in the written poem, but in the poet's voice speaking the verse aloud. Roger Caillois was lucky to be there that day in 1945, for as "litany followed upon invective and grief upon anger," he was hearing in Neruda's voice the formal and the emotional components of *Alturas de Macchu Picchu*. In more specific ways, a translator may also pick up vocal tones, intensities, rhythms, and pauses that will reveal how the poet heard a word, a phrase, a line, a passage. To get from the poet's voice into another language and into a translator's own voice is the business of translation. It depends on a moment-by-moment shuttle between voices, for what translating comes down to is listening— listening now to what the poet's voice said, now to one's own voice as it finds what to say.*

In order to go between but not get between the author and the reader, a translator constantly makes local choices in diction and phrasing that tune the new version as it goes. With *Alturas de Macchu Picchu* in particular, the choices matter because this poem marked "a new stage in my style and a new direction in

---

*I have used three recordings as aids in translating and interpreting. One is an Odeon recording of (I believe) 1955: Neruda's voice is often sonorous, slow, laden with emotion. The other, on tape, may be his earlier recording from 1947 (Santiago: Ibero-américa). In any case, it is a far more harsh, urgent, and compelling rendition. The third, probably from 1966, is a Caedmon recording, CDL 51215.

my concerns," as Neruda said.[1] But newness emerges from what came before. Into Neruda's long poem may have fed anything from his life up until August 1945—childhood, love, travel, politics, previous writings. A knowledge of these things should feed into the translator's work as well, if only to bring about some lexical echo, or shift in tone, or emphatic rhythm that shows what the newness actually consists of. This chapter recounts in detail the process of making an English version of *Alturas de Macchu Picchu*—that is, of creating yet another stage, another direction for the poem itself.[2]

To make a new version is to reimagine the original poem, and in this process the translator develops particular affinities with the author: a shared historical or philosophical perspective, a parallel emotional impetus, a kindred linguistic task. Occasionally one great poet translates another and brilliantly proves the affinity. Rilke translated Valéry's "Cimetière marin" into German with "an equivalence I scarcely thought could be achieved," he said; "my resources so corresponded with his great, glorious poems that I have never translated with such sureness and insight."[3] Or in the ultimate case, Samuel Beckett makes faithful but firsthand versions of Beckett's French—they are just what he would say in English.[4] When the translator is other than a great poet, those emotional and linguistic affinities are put to the test: each choice, each rendering attempts to realize in English what the author has said—that is, both to comprehend and to make actual. This is the heart of the process, this twofold incitement. Sometimes it strains the language of translation, whose words must keep to an original and yet set their own pace too. But often enough a happy chance will render the original fully and at the same time let the English verse do what it wants to.

The translator becomes obsessively alert to words, as certain of them spring into relief from the page or from the poet's recorded voice. Perhaps an ambiguous term in *Alturas de Macchu Picchu* occurred in earlier poems or prose in such a way as to clarify its present usage. In translating as prolific a writer as Neruda, one builds up a kind of concordance from work to work. A number of weighted words turn up more than once in *Alturas de Macchu Picchu*: *manantial* ("spring," "source"), *hundir* ("to sink," "plunge"), *entregar* ("to give up," "hand over"), and others become familiar tokens that keep their meaning. One can hear something slightly different in each context, but maybe those shadings signify less than the pattern and the resonance that emerge in translating the word identically as often as possible. There can be no hard-and-fast rules for deciding between the demands of the original and those of the translation. So I write from within the Spanish and without, feeling for the pulse and pressure of Neruda's verse but also keeping a distance at which my new version becomes just that—a new version of the story now discernible in both poems. What follows, then, is a close account of the translator's basic activity, the to-and-fro movement between Spanish and English.

CANTOS I, II: "THE EXHAUSTED HUMAN SPRING"

Opening the first half of the poem, the stage before his life brought him to Macchu Picchu, Neruda draws us right into that life, saying where he has been and when, how he has acted, and what he has missed so far. But with all that, his syntax and imagery still unfold somewhat obscurely:

> *Del aire al aire, como una red vacía,*
> *iba yo entre las calles y la atmósfera, llegando y despidiendo,*
> *en el advenimiento del otoño la moneda extendida*
> *de las hojas, y entre la primavera y las espigas,*
> *lo que el más grande amor, como dentro de un guante*
> *que cae, nos entrega como una larga luna.*

Even a close, practically word-for-word rendering requires a dozen decisions (some of them made while thinking out these paragraphs) that affect the sense and movement of the passage:

> From the air to the air, like an empty net,
> I went on through streets and thin air, arriving
>   and leaving behind,
> at autumn's advent, the coin handed out

in the leaves, and between spring and ripe grain,
the fullness that love, as in a glove's
fall, gives over to us like a long-drawn moon.

Other translations begin "From air to air."[5] Though it is often possible to drop the definite article when translating Neruda, here I think his opening movement belongs to "the air" we all live in. That movement also needs a protracted rhythm. He is dragging the air, as it were, searching his surroundings for something, coming to the fruits of summer and autumn but then leaving them behind.

The syntax of these lines has troubled readers and translators,[6] since *llegando y despidiendo* could make an independent unit, "arriving and saying goodbye." But *despedir* may have a stronger transitive meaning here, "dismiss" or "renounce." Perhaps "leaving behind" splits the difference between saying goodbye and renouncing. To settle then on *la moneda* ("the coin") as the object of *despedir*, a comma between *otoño* and *la moneda* would help: "leaving behind, / at autumn's advent, the coin." No editions have a comma there, but Neruda does pause markedly in two phonograph recordings (the third is noncommittal). So despite the pun, I think we see him leaving behind or forsaking the season's generosity, what the leaves and what love have to give. Not to relate him to them would ignore the emptiness of his net, the very need that set him writing this poem. In *Veinte poemas de amor* (1924) Neruda had said, "I cast my sad nets in your oceanic eyes."[7] That yearning for fulfillment, baffled for so many years, becomes the initial memory in *Alturas de Macchu Picchu*—a memory of failing to connect with nature and humankind.

Some of the translator's choices in these lines have a more local significance. Neruda's *moneda extendida*, the "extended" coin, calls not only for a visual image but also for a figurative sense, as in coin "handed out." And when love *nos entrega* (literally, "delivers to us"), which in the first of the *Veinte poemas de amor* suggests passive surrendering, Neruda's verb here can carry as well an active sense of giving. The phrase "give over" blends both ideas and also modulates away from the trivial rhyme of "glove" with "love." Within this same figure, the preposition *dentro* ("within") poses a more crucial question. If the fullness of love comes *dentro de un guante que cae*, literally "within a glove that falls," does it somehow come within the glove itself or—a more compelling thought—within a moment, "as in a glove's fall"? Neruda locates this experience, like the swelling calabashes of "Galope muerto" twenty years before, in high summer, "between spring and ripe grain." This is the kind of love we are offered but seldom grasp. It can concentrate and reveal itself in a moment, yet extend *como una larga luna*, "like a long-drawn moon"—*larga* implying duration rather than distance, as in *ese sonido ya tan largo*, "that sound so drawn out now," from "Galope muerto." In that poem Neruda perceived a kind of consummation that could seem a moment's doing yet stretch on endlessly. Both nature and passion gave him instances of it. Then *Alturas de Macchu Picchu* subjected that consummation to the demands of history.

After Neruda's "empty net" drifts through the streets, reaching then leaving behind seasons of ripeness, a sudden parenthesis interposes four images of forceful passion:

> (*Días de fulgor vivo en la intemperie*
> *de los cuerpos: aceros convertidos*
> *al silencio del ácido:*
> *noches deshilachadas hasta la última harina:*
> *estambres agredidos de la patria nupcial.*)

These images, with each phrase bearing four marked stresses, need the directest possible conveyance into English:

> (Days of live brilliance in the storm
> of bodies: steels transmuted
> into silent acid:
> nights raveled out to the final flour:
> battered stamens of the nuptial land.)

The figures surge up into Neruda's narrative from a deeper stratum than the lines around them. They all imagine a passion that is now only latently possible—is too brilliant, too consuming to take form yet as a clause or sentence. The last line, *estambres agredidos de la patria nupcial*, "battered stamens of the nuptial land," poses problems in translation. For one thing, "father-land" or even "homeland" at the end would dissipate the rhythm too much—why is it that English has nothing but compound words for this idea? And *estambres* can mean either "stamens" or "threads," which are both germane to the poem. Italian and French have cognates that retain both meanings, but the English word "stamen" has lost the root sense of "thread," and a choice must be made. Whereas "threads" would pick up "raveled" from the previous line, "stamens" does better by bringing out a regenerative potential in the "nuptial" land. But then why such violence in *agredidos* ("assaulted," "injured")? The previous figures embody a memory and a hope of sexual passion; in "battered stamens of the nuptial land" Neruda may momentarily be envisioning the damaged lives at Macchu Picchu and their difficult rebirth.

Following the parenthesis occurs a change of tense that can easily get lost in translation. Before, Neruda had said *iba yo*, "I was going" or "I went on" rather than "I went" through streets and air. Now he moves from the imperfect into a full sentence with preterite forms, *hundí, descendí, regresé*, "I plunged . . . dropped down . . . went back." The change marks a departure: from a drifting to a willed descent. Canto I, then, not only sets in motion the imagery of fruitless wandering but also imagines a decisive journey that will not actually occur until Canto VI— an ascent that requires descending because the site is buried, sunken out of consciousness. Having spoken of a *patria nupcial*, Neruda in this opening canto enters "a world like a buried tower," *un mundo como una torre enterrada*. Both *patria* and *torre* will come back later as epithets for Macchu Picchu, and the "human spring" Neruda seeks in this canto is echoed when he calls the city "High reef of the human dawn" (VI). In his beginning, Neruda's words prefigure his end.

Canto I also sets the poem's coordinates in time and space. Through the unfulfilling streets and seasons Neruda moves horizontally, but after imagining "days of live brilliance" he drops vertically like a buried tower, a sinking spiral, a sword, a plunging hand (the same verb, *hundir*, can yield both sinking and plunging in this sentence). *Hundí la mano turbulenta y dulce /en lo más genital de lo terrestre*, "I plunged my turbulent and gentle hand / into the genital quick of the earth." It seems a semantic windfall that the best rendering of *dulce*, "gentle," softens the sound of "turbulent" and then chimes etymologically with "genital." As for *lo más genital* (literally "the most genital"), "the genital quick" tunes up Neruda's Spanish slightly—I hope he would approve the change. Every quest is sexual, it seems, and so Neruda thinks of penetrating to some progenitive source beneath earth and ocean, even more purposefully here than in "Entrance into Wood." Because the source has been spent or forgotten, his descent along the vertical axis must also take him back in time, "back . . . to the jasmine / of the exhausted human spring." In the Caedmon recording, Neruda misreads *jazmín* ("jasmine") as *jardín*, as if it were the "garden" of the exhausted human spring, and that odd slip corroborates his return to some lost Eden. The *primavera humana*, being a natural as well as a historical source, may justify in translation the pun on "spring" as a fountain. Or perhaps that word needs capitalizing, so that other meanings of "spring" do not obscure Neruda's search for a season of renewal and rebirth.

His search has the elements of a mythic or ritual procedure, a spellbound underworld and undersea descent. To mark that quality throughout the canto's final lines, I give them more rhythmic shape than English free verse usually has, establishing an iambic pentameter base and varying it with anapests and dactyls:

> and deeper yet, in geologic gold,
> like a sword sheathed in meteors
> I plunged my turbulent and gentle hand
> into the genital quick of the earth.
>
> I bent my head into the deepest waves,
> dropped down through sulfurous calm

and went back, as if blind, to the jasmine
of the exhausted human spring.

Neruda himself recited much of the poem in an incantatory tone
and rhythm, as if conscious that only a heightened utterance
would carry him on this journey.

Having gone back to the "human spring," he begins Canto II,
Si la flor a la flor—echoing the poem's opening, *Del aire al aire*—
and then goes on to show why the human spring is exhausted.
The trouble lies in our dissonance with nature:

> *Si la flor a la flor entrega el alto germen*
> *y la roca mantiene su flor diseminada*
> *en su golpeado traje de diamante y arena,*
> *el hombre arruga el pétalo de la luz que recoge*
> *en los determinados manantiales marinos*
> *y taladra el metal palpitante en sus manos.*

> While flower to flower gives up the high seed
> and rock keeps its flower sown
> in a beaten coat of diamond and sand,
> man crumples the petal of light he picks
> in the deep-set springs of the sea
> and drills the pulsing metal in his hands.

The equation between natural and human existence, which is
lyric poetry's main source of metaphor, carries an inescapable
logic: instead of crumpling the flower, "man" (*el hombre*) should
conform to the example of nature's regenerative process. Neru-
da's clauses by their very placement reveal the crux of his meth-
od. Flowers give, but man crumples: what's broken is the meta-
phoric connection sought so avidly in Neruda's love poems.
That is, human life should be embodying and enacting meta-
phors from nature.

In translating *la flor entrega*, "flower gives up," it is worth
echoing Canto I, where love *nos entrega*, "gives over to us": our
own generousness and nature's ought to coincide. By the same
token Neruda's next line is crucial: *y la roca mantiene su flor disem-
inada*. Across the word *flor* a tensile arc gives shape to the line,

connecting two verbs whose meanings might be opposed: *mantener* ("maintain") and *diseminar* ("disseminate"). What holds them together is the idea that giving does not entail loss, that in spending passion and energy one need not lose substance or identity. Neruda's political exertions from 1936 to 1945 taught him this, and now on the way to Macchu Picchu he can put it in a single line.

That word *mantiene* marks Neruda's first use of the root *tener*, "to hold," which will occur in critical ways throughout the poem. Whether as "maintain," "sustain," "contain," or "detain," the root implies a dynamic form—some kind of matter or energy held in, yet holding its own. In translation, short Germanic verbs seem better than the Latinate words for holding this line's tensile shape: "and rock keeps its flower sown." "Sown" also lends a stronger sound and rhythm to the whole passage than "disseminated," and "keeps" has the sense of at once containing and prolonging. The rock that "keeps its flower sown" can give us intimations of Macchu Picchu, a stone structure that may have kept life stirring within it.

Since this first half of *Alturas de Macchu Picchu* essentially recapitulates the experience of Neruda's twenties, images of denatured life from his earlier poems keep turning up. The "clothing hung from a wire" in "Walking Around" can be seen here in "clothes and smoke" and "hostile trappings of the wire." The *amapola* ("poppy"), a frequent symbol for passion in his love poems, appears now in a striking figure from Canto II, where Neruda asks:

> *quién guarda sin puñal (como las encarnadas*
> *amapolas) su sangre?*

> who (like the crimson poppy) keeps
> no dagger to guard his blood?

In the earlier love poems it was usually enough to say something like "the color of poppies sits on your brow." Here, human and physical nature remain disjunct. Societal anxiety closes parentheses around the poppy, nature's example of passionate openness. More specifically, the word "guard" implies that we would lose less through openness than through constraint; that we might thrive within organic forms of existence rather than rigid forms of control.

In Canto II, nature provides the touchstone for sexual and social acts though not yet for political existence. The passage beginning "How many times in the city's winter streets" drifts with no verb through four long lines of loveless human scenes until *me quise detener*, "I wanted to stop." *Detener* ("stop," "pause," "arrest"), a common verb, was one Neruda often used revealingly. "Galope muerto" finds him *deteniéndose*—"in what's immobile, holding still, to perceive"—and in "Sonata y destrucciones" he is *detenido*, a journeyer "held" between shadows and wings. His prose also uses the word at important moments: in Spain "my poetry paused" amidst the anguish, and then "roots and blood began to rise through it"; and going home in 1943, he says, *Me detuve*, "In Peru I stopped and climbed to the ruins of Macchu Picchu."[8] Here in Canto II the verb *detener* interrupts a frustrating horizontal movement, what Eliot's *Four Quartets* calls "the waste sad time / stretching before and after," and creates, in Eliot's words, a "point of intersection of the timeless / with time":[9]

> *me quise detener a buscar la eterna veta insondable*
> *que antes toqué en la piedra o en el relámpago que el beso desprendía.*

> I wanted to stop and seek the timeless fathomless vein
> I touched in a stone once or in the lightning a kiss released.

Eliot's word "timeless" (for *eterna*) helps in translation, since both poets conceived of profound and heightened experience along a vertical axis, out of time. And because Spanish has another word for human veins (*vena*), my translation relies on "fathomless" to locate this mineral *veta* underground or perhaps undersea. In wanting to stop in mid-career and to descend, the poet recalls some early joy and anticipates in "a stone" some future one.

Right after Neruda recalls the stone and "the lightning a kiss released," an extended vision arises, showing what that vital touch was and what it might be like again. This vision arises between parentheses, as if caught and held against the stream of daily experience:

> (*Lo que en el cereal como una historia amarilla*
> *de pequeños pechos preñados va repitiendo un número*
> *que sin cesar es ternura en las capas germinales,*
> *y que, idéntica siempre, se desgrana en marfil*
> *y lo que en el agua es patria transparente, campana*
> *desde la nieve aislada hasta las olas sangrientas.)*

These lines, as the translator comes to realize, develop no main clause: beginning *lo que* ("that which"), they form a kind of instantaneous subliminal flash depicting what the poet stopped to seek:

> (Whatever in grain like a yellow history
> of small swelling breasts keeps repeating its number
> ceaselessly tender in the germinal shells,
> and identical always, what strips to ivory,
> and what is clear native land welling up, a bell
> from remotest snows to the blood-sown waves.)

Moving through progressive verb forms, a present tense, and the verb "is," this passage never resolves into a main verb but remains in suspension. Life given over to time and change ("history," "repeating," "ceaselessly," "germinal") is not exhausted, but through that very change keeps its form ("grain," "breast," "number," "shell").

The key phrase is the strangest, *idéntica siempre*, and needs close rather than interpretive translation. Tarn says that the grains shell "always the same way," but I think Neruda means they are "identical always": no matter how much generation the germ of life goes through, it keeps its essential identity, it remains one and the same.[10] Like the parenthesis in Canto I, which closes with "battered stamens of the nuptial land," this parenthesis closes with a presage of the mountain site: *y lo que en el agua es patria transparente, campana / desde la nieve aislada hasta las olas sangrientas.* No English verse could equal the way Neruda's *ah*-sounds move through *agua* to the *patria transparente*, then into the roundedness of *campana*, and finally resonate throughout the landscape of the last line. I have played with the sense a little to get rhyming vowel sounds—"clear native land welling up, a bell / from remotest snows to the blood-sown waves"—though that mixture may be somewhat rich.

The parenthesis closes and Neruda's narrative voice now returns, in the past tense again, saying he could not "touch," he could only "grasp" hollow faces or masks. In this alienation, he imagines finding some responsive touch in a place that will be either "running" or "firm":

> *No tuve sitio donde descansar la mano*
> *y que, corriente como agua de manantial encadenado,*
> *o firme como grumo de antracita o cristal,*
> *hubiera devuelto el calor o el frío de mi mano extendida.*

> I had no place to rest my hand,
> none running like linked springwater
> or firm as a chunk of anthracite or crystal
> to give back the warmth or cold of my outstretched hand.

The translation can, like the original, enrich its language by association: "my outstretched hand" reaches back to "the coin handed out in the leaves" in Canto I, as well as forward to moments when Neruda's hand will touch the city's stones and reach for the men who dwelt there. A place "running like linked springwater" will be found in Canto IX's epithet for the city, "wellspring of stone," *manantial de piedra*, and my word "linked," instead of the literal "chained" for *encadenado*, will again be heard when Neruda says to the Indian workers in Canto XII, "Tell me everything, chain by chain, link by link." I choose "linked" in Canto II because the word suggests controlling yet releasing a life-giving source: it anticipates the Incas' ingeniously stepped conduits and irrigation runnels at Macchu Picchu, which link the levels of the city, harmonizing hard natural fact with human need. One more phrase in this passage, *No tuve sitio*, also looks ahead through the poem as if through the years. Here Neruda says, "I had no place" to rest, and the need for one is so sharp that it carries through to Canto VI, where he will announce simply: *este es el sitio*, "this is the place."

CANTOS III, IV, V: "WHAT COULD NOT BE REBORN"

Because this poem prepared a new stage in his work, it "came out too impregnated with myself," Neruda said. "The beginning is a series of autobiographical recollections. I also wanted to touch for the last time there upon the theme of death."[11] He said this after being exiled as a Communist between 1948 and 1952, during which time he was welcomed throughout the Soviet orbit and in China, saw *Canto general* translated into twenty-five languages, and felt persuaded that poetry's task was to hearten the common struggle.[12] These conditions made him sensitive to the poem's subjective, dispirited vein. Yet it is hard to imagine *Alturas de Macchu Picchu* without Neruda's presence, particularly the constantly inquiring force of his voice.

"What was man?," Neruda cries at the close of Canto II, and the next canto opens with another figure from nature:

> Lives like maize were threshed in the bottomless
> granary of wasted deeds . . .
> and not one death but many deaths came each man's way.

What troubles Neruda most about this way of living, which feels like a "lamp snuffed out in suburban mud, a petty fat-winged death," is that such dwindling and death have no communal matrix, no shared vision, no common *logos* to redeem them. "Alone," he says in Canto IV, "I roamed round dying of my own death." Even the workers whom he evokes fairly strongly, "the drover, the son of seaports, the dark captain of the plow," remain isolated as *cada ser* or *cada uno* or *cada hombre*: "each being," "each one," "each man." One can question whether Neruda's vision really is shared commonly. In translating, it is hard to see *hijo* ("son" or "child"), *uno*, and *hombre* as generic rather than gender-linked: this canto does not suggest that for women, as for drovers and sailors and farmers, "their dismal weariness each day was like / a black cup they drank down trembling."

Canto IV opens with *La poderosa muerte*. Whether a "powerful," "mighty," "irresistible," or "overmastering" death, as translators have heard it,[13] it is in any case the "one death," which Canto III opposed to the "many deaths" that isolated men die day after day. By complex figures of speech—death was like salt in the waves, like sinking and height—Neruda connects this *poderosa muerte* to other ideas in the poem. It is not simply that his writing runs to figures of speech, but that in those figures he evolves the deeper-than-narrative structure of his poem, particularly through words the translator has noticed and will come upon again:

> *La poderosa muerte me invitó muchas veces:*
> *era como la sal invisible en las olas,*
> *y lo que su invisible sabor diseminaba*
> *era como mitades de hundimientos y altura.*

> The mightiest death invited me many times:
> like invisible salt in the waves it was,
> and what its invisible savor disseminated
> was half like sinking and half like height.[14]

The literal sense of *diseminaba* seems called for (and enriches the sound) in this instance. Along with its corrosiveness, salt has enhancing and preserving qualities, and these fit Neruda's idea of a death that sustains the potential for rebirth. In Canto XII, for instance, he will say to the buried American, "Give me your hand out of the deep / region seeded by all your grief"—your *dolor diseminado*. The analogy in Canto IV imagines death *como mitades de hundimientos y altura*—literally, "like halves of sinkings and height." The available verse translations miss Neruda's drift, I think. Belitt's "height, or the ruin of height, a plenitude halved" eludes my understanding, and Tarn's "fragments of wrecks and heights" skirts the exact sense of *mitades* ("halves"), the idea that death is a whole made up equally of what sinking and height connote.[15] The image of sinking need not have negative force, as Belitt and Tarn imply; for Neruda it leads to the deep pole, the basis, the root. The words *hundir* and *altura* take various forms both early and late in the poem, suggesting that an encounter with Macchu Picchu involves the full scale of what we can experience: from the unconscious to the spirit, from sexual earthiness to transcendent ecstasy, from past to future, from death to renewal.

Even when a profuse and vaguely symbolic imagery in *Alturas de Macchu Picchu* makes translating uncertain, it is well to trust rather than paraphrase Neruda, for a logic usually underlies what he says. In the poem's opening image he had stopped wandering through the streets to sink into earth and sea. Now in "suburban mud" or "cluttered streets" (III) he looks for the dimension that people lack, crying out to it *ancho mar, oh muerte!*, "broad sea, oh death!" (IV). Then a little later he says: *quise nadar en las más anchas vidas, / en las más sueltas desembocaduras.* The choice of rendering *anchas* again as "broad"—"I wanted to swim in the broadest lives, / in the openest river mouths"—indicates that life can have great breadth, like that of death.

Neruda is seeking a consummation in the "openest river mouths" and the undifferentiated primal element from which life emerged and to which it returns. A source for this idea can be found in some impressions he sent from Ceylon to a Chilean newspaper in 1929, during the period these early cantos represent. He was talking about the effect of Hindu belief on life in the Orient:

Origin and duration are antagonistic states: original being is still immersed in spontaneousness, in the creative and destructive element, while day-to-day lives go on abandoned, deprived of beginning or end. With no loss of itself, and losing itself, being goes back to its creative origin, "like a drop of seawater to the sea," says the *Katha Upanishad*.[16]

In 1929, trying to find some meaning in his own day-to-day life, Neruda saw this potential immersion in the primal sea of being as "a source of impossible and fatal obscurities." But what he called "duration" or daily life had by 1945 come to be in need of "its creative origin." Having seen so many abandoned, deprived lives around him, and seeking to recover an American genesis, Neruda at Macchu Picchu felt impelled to plunge his hand or sink like a drop through earth and sea to the human spring.

The poet's "turbulent and gentle hand," from Canto I, now in Canto IV has found men denying him as if he made a Christ-like demand on them: they shut themselves off "so I would not touch / with my streaming hands their wound of emptiness," *para que no tocaran / mis manos manantiales su inexistencia herida*. There seems no good way to specify in translation the recurrent image of *manantial* ("source," "spring"), as here in *manos manantiales*, though Tarn's "divining fingers" hits on an ingenious solution. As "streaming hands" they could easily be Walt Whitman's hands touching his fellow creatures or dressing the wounded, and in fact another passage, from Canto V, also begins much like Whitman:

> I lifted the iodine bandages, plunged my hands
> into meager griefs that were killing off death,
> and all I found in the wound was a cold gust
> that passed through loose gaps in the soul.

It begins like Whitman, at least, but ends more like Eliot, whose vision of urban and suburban spiritlessness in *Four Quartets*— "men and bits of paper, whirled by the cold wind / . . . Wind in and out of unwholesome lungs"—is strikingly akin to Neruda's.[17]

Eliot would never play the healing or suffering servant of humanity as Whitman and Neruda do, and they in turn could hardly live with Eliot's austere deprecation of sensuality. Yet Neruda's and Eliot's ideas share similar forms, if they differ in substance and tone. Eliot's sense of a "darkness to purify the soul," where "the darkness shall be the light"[18] (which in fact derives from the Spanish mystic San Juan de la Cruz), resembles Neruda's vision of death as a "gallop of nighttime clarity" (IV), except that Neruda's paradox seems homemade, instinctive. And in Canto V Neruda's formula for the empty human shuffle around him—*Era lo que no pudo renacer*, "It was what could not be reborn"—might well be translated by Eliot's fine discrimination of what keeps humankind from spiritual rebirth: "that which is only living / Can only die."[19] What distinguishes Neruda from Eliot, at least in *Alturas de Macchu Picchu*, is that finally he aims at a secular rebirth and makes himself the agent of it.

CANTOS VI, VII: "LIVING, DEAD, SILENCED, SUSTAINED"

Entonces—in Neruda's recordings the word is weighted, slow, sonorous:

> *Entonces en la escala de la tierra he subido*
> *entre la atroz maraña de las selvas perdidas*
> *hasta ti, Macchu Picchu.*

Our word "then" sounds too thin and brief for such a crucial moment. "Then, then" (depending on how it's spoken) might get a dramatic emphasis at this point, but once one begins such compensating for an adequate English rendering, the door opens too wide.

> Then on the ladder of the earth I climbed
> through the lost jungle's tortured thicket
> up to you, Macchu Picchu.

This is the watershed of the poem, as of Neruda's entire poetry, and it makes a beautifully timed cadence. For *hasta ti, Macchu Picchu*, I am tempted to say "up to thee, Macchu Picchu," to preserve the Spanish form used with one's intimates or when praying to God. Even without that archaism in English, we can hear Neruda speaking to Macchu Picchu in the directly personal way he spoke a canto earlier to death: "Solemn death it was not you," *No eras tú, muerte grave.* He may feel equally close to both and may also in some way mean to identify the two.

Another small semantic event in Canto VI's opening lines has larger implications that might go unnoticed or remain vague without the specific focus that occurs in translation. Neruda climbs *en la escala de la tierra*, "on the ladder of the earth," and immediately invokes Macchu Picchu as *Alta ciudad de piedras escalares*—High city of laddered stones," as a Spanish ear might hear the phrase, though "stepped" or "scaled" describes the actual construction more closely. By echoing *escala* in *escalares*, Neruda makes the cut stone and the earth congruent with each other. A human construction conforms superbly to raw, ineluctable nature: this is what gives Macchu Picchu its mythic aura.* The physical site and the city do exhibit this conformity in the way the steep, rocky slopes give rise to flights of stone steps and mortarless walls as smooth as the day they were fitted. Unlike the urban scene in "Walking Around," with its "hideous intestines hanging from the doors of houses I hate," Neruda finds stone buildings that fuse the primordial presence of the Andes with the aspirations of an indigenous people.

That fusion of nature and history explains another image from the beginning of Canto VI. *En ti*, Neruda says to the site,

> *En ti, como dos líneas paralelas,*
> *la cuna del relámpago y del hombre*
> *se mecían en un viento de espinas.*

> In you like two lines parallel,
> the cradles of lightning and man
> rocked in a wind of thorns.

Tarn interestingly chooses the figurative sense of *línea* and has two "lineages" issuing in one "cradle both of man and light." His choice of "light" for Neruda's *relámpago* ("lightning flash") tends to assimilate this image to a biblical genesis. "Lightning," on the other hand, not only recalls Neruda's glimpse of ecstasy

*In 1929 in Ceylon, Neruda visited the site of Sigiriya, a ruined palace built in A.D. 477 atop a granite rock of great height. His impressions of the place, written for the Santiago newspaper *La Nación* (Nov. 17, 1929) and entitled "Ceylán espeso" ("Dense Ceylon"), show some of the same imagery and ideas that emerged from his visit to Macchu Picchu: "The grey shells of slender stone capitals buried for twenty centuries loom up among the plants; demolished statues and stairways, immense pools and palaces that have returned to the soil, their progenitors now forgotten. . . . In the center of dense jungle, an abrupt, immense hill of rock, barely accessible by insecure, dangerous steps cut in the great stone; on its height the ruins of a palace and the marvelous Sigiriyan frescos intact despite the centuries . . . everywhere the ruins of what disappeared, covered by plant growth and oblivion." The entire article is reprinted in Juan Loveluck, ed., "Neruda en *La Nación* (1927–1929): prosa olvidada," *Anales de la Universidad de Chile*, 129, nos. 157–60 (Jan.–Dec. 1971), 78.

in Canto II, "the lightning a kiss released," but finds a dazzling, threatening energy at the cradle of a cosmos more secular than biblical. Neruda's cradles identify Macchu Picchu as a remote source of both natural and human phenomena, of "lightning and man." In the scheme of *Canto general* (1950), Neruda used *Alturas de Macchu Picchu* as the second of fifteen books, thus placing it far back in the epic's chronology. It follows directly upon the poems about untouched minerals, wild plants, solitary birds, and invisible Arauco, and it comes before the third book, *The Conquistadors*. In effect, then, Macchu Picchu occurs between a Creation and the first human cataclysm. It stands suspended, untouched (as was indeed the case) by the incursions of history.

The poet in Canto VI continues invoking this place with honorific yet pointed epithets:

> Mother of stone, spume of condors.
> High reef of the human dawn.
> Spade lost in the primal sand.

Catalogs of attributes are a vital convention in medieval oral poetry: addressed to a god, a ruler, a sacred place, they establish the qualities or powers that a people value. Here Neruda, whose emphatic, alliterated lines sound rather like Anglo-Saxon verse, reinforces Macchu Picchu's twofold aspect as a human construction and a fact of nature by calling to the "Mother of stone" alongside the "spume of condors." His second epithet does much the same: "High reef of the human dawn"—a natural metaphor for a primal history. But if he sees the city as a reef, long-lasting and visible, he also imagines it as a spade lost in the sand: Macchu Picchu appears emergent and yet buried. In Neruda's next line the verb tenses embody a similar double vision: *Ésta fué la morada, éste es el sitio*, "This was the dwelling, this is the place." *Sitio* could of course be translated as "site," but that risks giving it a merely archaeological significance. The past tense balanced against the present and the matching half-lines divide Macchu Picchu's genius equally between the city that people formerly dwelt in and the natural site a poet now announces.

Neruda's assurance that past and present time can fuse through the poet's agency takes even more concrete form later in Canto VI, in a particular sequence of tenses:

> Miro las vestiduras y las manos,
> el vestigio del agua en la oquedad sonora,
> la pared suavizada por el tacto de un rostro
> que miró con mis ojos las lámparas terrestres,
> que aceitó con mis manos las desaparecidas
> maderas.

As it happens, the first-person, present-tense *miro* ("I look at") takes only a change in accent to become, three lines later, the third-person past, *miró* ("looked at"). English cannot quite match that economy:

> I look at clothes and hands,
> the trace of water in an echoing tub,
> the wall brushed smooth by the touch of a face
> that looked with my eyes at the lights of earth,
> that oiled with my hands the vanished
> beams.

Using one English verb for *miro* and *miró* helps in recognizing Neruda's presence as both a pilgrim now and a native then. Tarn varies the verb, saying "I gaze" and then "a face that witnessed," because "gaze" has a strength that is needed here and "witness" has suggestive overtones. Neruda's kind of witness can also gain from simplicity and immediacy. His double residence at Macchu Picchu, in the present and the past, can bear every possible emphasis in translation, for it matters vitally to him. (In his urgency Neruda even says that the face not only looked, it also "oiled.") He recited these lines passionately, putting unusual stress on *mis ojos* and *mis manos*: "that looked with *my eyes*," "that oiled with *my hands*."

This emphasis also clarifies Neruda's surprising use of *porque* ("because") in the very next line. Why does he look at the trace of water, the vanished beams, the wall brushed by "a face / that looked with my eyes"?

> . . . *porque todo, ropaje, piel, vasijas,*
> *palabras, vino, panes,*
> *se fué, cayó a la tierra.*

> . . . because everything, clothing, skin, jars,
> words, wine, bread,
> is gone, fallen to earth.

Having for years let my translation of *porque todo . . . se fué* remain as "for everything . . . is gone," I now see it fails to intensify the logic of Neruda's statement. Precisely "because" every rudiment of that previous life is now gone, he says "my" eyes long ago looked and "my" hands worked. We may not want to assent to that illusion, but it fosters a crucial idea. Unless renewed in the person of the poet, these beams, jars, and wine remain utterly lost to us now. To redeem the past, to translate it over the centuries into his own eyes and hands, requires an act of imagination—not, as ultimately for Eliot, an act of religious faith. Neruda does allow a hint of resurrection (or transubstantiation) by including *palabras, vino, panes,* "words, wine, bread," among the things we may have lost. Tarn calls the *panes* "loaves," giving a more specific Christian coloring to Neruda's redemptive mission.

To translate *panes* as "loaves," the way Tarn does, and in the next canto *vaso* ("glass" or "vessel") as "chalice," accentuates an already difficult question. Neruda has been faulted for making use of his Spanish Catholic heritage while at the same time lamenting the Conquest, and no doubt that is a real split in him as in many Latin Americans.[20] In *Alturas de Macchu Picchu*, I think he deliberately highlights neither Christian nor indigenous imagery because he is addressing a general audience, both Latin and American. It is also held against him that he speaks for pre-Columbian peoples while ignoring present-day Indians— another tendency in countries such as Peru and Mexico. He calls up slaves from the Inca past without a word for modern Quechua speakers, but here again I believe he does so to be heard by modern workers in general, for whose plight he finds a deep basis at Macchu Picchu.

Eliot's *Four Quartets* (1943), published a few years before Neruda's poem, also doubles back to a neglected site and summons forgotten ancestors. In "East Coker," he revisits the village his forebears emigrated from, and we see the dancing of sixteenth-century rustic feet "long since under earth / Nourishing the corn." This scene shares with the return to Macchu Picchu an assumption that, in Eliot's words, "We are born with the dead"; that we need the past just as the past needs us. Eliot's third quartet, "The Dry Salvages," evokes scenes from his childhood but—tellingly enough—does not try specifically to recover any American place or time from oblivion. The final poem, "Little Gidding," locates in England a site essentially like Macchu Picchu: a seventeenth-century Anglican chapel and refuge from civil war, later destroyed by Cromwell's Puritans. Eliot shows the way there, telling us "to kneel / Where prayer has been valid. . . . / And what the dead had no speech for, when living, / They can tell you, being dead."[21] Although Neruda says as much of the dead at Macchu Picchu, the effect of their message differs radically. Eliot leads us—or rather, he leads the English in wartime—to reconcile past with present strife and suffering in a formal pattern, and thus to approach a purified condition founded on Christ's. Neruda, though he also imagines transfiguring past and present agonies, would do so by questioning, by refusing to accept the hunger and toil of South American Indians. And where Eliot wants the poets in his tradition, such as Dante, to infuse his own language, Neruda would speak for the voices utterly lost.

The communication Neruda feels he has opened at Macchu Picchu lets him, in Canto VII, directly and collectively address those who died there as *vosotros* (in this case, *os*). A translation cannot pick up that sound, which Latin Americans associate mainly with the way they are spoken to in church or at political rallies, but I would borrow Tarn's excellent solution, "You dead":

> *Muertos de un solo abismo, sombras de una hondonada . . .*
> *desde los capiteles escarlata,*
> *desde los acueductos escalares*

os desplomasteis como en un otoño
en una sola muerte.

You dead of a single abyss, shadows of one ravine . . .
from the red-topped columns,
from the laddered aqueducts
you plummeted as in autumn
to one sole death.

It would help to hear the plural pronoun and verb (*os desplomasteis*), for Neruda now believes that these dead in "a single abyss" died the consuming and unifying death barred to the isolated individual today.

They "plummeted," Neruda says, calling to mind the city's sheer architectural lines. This powerful vertical movement again signals a revelatory event. At first the poet dropped as if blind through the deepest waves, and then on reaching Macchu Picchu he said: "Here the broad grains of maize rose up / and fell again like red hail" (VI). Now the inhabitants themselves take part in this archetypal movement. Neruda speaks in this canto of an *árbol poderoso*, a "mighty tree" cut down, and throughout *Canto general* an *árbol* stands for a race of people (often Araucanians) arisen from the earth.[22] Here the tree *sostuvo una mano que cayó de repente / desde la altura hasta el final del tiempo*: it "held up a hand that fell suddenly / down from the height to the end of time." Neruda's image implies that the people as an organic entity sustained this individual hand. Then the hand "fell," and in translation that common word allows not so much an allusion to Adam's fall as an association of Neruda's story with the most elemental and familiar events: leaves fall, rain falls, towers fall, Rome falls. Tarn sees instead "a hand that suddenly pitched / from the heights to the depths of time." Although "pitched" has more force than "fell," it does not pick up the lament from Canto VI, where "everything . . . is gone, fallen to earth"; nor does it anticipate a later moment in Canto VII, where Neruda will say to the dead: *cuanto fuisteis cayó*, "whatever you were fell away." Tarn's "depths of time" makes sense, but in fact Neruda used a more surprising image: the hand fell from the height to *el final del tiempo*, "the end of time." If ordinarily we imagine time stretching horizontally to its end, *Alturas de Macchu Picchu* reaches down to that end along a vertical axis.

In ritual response to the fall of an entire community, the next lines begin: *Pero una permanencia*, "Yet a permanence . . . rose up in the hands / of all." These lines contain essential statements within ambiguous syntax, so that translating them requires more decisions than usual about what the lines really mean:

> *Pero una permanencia de piedra y de palabra,*
> *la ciudad como un vaso, se levantó en las manos*
> *de todos, vivos, muertos, callados, sostenidos,*
> *de tanta muerte, un muro, de tanta vida un golpe*
> *de pétalos de piedra.*

I have restored three commas from the poem's first appearance in a Venezuelan magazine (1946), putting them after *palabra* ("word"), where *Obras completas* has a colon, and after *vaso* ("bowl") and *sostenidos* ("sustained"), where there is no punctuation.[23] The pauses in Neruda's recordings of the poem support these changes, and his meaning gains as well:

> Yet a permanence of stone and word,
> the city like a bowl, rose up in the hands
> of all, living, dead, silenced, sustained,
> a wall out of so much death, out of so much life a shock
> of stone petals.

Those commas after "word" and "bowl" bring the permanence of stone and word right into apposition with the city. After all, the whole poem depends on such a possibility. The city's physical buildings have persisted, yet the permanence the poet claims for them depends on the word as well as the stone. Neruda's genius in alliterating *permanencia* with both *piedra* and *palabra* gets washed away in translation, but even without it a new idea comes clearly into view. This *palabra* belongs not only to the poet but to Macchu Picchu's inhabitants, whose "words, wine, bread" have fallen to earth. His advent and response, his words, now form part of the city's permanence.

Neruda introduces this idea momentarily and passes on to *la ciudad como un vaso*, "the city like a bowl." Taken strictly, *vaso* denotes "glass" or "vessel," but a more formal vessel (*vasija*) occurs in the next passage, and "glass" seems inappropriate to the place and the occasion. Other translators use "cup" or "goblet," and Tarn elects "chalice," which sounds Eucharistic. Like *vaso*, "bowl" implies a cavity that might contain much life and death, and the word also resonates with "stone" and "rose" on either side of it. Neruda's image suggests both that the people's hands held the city up and that in turn the city holds on to its people—*vivos, muertos, callados, sostenidos*, "living, dead, silenced, sustained." A comma after *sostenidos* balances this sequence so that those in the true city, the one Neruda's poem re-creates, are living though dead, silenced yet sustained. (Semantically I would prefer "held fast," but "sustained" does more for the verse.) After *sostenidos*, the next phrases articulate so loosely that they are practically impossible to render with any confidence: *de tanta muerte, un muro, de tanta vida un golpe / de pétalos de piedra*. The preposition *de* covers many relationships; here it is probably "out of" or "from": "a wall out of so much death, out of so much life a shock / of stone petals." Perhaps Neruda means that with so much labor and death in it the city has become a wall, sealed off yet buttressed against further loss; and that latent with so much life, it has the energy to shock or to flower. But finally the line is anyone's guess.

Throughout the last verse paragraph of Canto VII, hints of ambivalence and irony continue to tug at Neruda's language, making the city more than simply a vanished glory. Its "dead of a single abyss" he now sees as man "all tangled in his hole," over which the unpeopled city remains an *exactitud enarbolada*, an "upraised exactitude." If the root *árbol* ("tree") could survive translation, it would recall the growth and wholeness of an indigenous people, but against that sense Neruda's word "exactitude" begins to suggest the exactions of life under Inca rule and the human cost of perfecting that city. Two lines later Neruda's epithet for the city has an even darker coloring: *la más alta vasija que contuvo el silencio*, "the highest vessel that held silence in."

Whereas the verb *sostener*, however translated, carries a sense of supporting, prolonging, or holding on, by *contener* Neruda means something more constraining—not the vessel's openness but its enclosure. And another crucial word in this line can come through whole, for once, into English: *silencio*. But the silence that the city held in remains profoundly ambiguous: is it a kind of purified suffering or a mute defeat? Canto VII then closes with an entire line that presents absolutely no problem in translation, a line whose simplicity offers the clearest kind of insight into what Macchu Picchu means: *una vida de piedra después de tantas vidas*, "a life of stone after so many lives."

CANTOS VIII, IX: "THE DEAD REALM LIVES ON STILL"

If tragic affirmation could sum up Neruda's quest, the poem might have ended there, with "a life of stone after so many lives." But he had still to come at Macchu Picchu in different ways: a prolonged interrogation in Canto VIII, a sequence made purely of epithets in IX, a radical revision of the city's human story in X through XII. These cantos do what only a long poem like Neruda's or Eliot's can do: they take varying perspectives on a subject, they move from narrative to lyric and other forms, they take on new voices and tones of speech. As a long poem, *Alturas de Macchu Picchu* develops the reach of an epic without losing the intensity of lyric verse. And by personifying the city, evoking its people, and persisting in his own voice and person, Neruda also creates an unusual dramatic form that finally governs our experience of the poem.

In Canto VIII a new mood, the imperative, along with a series of insistent questions, begins to draw us into a tighter relation with Macchu Picchu. The same verb with which Neruda first says "I climbed" (*he subido*) through the lost jungle, he now uses in a new way: *Sube conmigo, amor americano. / Besa conmigo las piedras secretas*, "Climb up with me, American love. / Kiss the secret stones with me." The "love" Neruda addresses is not a consort but a kind of pilgrim, who like himself once probed the unloving world alone and now has a strange community to encounter. Perhaps Neruda is also summoning the reader—ourselves—into intimate touch with Macchu Picchu. Yet the poet in his own person continues to provide our only perspective. In this canto he confronts the river, the Urubamba winding down through its gorge two thousand feet below the peaks that flank the city: *La plata torrencial del Urubamba / hace volar el polen a su copa amarilla*, "The torrential silver of the Urubamba / sends pollen flying to its yellow cup." Like the grain's "yellow history" in Canto II, this image would seem to indicate a life-giving source, but it is hard to tell, since Neruda also describes the river as "crystal and cold, a buffeted air / dividing the clash of emeralds." Other ornate figures follow as the poet says to his companion, "Love, love, . . . study the blind child of the snow," and then begins a long interrogation of the river's "arterial waters" and "rapid swords" and "tormented flashings."

Besides using heavily figurative language, Neruda also composed this canto wholly in the classic Spanish eleven-syllable meter. To carry over that formalness, I keep mainly to four-stress lines in translation, but not to the extent of padding them. With this canto, the poem's longest by far, I find myself awkwardly situated as a translator. It seems bloated, its metaphors merely jostling each other. Yet one engages to make as vital and convincing a version as possible—which is, after all, the only thing to do, short of impermissible cutting or "tuning up."

My sense, then, is that in Canto VIII Neruda pulled out the stops on his verse without yet having a distinct dramatic purpose. Why is it that "the empty vine goes flying"? Why does "the blind child of the snow" have "rapid swords"? Neruda's metaphors typically take one of three forms, with which the translator becomes quite familiar, especially in this canto. He will speak of the river's "war-worn stamens," where neither term, "war-worn" or "stamens," suggests the tenor of the metaphor; or he will combine adjective and noun so that one term analogizes while the other specifies the river, as in "arterial waters" or "cascading hands"; or he will create metaphors with a genitive link, such as "the bitter greeting of the dew." All these examples show Neruda instinctively linking natural with human life, and in that sense they have some point. But often his metaphors come to hand too readily, in translation as well. They are surprising but not surprisingly true, and at such times Neruda virtually parodies himself. In this canto a spate of images makes the reader, like the would-be translator, careless of what they signify and whether they add up. Such is not the case in Canto II, whose extended analogy between flowers, rocks, and people develops their critical relationship; or in Canto IX, whose sheer accumulation of epithets demonstrates in itself the poet's hold on the city.

Canto VIII does serve to begin Neruda's questioning of Macchu Picchu, though his vague "American love" has little purpose as a companion—the speaker himself ends up asking all the questions. He calls on the Incas' sacred river, changing from "Urubamba" to a more ancient Quechua name as if to trigger deeper truths about the city's original condition:[24]

> Oh Wilkamayu of resonant threads,
> when you shatter your bands of thunder
> into white spume, like wounded snow,
> when your steep gale
> sings and slashes arousing the sky,
> what language do you bring to the ear
> barely uprooted from your Andean foam?

It is a dire view of the sacred river. Possibly I have injected more violence into Neruda's question than he intended: my word "shatter" (*rompes*) could be "break," and "slashes" (*castiga*) could be "punishes." Yet he does seem to have displaced the breakdown of a city and a people onto the everlasting river below them. His question also suggests that the river in some way acts to translate that breakdown to the listener: *qué idioma traes a la oreja*, "what language do you bring to the ear."

Then Neruda makes it clear that Macchu Picchu's ruin involved the essence of a people, their voice. The river manifests a breakdown in the power of speech, of self-expression:

What do your tormented flashings say?
Your secret insurgent lightning—did it
once travel thronging with words?
Who goes on crushing frozen syllables,
black languages, banners of gold,
bottomless mouths, throttled shouts
in your slender arterial waters?

The Incas had neither written language nor picture writing like that of Central America, which makes the fall of their civilization even more drastic and irrevocable.[25] Whatever songs, whatever oral tradition they had, lapsed utterly. It is a painful thought for a poet.

The canto's final imperative says: *Ven a mi propio ser, al alba mía / hasta las soledades coronadas*, "Come to my very being, to my own dawn, / up to the crowning solitude." (In the first line I have adopted Tarn's good rendering.) Apparently Neruda situates his own dawn on the heights of Macchu Picchu—a fairly ambitious conceit. His next line, however, objectifies that thought with lapidary compactness: *El reino muerto vive todavía*. English can compact it further—"The dead realm still lives"—but that aborts the rhythm and fails to set life against death as directly as *muerto* and *vive* do, or to prolong a keen sound the way *vive* feeds into *todavía*. Saying "The realm that died is still alive" slips into singsong, and Tarn's "The fallen kingdom survives us all this while" imports something new. Perhaps to suggest Neruda's rhythm and cleave to his idea a simple sentence will do: "The dead realm still lives on." But that lightens the accent on "lives," whereas Neruda's strongest accent falls on *vive*: *El reino muerto vive todavía*. I will leave it at this: "The dead realm lives on still," and let Neruda's vigor remain in Spanish, where anyway the reader has probably absorbed it by now. Yet given Neruda's earlier questioning, the canto cannot close there, on an affirmative note. His final image, which I think refers to a stone altar for sun worship at Macchu Picchu, reminds us that this dead realm still lives in a threatened time: "And across the Sundial like a black ship / the ravening shadow of the condor cruises."

In contrast to this canto's ornate questioning, Canto IX shores up the ruined city with a series of terse, impersonal metaphors. It makes a unique text for translation: forty-three lines, again in strict hendecasyllables, with no stanza break, each line stopped at the end and containing one or more often two epithets addressed to Macchu Picchu. The canto opens:

> *Águila sideral, viña de bruma.*
> *Bastión perdido, cimitarra ciega.*
> *Cinturón estrellado, pan solemne.*
> *Escala torrencial, párpado inmenso.*
> *Túnica triangular, polen de piedra.*

As pure invention, Neruda's phrases call for literal English renderings; that is, anything idiomatic or interpretive would belie them. They call as well for the balanced stresses—two in each half-line—of ritual invocation:

> Sidereal eagle, vineyard of mist.
> Bulwark lost, blind scimitar.
> Starred belt, sacred bread.
> Torrential ladder, giant eyelid.
> Triangled tunic, pollen of stone.

Because many of these words have occurred before in contexts closer to narrative—eagle, mist, lost, blind, bread, torrential, ladder, pollen, stone—their reappearance here in set formulas shows Neruda gathering fragments that were dispersed, so as to sustain and maybe even reconstruct the city with his words. The half-lines abut each other, and one measured verse is set upon the next like fitted stones. In fact, near the beginning, seven successive lines close with something made *de piedra*: "pollen of stone . . . bread of stone . . . rose of stone . . . wellspring of stone . . . light of stone . . . vapor of stone . . . book of stone." In opening the whole *Canto general*, Neruda dedicates himself to "my land without name, without America," and here in Canto IX he makes the poet's primary activity that of naming.[26]

Manantial de piedra, and the English "wellspring of stone," call the unmoving stone city a vital, fluent source, and *Madrépora del*

tiempo sumergido, "Coral of sunken time," sees it growing dura-
bly though invisibly. Two other images in this canto imply
something essential about Macchu Picchu. *Vendaval sostenido en
la vertiente*, "Gale sustained on the slope," describes a force,
both violent and elemental, that would naturally have spent it-
self but for something holding it up, some vital collective spirit
as in the earlier uses of *sostener*. The epithet that follows, *Inmóvil
catarata de turquesa*, suspends "cataract" between "immobile"
and "turquoise": as "immobile" keeps it from perishing, the
forceful fall of water takes on the formal beauty and stillness of a
precious stone, giving a dynamic form to the ruined city.

Not every epithet here makes so condensed or original an in-
sight. *Torre sombrera, discusión de nieve*, sounds impressive as
"Shading tower, dispute of snow," but hasn't very much mean-
ing. *Cúpula del silencio, patria pura*, could be "cupola" or "vault"
or "Dome of silence, purebred homeland," but *patria* does not
gain much in that combination. *Bastión perdido, cimitarra ciega*,
enlists the somewhat suggestive adjectives "lost" and "blind,"
but what is gained by "bastion" and "scimitar," notions alien to
the Inca city? A few of Neruda's paired epithets could even be
scrambled mischievously in translation without much damage:
Serpiente andina, frente de amaranto, could come out "Serpent of
amaranth, Andean brow," and go unnoticed; *Serpiente mineral,
rosa de piedra*, might as well be "Serpent of stone, mineral rose."
This interchangeability demonstrates the random process by
which Neruda sometimes finds his metaphors. A hostile critic
of his, the Spanish poet Juan Larrea, makes this point and goes
so far as to "continue the game" of Canto IX by composing an
even longer syllabic sequence but with images more endemic to
Inca civilization.[27] Larrea calls Neruda's canto a dadaist grab
bag, which is only partly so, and says that it parodies the litany
to the Blessed Virgin, which may in a sense be true. Neruda
does exploit the cumulative and attributive qualities of litany; he
may also be playing on a Catholic rhythm to tantalize and shock
the reader into regarding Macchu Picchu sacredly. More se-
riously, Larrea faults him for a lack of interest in Macchu Picchu
itself. Why aren't such terms as *quipu* (the Incas' knotted-cord

system of communication), *amauta* (a sage), *quena* (an Andean flute), *chicha* (fermented maize), *coca*, and others present in the canto? One reason may have been that Neruda, as he once said, felt "Chilean, Peruvian, American," in Macchu Picchu: he had the Araucanian past along with all of Latin America's past and present in mind when he wrote.

Apart from this complaint, Larrea does have a point. The ruined city acted strongly as a catalyst for Neruda's poetic development, and particularly in later cantos where the theme of hunger emerges, he projects his ideas onto Macchu Picchu rather than trying to do justice to the place itself. Whether this invalidates the poem's redemptive treatment of American place and time, as Larrea also claims, is another question. Canto IX's closing lines provide both strong and weak examples of that treatment:

> *Volcán de manos, catarata oscura.*
> *Ola de plata, dirección del tiempo.*

"Volcano of hands" puts an eruptive force (familiar in Mexico and Chile if not in Peru) into human hands, which might emblematize a workers' revolution, but "dark cataract" is vague and reiterative. *Ola de plata*, "Silver wave," also seems an empty gesture, but not *dirección del tiempo*, which a motto from *Four Quartets* might serve to gloss if not actually to translate: "In my end is my beginning."[28] Three ways of envisioning time converge in Neruda's epithet: *dirección*, meaning "guidance," "route," or "aim, address," places the city in the beginning, along the way, and at the end of American history. Probably the truest choice for *dirección del tiempo* is the literal one, "direction of time," which fits all three meanings, but Tarn's "destination of time" is more compelling.

CANTOS X, XI: "LET ME GRIND STONE STAMENS"

These cantos gather to a climax everything that *Alturas de Macchu Picchu* has ventured so far: the poet's personal stake, his dismay at a sick, isolated human condition, the contrast between this moribund existence and a communal amplitude of life and death, the inspiration of a towering site whose people worked and then fell silent. After interrogating the river's "bottomless mouths" in Canto VIII and then reciting an impersonal litany to the city in IX, Neruda himself now totally pervades the last quarter of the poem. His voice and presence animate every passage, indeed every line, which means that his reader is more than usually governed by the poet's disposition. It also means that the translator's attempt to find in English an authentic idiom and tone, a voice that feels right, becomes an oddly subjective experience—one of possessing and being possessed, which may be just what the poem requires.

Canto X begins outright with a question: *Piedra en la piedra, el hombre, dónde estuvo?*, "Stone upon stone, and man, where was he?" The speaker makes a more direct demand than in Canto VIII, and where the epithets of Canto IX touched mainly on Macchu Picchu's natural or man-made aspects ("vineyard of mist. / Bulwark lost"), this canto concerns the people themselves. In the first line *el hombre* is strung syntactically between *la piedra* and a question, "where was he?" Suddenly it occurs to Neruda that the city's inhabitants may not have "plummeted as in autumn to one sole death" (VII): perhaps they ground their lives away in 1445 no less tediously than people do in 1945. To a translator, that thought occurs in rendering the imagery from Canto X in such a way as to recall the poem's earlier images of human attrition: "Were you too then the broken bit / of half-spent humankind," Neruda asks in X, recalling "a bit of petty death" (V); "your empty mouth" in X recalls "his empty skin" (V). And the wasted "days of unraveled light" that Neruda now attributes to Macchu Picchu recall ironically the passionate "nights raveled out" that he had hoped for in Canto I. These verbal recurrences along with many others bring about the twofold vision of *Alturas de Macchu Picchu*, which is the poem's reason for being. Neruda, having known contemporary misery such as he found in northern Chile's bleak mining region, focuses both on the society around him and on the misery of Macchu Picchu's forgotten inhabitants: one vision responds to the other. It is a difficult but desirable historical perspective—one which compels him to question the magnificent city.

That Neruda's tone and the very shape of his verse have changed in Canto X immediately affects the job of translation. Most noticeably, the sixteen sentences that make up the canto are without exception questions and imperatives. Ranging from one to eleven lines long, they either ask or demand to know something the city has not revealed:

> Hunger, coral of humankind,
> hunger, hidden plant, root of the woodcutter,
> hunger, did your reef-edge climb
> to these high and ruinous towers?

The shock of this question in Spanish is its message to the ear and the eye that nothing keeps *hambre* ("hunger") from *hombre* ("man") but one small vowel:

> *Hambre, coral del hombre,*
> *hambre, planta secreta, raíz de los leñadores,*
> *hambre, subió tu raya de arrecife*
> *hasta estas altas torres desprendidas?*

In this triple invocation of "hunger," Neruda seems to be calling an oracle out of the city, an unwilling or clandestine oracle. To ask if hunger "climbed" to the city he uses *subir*, the same verb he used when he himself climbed "through the lost jungle" (VI) and when he bid his *amor americano* "climb up with me" (VIII). By that measure, hunger retains as active a presence, as dramatic a role, at Macchu Picchu as the poet does. What's more, by calling hunger both a "root" and a "reef," he makes it organic to the site and also gives it another lexical hold on Macchu Picchu, the "high reef of the human dawn" (VI).

Neruda has moved past the spectacle of "stone upon stone" to the lives beneath them. At this moment, one of the poem's most intense, he presses his interrogation into an imperative mood that would commit him bodily to the human fact at Macchu Picchu:

> Yo te interrogo, sal de los caminos,
> muéstrame la cuchara, déjame, arquitectura,
> roer con un palito los estambres de piedra,
> subir todos los escalones del aire hasta el vacío,
> rascar la entraña hasta tocar el hombre.

> I question you, salt of the roads,
> show me the trowel; architecture, let me
> grind stone stamens with a stick,
> climb every step of air up to the void,
> scrape in the womb till I touch man.

Something about our word "architecture," probably its flat ac-
centing and dim vowel sounds, makes it much less potent than
arquitectura to stand as the poet's interlocutor, so I shift its posi-
tion a little to help my "I" confront the city's monumental form.
In almost any other context, grinding "stone stamens with a
stick" would create an inexcusable alliteration, but here that
very insistence reinforces Neruda's need to work his way into
the makings of the city. Now it is not the *alturas* of Macchu Pic-
chu he reaches but *la entraña*. Although the word means "en-
trail" or "inmost recess," I would risk translating *rascar la entraña
hasta tocar el hombre* as "scrape in the womb till I touch man,"
because Neruda has penetrated to the origin, the "mother of
stone" whose sons lie buried in her. (I also have the best prece-
dent for hearing *entraña* as "womb": Neruda himself translated
a phrase from Blake—"the virgin . . . shall awaken her womb"
—with the word *entraña*.)[29] With this quasi-filial yet sexually in-
vasive entrance into Macchu Picchu, he can now "touch man"
where before he could not "touch with my streaming hands"
(IV) those who denied him. What's more, in asking to grind the
stones he comes to delve in the womb: that is, by committing his
own handwork to the ruined city, he discovers its human basis.

Further questions—were rags, tears, and blood the human
lot?—lead to Canto X's strongest imperative: *Devuélveme el escla-
vo que enterraste!* Anything but the directest possible version—
"Give me back the slave you buried!"—would vitiate the anger
audible in Neruda's voice when he reads this line. Larrea, as-

suming Inca governance to have been provident, disallows the
assumption of misery and exploitation behind *esclavo*. Even if he
is right, for Neruda it matters more to create a continuum be-
tween then and now, a deep-seated incentive behind the pres-
ent struggle for social justice. Though his Mexican and Peruvian
friends, such as Diego Rivera and Uriel García, found inspira-
tion in a specifically Indian heritage, Neruda could make more
human contact and moral cause with the poor as such, with the
worker. It matters most to him that the worker at Macchu Picchu
was undeniably anonymous and is now forgotten. "Tell me how
he slept," Neruda asks, and "if every course of stone / weighed
down his sleep, and if he fell underneath."

Then he turns and speaks to another face of Macchu Picchu:
Antigua América, novia sumergida, "Ancient America, sunken
bride." It is not a mother now, or a slave, but some potential
innocence that Neruda imagines was exposed to the "empty
height of the gods," the "bloodstained body of the new grain."
These forces—perhaps they signify Inca religion and forced la-
bor—provoke the canto's final question to a "buried America":

> . . . *América enterrada, guardaste en lo más bajo,*
> *en el amargo intestino, como un águila, el hambre?*

> . . . buried America, did you keep in the deepest part
> of your bitter gut, like an eagle, hunger?

Again the tolling word is *hambre*, but unlike the previous lines,
which began *Hambre, coral del hombre*, these prolong the ques-
tion until its last word is inevitable. In Spanish the ear does not
notice an unstressed syllable at the end, as in *hambre*, because
virtually every line has one. In English the ear does mind it. I
could end emphatically on "your bitter gut," but would rather
let Neruda's accusation reach its true close with a slightly trou-
bling sound and rhythm: "like an eagle, hunger."

No more questions are needed. Now an imperative based on
Neruda's key preposition, *a través* ("through," "across"), finally
completes the gesture begun in Canto I when he plunged his
hand into the earth. Canto XI opens:

A través del confuso esplendor,
a través de la noche de piedra, déjame hundir la mano
y deja que en mí palpite, como un ave mil años prisionera,
el viejo corazón del olvidado!

Through the dazing splendor,
through the night of stone, let me plunge my hand
and let there beat in me, like a bird a thousand years
    imprisoned,
the old forgotten human heart!

To make the kind of rolling rhythm that Whitman's poems often
start with, this passage could have gone: "Down through the
dazing splendor, / down through the night of stone let me
plunge my hand." I still regret not letting it go that way, but *a
través* alone does not quite justify "down," even if the verb *hun-
dir* ("plunge") might. (Now and then, in an account such as
this, one can have one's cake and eat it too, by being discreet in
translation and then reckless in commentary.) In Canto I, Ne-
ruda had moved instinctually down to the genital quick. Now,
having found hunger in America's "deepest part" (X), he de-
scends into history with the same gesture of plunging his hand
—and with ambiguous suggestions of the Aztec ritual in which
an Indian's heart was cut out alive. The human heart Neruda
seeks is "a thousand years imprisoned," or might I have said
"arrested"? Though that word takes *prisionera* too literally and
makes an unwanted pun on cardiac arrest, it would suggest the
working of history in *Alturas de Macchu Picchu,* where an origi-
nal American life, arrested for centuries as if frozen in stone,
needs the poet to release it.

Neruda's next passage, another four-line imperative, moves
toward the verb *caer* ("fall"). In "Galope muerto," "Agua sexu-
al," and throughout most of *Residencia en la tierra,* the word had
signaled a kind of dripping away, a decadence or death that the
poet had somehow to counter. Only in "Entrada a la madera"
could he "fall . . . / to a forgotten room in ruins" and still come
up with new life. Earlier in *Alturas de Macchu Picchu,* Neruda
says twice that everything that used to support the city's life is

fallen. Now *caer* occurs to him as he makes a vital descent from
the splendid structure down into human nature:

> *Déjame olvidar hoy esta dicha, que es más ancha que el mar,*
> *porque el hombre es más ancho que el mar y que sus islas,*
> *y hay que caer en él como en un pozo para salir del fondo*
> *con un ramo de agua secreta y de verdades sumergidas.*

> Let me forget today this joy that is broader than the sea,
> because man is broader than sea and islands
> and we must fall in him as in a well to rise from the bottom
> with a branch of secret water and sunken truths.

The verb *caer* comes almost to signify plunging rather than laps-
ing, as if by some mythic, pre-Christian descent and return,
Neruda would redeem the life that fell away at Macchu Picchu.
Still, this passage poses a puzzling choice. The third-person
construction, *hay que caer en él como en un pozo*, means "it is nec-
essary to," "one must fall in him as in a well," but that sounds
too impersonal at such a juncture. The question is whether
Neruda wants to instruct or to include the reader: "you must" or
"we must"? It would thicken the poem's dramatic plot to have
him turn here and say "you must," addressing us directly for
the first time. But I think he means to involve himself (and the
reader no less) by saying that "we" must fall into humankind to
rise with sunken truths. These *verdades sumergidas* are sunken in
the sense of being forgotten, out of reach, but also latent—we
remember the inchoate energy that "Galope muerto" locates in
a *sumergida lentitud* or "sunken slowness," and the germinal
core of things to which Neruda falls in "Entrada a la madera."
We risk falling in order to discover these truths.

   A startlingly kindred idea to Neruda's exists in North Ameri-
can poetry—not in Eliot, for whom descent usually meant pur-
gation, but in William Carlos Williams. A brief, little-noticed
chapter from *In the American Grain* (1925), entitled "Descent,"
honors Sam Houston for leaving civilization to spend many
years among the Cherokee Indians. "It is imperative that we
sink," says Williams, giving us a perfect English equivalent for

Neruda's *hay que caer.*[30] Both poets decried any system that either repressed or transcended human sensuality and suffering. Both sank a taproot into the common clay where they lived.

Something must be keeping Neruda from reaching mankind's sunken truths if it takes so many imperatives to get him released: "let me grind stone stamens . . . let me plunge my hand . . . let there beat in me . . . let me forget." It is in fact the sublimity of Macchu Picchu, which gave his poem its title and which here he calls "this joy" and "dazing splendor," that now keeps him from the city's human basis. Canto XI goes on:

Déjame olvidar, ancha piedra, la proporción poderosa,
la trascendente medida, las piedras del panal,
y de la escuadra déjame hoy resbalar
la mano sobre la hipotenusa de áspera sangre y cilicio.

Let me forget, broad stone, the sovereign symmetry,
transcendent measure, honeycombed stones,
and from the square edge let me this day slide
my hand down the hypotenuse of haircloth and bitter blood.

He has been fascinated, gratified, exalted, but is now not to be confined by the architectonics of Macchu Picchu, its harmonious geometry of rectangles, squares, trapezoids, triangles, polygons, diagonals, perpendiculars, slopes, and curves. If Neruda did not turn on the city this way, demanding to forget the unforgettable stature of it, *Alturas de Macchu Picchu* would remain a powerful but conventional meditation. As it is, he hits on an astonishing image that ties the great structure to its invisible human cost: "and from the square edge let me this day slide / my hand down the hypotenuse of haircloth and bitter blood." Since we share a common geometry with Neruda, his image loses nothing in translation. "Hypotenuse"! What a word for this poem—something that connects the stone's square sides, opposes their perfect angle, and remains unseen by onlookers until the poet traces it with his hand.

The compassion generated in this image leads Neruda back to the bodies of men and women asleep or dead at Macchu Picchu.

He names three of them: Juan Cortapiedras, Juan Comefrío, Juan Piesdescalzos. Some translators retain "Juan," but since Neruda has given the Indians a common Spanish name, an English one seems called for. "John" sounds too formal. For an everyday worker's name, maybe "Jack" will do. Jack Stonebreaker, Jack Coldbiter, Jack Barefoot. These nuances matter because the act of naming must bring Neruda face to face with his predecessors. He ends the canto by calling them up, reclaiming (only male, it seems) Indians from the bitter gut: "rise to be born with me, brother."

CANTO XII: "AS IF I WERE ANCHORED HERE WITH YOU"

Eliot puts it this way: "We are born with the dead: / See, they return, and bring us with them." [31] Neruda brings them with himself, so that his far and near visions coalesce. When the poet says "rise to be born with me, brother," he is not only summoning the past into the present but urging the present into the future. *Sube a nacer conmigo, hermano*: that simple imperative addressed to Indian workers also opens the final canto, and bristles with chances and disappointments for the translator. *Subir* has meant "climb" in this poem: the poet climbed to Macchu Picchu, and so did hunger. Now Neruda is asking a dead man to climb up to him, but I hear something more solemn, probably not "climb" but "rise to be born with me, brother." Tarn avoids the revolutionary jargon of "rise" and "brother" by having Neruda say, "Arise to birth with me, my brother," but possibly it should not be avoided. And though it weakens *nacer* to have to translate it as "to be born," changing Neruda's verb into the noun "birth" partly frustrates his call for a momentous act, an act in which the poet is also "to be born." English lacks an active verb for the process of coming to birth, but Neruda had *nacer* and used it throughout his poetry. Perhaps the death of his own mother when he was born and the distressful birth of his only child made him cherish the word, since he attached it to plants, birds, waves, nations, poems, all the things he valued most.

The verb *nacer*, carrying a personal weight as well as a political metaphor, brings Neruda to the critical moment of his American genesis—a moment in which personal and political motives are united. "Rise to be born with me," *Sube a nacer conmigo*: in renewing himself, the poet would bring others to a kind of rebirth. This double process belongs to the poem's broadly sexual configuration, in which Neruda blends the impulses of a son and a lover. Through the early cantos he has been probing a loveless quotidian world for some passionate response to his "streaming hands" (IV), some consummation, some *patria nupcial* (I). Then he climbs to the site through "lost jungles," *selvas perdidas* (VI)—they are words he often used for the ambience of his childhood—and reaches the "mother of stone." She is now to be delivered of his brothers, as he scrapes the womb and plunges his hand toward forgotten man. "Look at me from the bottom of earth," Neruda says to him in Canto XII, *Mírame desde el fondo de la tierra*, and the translator (in a state of ideal alertness) will recall having dealt with that phrase somewhere before. In the opening lyric of *Veinte poemas de amor* (1924), Neruda had told his woman that he digs in her "and makes a son leap from under earth," from *el fondo de la tierra*—the same phrase as in *Alturas de Macchu Picchu*. I translate it differently because in 1924 the lover as husbandman is speaking, in 1945 the visionary pilgrim, but over the years Neruda's impulse remained much the same. As he grounded himself in all of American place and time, the sexual impulse had more to work on. Here in Canto XII it makes him reach into the recesses of Macchu Picchu for a passionate connection with his fellow beings.

Dame la mano desde la profunda / zona de tu dolor diseminado, "Give me your hand out of the deep / region seeded by all your grief." For the demands of this canto, Neruda adopts the eleven-syllable line again, which can be matched by four-stress (and often eight-syllable) English lines. And by this time, a semantic depth can be felt behind the poem's words. Hands of modern man that drilled the pulsing metal; the poet's hands plunging into earth, lifting bandages, looking for love or rest, oiling the vanished beams; the Indians' "spidery hands" that suddenly fell but hold up the city like a bowl—all these hands join in the simplest of utterances, *Dame la mano*, "Give me your hand." In Canto VII Neruda imagined Macchu Picchu's dead united in "the deepest" ravine. Now in that depth he can see not only their unity but their *dolor diseminado*, and the memory of a rock that generously "keeps its flower sown" (*diseminada*), in Canto II, offsets this later suggestion of Christian suffering in *dolor.*

"Give me your hand": Neruda reaches for his *hermano*, but then breaks that movement with startling honesty:

> No volverás del fondo de las rocas.
> No volverás del tiempo subterraneo.
> No volverá tu voz endurecida.
> No volverán tus ojos taladrados.

English can only barely approximate those primary negative stresses, much less the multiple assonance in Neruda's lines:

> You won't come back from bottom rock.
> You won't come back from time under ground.
> No coming back with your hardened voice.
> No coming back with your drilled-out eyes.

The repeated pulse of "You won't come back" and the idiomatic abruptness of "No coming back" can help enforce the blank fact of this loss. To redeem the loss, Neruda asks various laborers at Macchu Picchu to look at him "from the bottom of earth, / plowman, weaver, voiceless shepherd." He still speaks to them as *tu*, as individuals, but then at the end of a long appeal he shifts to the second-person plural: *traed a la copa de esta nueva vida / vuestros viejos dolores enterrados*, "bring all your age-old buried / griefs to the cup of this new life." In widening his voice to address them all, Neruda effects a stirring change. All of them fell, died a like death, are equally forgotten, and now can be called back collectively. From here until the end of the poem, a sequence of sixteen such imperatives summons the dead as well as their painful labor: "Show me your blood and your furrow," the old lamps and flints, the stumbling, the whips. Once, even though he has said there is "No coming back with your hardened voice," the poet prompts them to speech:

> decidme: aquí fui castigado
> porque la joya no brilló o la tierra
> no entregó a tiempo la piedra o el grano.

The verb *entregar* ("give up," "hand over") rings deeper now, thanks to earlier uses when Neruda was reaching out to his fellow creatures for love. Now he has found what he was after all those years:

> say to me: here I was punished
> when a gem didn't shine or the earth
> give forth its stone or grain on time.

He wants to bear it all in mind, including *la madera en que os crucificaron*, "the wood they crucified you on."

Neruda's voice takes on a terrific plangency in reading this section aloud. We hear why in a line the poem has been heading for all along: *Yo vengo a hablar por vuestra boca muerta*, "I come to speak through your dead mouth." Since *por* can signify either "through" or "for" their dead mouths, he may mean to speak both on their behalf and in place of them, though that would preclude his taking on their pain directly. What is not ambiguous is Neruda's phrase *vuestra boca muerta*. Since *vuestra*, the possessive of *vosotros*, modifies *boca*, a singular noun, the dead all have one mouth (thanks to a grammatical twist unavailable in English). Neruda convokes them as a unified community, relying now on the essential medium of speech as the poem's final period begins:

> A través de la tierra juntad todos
> los silenciosos labios derramados
> y desde el fondo habladme toda esta larga noche
> como si yo estuviera con vosotros anclado.

All through the earth join all
the silent wasted lips
and speak from the depths to me all this long night
as if I were anchored here with you.

"All through," which combines the senses of *a través* as both "through" and "across," helps a new idea emerge at this point: the idea that communicating down through the earth with humanity's past puts him in touch across present time as well, with "all / the silent wasted lips." Neruda's twofold presence at Macchu Picchu, in pre-Columbian and mid-twentieth-century time, gives him this privilege and lets him speak "as if I were anchored here with you": the subjunctive "as if I were" says he is and he isn't there, he shares their plight and at the same time his voice translates it into present terms.

"Through me many long dumb voices," Neruda might have been saying.[32] Possibly it seems strange that a line from *Song of Myself* should provide the kind of free translation for *Alturas de Macchu Picchu* that Eliot's *Four Quartets* sometimes provides, since between Eliot and Whitman so little affinity exists. Neruda needed a way of moving through time and place, evoking the past so that at certain points it might come up into the present with a rising, regenerative force: this is the way Eliot moves in *Four Quartets*. Within such a pattern, though, the quality of Neruda's voice and feeling recalls Whitman's: the plasmic human sympathy, the welcoming of materiality and sensuousness, the awareness of common lives and labor, the openness toward the human prospect, the poet's volunteering himself as a redeemer.

Contadme todo, cadena a cadena, / eslabón a eslabón, y paso a paso: "tell me everything, chain by chain, / link by link, and step by step." By this point a full set of related terms has developed within the poem: tell, say, speak, sing, language, word, syllable, lips, mouth, voice, shout, silent, silenced. So much is vested in the act of speech that a reader must ask what connection speech has with other actions and passions. The question, on which theories of language and literature turn, touches *Alturas de Macchu Picchu* in two ways. First, because Neruda moves indistinguishably between actual and symbolic narrative, each kind of narrative shares its virtue with the other: his climb to the ruins goes beyond mere credible fact, while plunging his hand to the earth's quick keeps a physical credibility about it. Second, speech enables the poet to forge a collectivity. Neruda prized the oral, communal nature of poetry and recognized the voice-less anonymity of the poor: in *Alturas de Macchu Picchu* he calls attention to the need for voice-to-voice contact between himself and the city's inhabitants. Perhaps even more critically, he is aware of being a poet, not a worker, and of dealing with workers who are not poets. By establishing speech as an authentic medium between him and them, he can turn his words —"let me grind stone stamens"—into a virtual action, just as the voiceless workers can "tell me everything."

The lines beginning *contadme todo*, "tell me everything," go on immediately to say *afilad los cuchillos*, "file the knives," as if both kinds of activity, telling and filing, came from the same sphere and followed the same laws. Neruda not only speaks "as if" he were at Macchu Picchu, he identifies what can be told with what can be done:

> *afilad los cuchillos que guardasteis,*
> *ponedlos en mi pecho y en mi mano,*
> *como un río de rayos amarillos,*
> *como un río de tigres enterrados.*

> file the knives you kept by you,
> drive them into my chest and my hand
> like a river of riving yellow light,
> like a river where buried jaguars lie.

A passage like this never ceases to need translating, partly because it makes so terrifying a gesture. The knife an Indian would have kept for handwork and for protection against animals or other people—is it to be used on an advocate, the poet exposing himself to whatever energy remains at Macchu Picchu? In the United States we have little precedent for this kind and degree of a poet's commitment, except for Whitman's "I am the man, I suffer'd, I was there."[33] So it challenges our resources to make a viable translation.

Take the four lines beginning *afilad los cuchillos*, "file the knives." The music in them, the mesh of sound in rhythm, comes from Neruda's brilliant *e*-sounds, two per line, moving through patterns of alliteration and assonance. In English a corresponding music can emerge from bright *i*-sounds—"file the knives you kept by you, / drive them into my chest and my hand"—thanks to the (etymologically unrelated) "file" for *afilad*, instead of the more usual "sharpen." For *ponedlos en mi pecho y en mi mano*, the fairly bland *ponedlos* literally means "place them," but if Neruda wants to be given knives to defend the helpless dead, why *en mi pecho*, in his chest? Does *pecho* here carry its figurative sense of "courage"? Since the preposition *en* can mean either "in" or "into" his chest, Neruda's line is ambiguous. Rather than leave it that way, I make the decision—a risky one, considering how much depends on it—that he wants to suffer the knives, not use them.[34] Clearly Neruda desires to take onto himself the pain of those he is addressing—he has even asked to see the wood they were crucified on. So there is virtual truth in the imperative as I translate it. I hope I am not too influenced by the fact that "drive" resonates with "knives."

What effect has the double simile that follows this image of knives? Neruda's line, *como un río de rayos amarillos*, forms such a tense arc of sound that it virtually eclipses the meaning of the words, let alone any equivalent translation of them. What occurs to me is an etymological deepening of "river" into "riving" —"like a river of riving yellow bolts" or "riving yellow light"— since *rayo* means "lightning bolt" or "ray of light." In the second simile, *como un río de tigres enterrados*, "tigers" would prolong the bright sound, but *tigres* in South America refers to jaguars. I have felt for years that my literal translation—"like a river of buried jaguars"—needed lengthening into pentameter like the line above it, and needed intensifying as well. Now I see a change that will do it: "like a river where buried jaguars lie." The *i*-sound gets prolonged in "lie," and that word sustains—as the whole poem sustains—an energy not merely buried but latent, recoverable.

When the poet's secular voice asks an ancient people to give their pain to him, saying "file the knives you kept by you, / drive them into my chest and my hand," these wounds (if they really are a kind of stigmata) must seem strangely familiar to any reader of the New Testament. Then two similes extend and sharply modify this image, recasting it in a native milieu: the pain Neruda takes on will be "like a river of riving yellow bolts, / like a river where buried jaguars lie." The Urubamba River sends up sound and mist around Macchu Picchu; from the city you see it two thousand feet below like a yellow ribbon gleaming and twisting. In this image, the river lends the raw force of nature to the poet's agony. So does the underworld presence of jaguars, perhaps the most powerful cult god of the Central Andes.[35] For the North American and even the Latin American reader, then, these two similes carry Neruda's Christ-like assumption of responsibility beyond familiar ground. They also resist the tendency that any translation has, by virtue of its being in one's native tongue, to assimilate what is strange.

Five appeals to the silent lips bring Neruda's poem to a close.* The first two,

> *Dadme el silencio, el agua, la esperanza.*
> *Dadme la lucha, el hierro, los volcanes,*

do not demand much energy to translate, which could indicate a hollowness in them—it depends on your mood:

> Give me silence, water, hope.
> Give me struggle, iron, volcanoes.

The next two are astir with possibilities:

> *Apegadme los cuerpos como imanes.*
> *Acudid a mis venas y a mi boca.*

Now and then a lucky or last-ditch thought turns up a likely word. For *apegad*, not "attach" or "cling" but "fasten" seems right to me: its sound attracts it to "magnets" (*imanes*) and then to "hasten" (*acudid*) in the next line:

---

*After the poem's first appearance, besides minor changes in punctuation and spacing, Neruda made one omission. Following *como un río de tigres enterrados,* this line originally appeared: *y dejadme llorar antes de que hable,* "and let me weep before I speak." Perhaps he took it out to maintain the impression that in essence the workers were speaking through him.

> Fasten your bodies to me like magnets.
> Hasten to my veins to my mouth.

These lines embody the kind of adhesive fellow-feeling that Neruda found in Walt Whitman, and they do more than that. Having taken the forgotten workers' knives in his chest and hand, Neruda now wants their flesh and blood transfused into him. Lives that were stifled in the mother of stone can rise to be born through him—through his veins, because some lamb's blood he swallowed as a child and some children's blood he saw flowing in Madrid's streets have brought him to a consanguinity with those who worked and died at Macchu Picchu; and through his mouth, because this genesis begins with a voice, Pablo Neruda's voice. *Yo vengo a hablar por vuestra boca muerta*, he had said, "I come to speak through your dead mouth." Now the current of speech shifts the other way at last. Neruda asks his American predecessors, much as the translator asks the poet, to

> Speak through my words and my blood,

and this final appeal the poem itself has by now fulfilled:

> *Hablad por mis palabras y mi sangre.*

AFTERMATHS OF TRANSLATION

Pablo Neruda died on September 23, 1973, twelve days after the military coup in Chile. There was occasion to recite his poetry in translation, to bring North Americans closer to Chile in whatever way possible. At one point, I discovered a strange side effect of translating at its most earnest: the experience of being possessed, the illusion that the lines you've translated are speaking through you and for you. I had memorized passages from my version of *Alturas de Macchu Picchu* without intending to. There is, I found, a great difference between writing down translations on the page and speaking the lines to expectant faces:

I bent my head into the deepest waves,
dropped down through sulfurous calm
and went back. . . .

One naturally feels an empathy with first-person narrative and lyric speech. As a translator I have felt something more: a strange sense of having authored the lines I am speaking. Maybe this illusion is necessary to generate in English an idiomatic, life-giving voice.

From the illusion of authorship an even stranger illusion or self-deception follows, as a kind of occupational hazard. After steeping myself in Neruda's Spanish, I set it aside and focus for days on my English version to make it as authentic as possible. Eventually in turning back to the Spanish, I may by this time have forgotten its exact wording and configuration. I am astonished to find that somehow it now sounds like an uncannily good translation of my own poem, with perhaps a few odd spots: *descendí como gota*—that's very good, for "dropped down," but perhaps *lo más genital* seems a little disappointing, after "genital quick." This illusion does not last long, but in a deeper sense it does last, and for the engaged reader as well as for the translator. It means that we are liable for what the words have to say.

One last cautionary tale on the hazards of translating Neruda also stems from September 1973. On September 17, a poem was circulated by international wire services in which Neruda was heard to denounce violently Nixon and Pinochet, among others, as "hyenas ravening / our history . . . satraps bribed a thousand times over / and sellouts, driven / by the wolves of Wall Street, / machines starving for pain." [36] I couldn't see how Neruda, extremely ill at the time, could have produced such a concerted outburst. But after hesitating for fear of endangering his position, I was persuaded to translate the poem. It was published immediately on the Op-Ed page of the *New York Times*, carried in many other periodicals, and used as a poster. [37] Then I learned that "The Satraps," as it was called, was actually written by Neruda twenty-five years earlier, about Central American dictatorships backed by the United States. It seems that a Jewish literary magazine in Buenos Aires had adjusted the dictators' names to apply to 1973.[38]

I am chagrined at not having recognized the poem, but feel a good deal more satisfied that I and others were deceived—that Neruda's anger had its impact at another moment of Latin American history. Thousands were being killed in Chile, as that poem says, "with no other law but torture / and the lashing hunger of the people." On looking up the original poem I found that one line had been garbled over the wires. It was not *máquinas hambrientas de dolores*, but *dólares*—not machines starving for pain, but for dollars. But the mistranslation had its own truth and I let it stand.

ALTURAS DE MACCHU PICCHU

HEIGHTS OF MACCHU PICCHU

ALTURAS DE MACCHU PICCHU

I

Del aire al aire, como una red vacía,
iba yo entre las calles y la atmósfera, llegando y
    despidiendo,
en el advenimiento del otoño la moneda extendida
de las hojas, y entre la primavera y las espigas,
lo que el más grande amor, como dentro de un guante
que cae, nos entrega como una larga luna.

(Días de fulgor vivo en la intemperie
de los cuerpos: aceros convertidos
al silencio del ácido:
noches deshilachadas hasta la última harina:
estambres agredidos de la patria nupcial.)

Alguien que me esperó entre los violines
encontró un mundo como una torre enterrada
hundiendo su espiral más abajo de todas
las hojas de color de ronco azufre:
más abajo, en el oro de la geología,
como una espada envuelta en meteoros,
hundí la mano turbulenta y dulce
en lo más genital de lo terrestre.

Puse la frente entre las olas profundas,
descendí como gota entre la paz sulfúrica,
y, como un ciego, regresé al jazmín
de la gastada primavera humana.

HEIGHTS OF MACCHU PICCHU

I

From the air to the air, like an empty net,
I went on through streets and thin air, arriving and
    leaving behind,
at autumn's advent, the coin handed out
in the leaves, and between spring and ripe grain,
the fullness that love, as in a glove's
fall, gives over to us like a long-drawn moon.

(Days of live brilliance in the storm
of bodies: steels transmuted
into silent acid:
nights raveled out to the final flour:
battered stamens of the nuptial land.)

Someone expecting me among violins
met with a world like a buried tower
sinking its spiral deeper than all
the leaves the color of rough sulfur:
and deeper yet, in geologic gold,
like a sword sheathed in meteors
I plunged my turbulent and gentle hand
into the genital quick of the earth.

I bent my head into the deepest waves,
dropped down through sulfurous calm
and went back, as if blind, to the jasmine
of the exhausted human spring.

II

Si la flor a la flor entrega el alto germen
y la roca mantiene su flor diseminada
en su golpeado traje de diamante y arena,
el hombre arruga el pétalo de la luz que recoge
en los determinados manantiales marinos
y taladra el metal palpitante en sus manos.
Y pronto, entre la ropa y el humo, sobre la mesa hundida,
como una barajada cantidad, queda el alma:
cuarzo y desvelo, lágrimas en el océano
como estanques de frío: pero aún
mátala y agonízala con papel y con odio,
sumérgela en la alfombra cotidiana, desgárrala
entre las vestiduras hostiles del alambre.

No: por los corredores, aire, mar o caminos,
quién guarda sin puñal (como las encarnadas
amapolas) su sangre? Lo cólera ha extenuado
la triste mercancía del vendedor de seres,
y, mientras en la altura del ciruelo, el rocío
desde mil años deja su carta transparente
sobre la misma rama que lo espera, oh corazón, oh frente triturada
entre las cavidades del otoño.

Cuántas veces en las calles de invierno de una ciudad o en
un autobús o un barco en el crepúsculo, o en la soledad
más espesa, la de la noche de fiesta, bajo el sonido
de sombras y campanas, en la misma gruta del placer humano,
me quise detener a buscar la eterna veta insondable
que antes toqué en la piedra o en el relámpago que el beso desprendía.

(Lo que en el cereal como una historia amarilla
de pequeños pechos preñados va repitiendo un número
que sin cesar es ternura en las capas germinales,
y que, idéntica siempre, se desgrana en marfil
y lo que en el agua es patria transparente, campana
desde la nieve aislada hasta las olas sangrientas.)

II

While flower to flower gives up the high seed
and rock keeps its flower sown
in a beaten coat of diamond and sand,
man crumples the petal of light he picks
in the deep-set springs of the sea
and drills the pulsing metal in his hands.
And soon, among clothes and smoke, on the broken table,
like a shuffled pack, there sits the soul:
quartz and sleeplessness, tears in the ocean
like pools of cold: yet still
man kills and tortures it with paper and with hate,
stuffs it each day under rugs, rends it
on the hostile trappings of the wire.

No: in corridors, air, sea, or roads,
who (like the crimson poppy) keeps
no dagger to guard his blood? Anger has drained
the tradesman's dreary trafficking in lives,
while in the height of the plum tree the dew
leaves its clear mark a thousand years
on the same waiting branch, oh heart, oh face ground down
among deep pits in autumn.

How many times in the city's winter streets or in
a bus or a boat at dusk, or in the densest
solitude, that of night festivity, under the sound
of shadows and bells, in the very cave of human pleasure,
have I wanted to stop and seek the timeless fathomless vein
I touched in a stone once or in the lightning a kiss released.

(Whatever in grain like a yellow history
of small swelling breasts keeps repeating its number
ceaselessly tender in the germinal shells,
and identical always, what strips to ivory,
and what is clear native land welling up, a bell
from remotest snows to the blood-sown waves.)

No pude asir sino un racimo de rostros o de máscaras
precipitadas, como anillos de oro vacío,
como ropas dispersas hijas de un otoño rabioso
que hiciera temblar el miserable árbol de las razas asustadas.

No tuve sitio donde descansar la mano
y que, corriente como agua de manantial encadenado,
o firme como grumo de antracita o cristal,
hubiera devuelto el calor o el frío de mi mano extendida.
Qué era el hombre? En qué parte de su conversación abierta
entre los almacenes y los silbidos, en cuál de sus movimientos
    metálicos
vivía lo indestructible, lo imperecedero, la vida?

I could grasp only a clump of faces or masks
thrown down like rings of hollow gold,
like scattered clothes, daughters of a rabid autumn
that shook the fearful races' cheerless tree.

I had no place to rest my hand,
none running like linked springwater
or firm as a chunk of anthracite or crystal
to give back the warmth or cold of my outstretched hand.
What was man? Where in his simple talk
amid shops and whistles, in which of his metallic motions
lived the indestructible, the imperishable—life?

III

El ser como el maíz se desgranaba en el inacabable
granero de los hechos perdidos, de los acontecimientos
miserables, del uno al siete, al ocho,
y no una muerte, sino muchas muertes llegaba a cada uno:
cada día una muerte pequeña, polvo, gusano, lámpara
que se apaga en el lodo del suburbio, una pequeña muerte de alas
*   gruesas*
entraba en cada hombre como una corta lanza
y era el hombre asediado del pan o del cuchillo,
el ganadero: el hijo de los puertos, o el capitán oscuro del arado,
o el roedor de las calles espesas:
todos desfallecieron esperando su muerte, su corta muerte
*   diaria:*
y su quebranto aciago de cada día era
como una copa negra que bebían temblando.

III

Lives like maize were threshed in the bottomless
granary of wasted deeds, of shabby
incidents, from one to sevenfold, even to eight,
and not one death but many deaths came each man's way:
each day a petty death, dust, worm, a lamp
snuffed out in suburban mud, a petty fat-winged
    death
entered each one like a short spear
and men were beset by bread or by the knife:
the drover, the son of seaports, the dark captain of the plow,
or those who gnaw at the cluttered streets:
all of them weakened, waiting their death, their brief death
    daily,
and their dismal weariness each day was like
a black cup they drank down trembling.

IV

La poderosa muerte me invitó muchas veces:
era como la sal invisible en las olas,
y lo que su invisible sabor diseminaba
era como mitades de hundimientos y altura
o vastas construcciones de viento y ventisquero.

Yo al férreo filo vine, a la angostura
del aire, a la mortaja de agricultura y piedra,
al estelar vacío de los pasos finales
y a la vertiginosa carretera espiral:
pero, ancho mar, oh muerte!, de ola en ola no vienes,
sino como un galope de claridad nocturna
o como los totales números de la noche.

Nunca llegaste a hurgar en el bolsillo, no era
posible tu visita sin vestimenta roja:
sin auroral alfombra de cercado silencio:
sin altos y enterrados patrimonios de lágrimas.

No pude amar en cada ser un árbol
con su pequeño otoño a cuestas (la muerte de
     mil hojas),
todas las falsas muertes y las resurrecciones
sin tierra, sin abismo:
quise nadar en las más anchas vidas,
en las más sueltas desembocaduras,
y cuando poco a poco el hombre fue negándome
y fue cerrando paso y puerta para que no tocaran
mis manos manantiales su inexistencia herida,
entonces fui por calle y calle y río y río,
y ciudad y ciudad y cama y cama,
y atravesó el desierto mi máscara salobre,
y en las últimas casas humilladas, sin lámpara, sin fuego,
sin pan, sin piedra, sin silencio, solo,
rodé muriendo de mi propia muerte.

IV

The mightiest death invited me many times:
like invisible salt in the waves it was,
and what its invisible savor disseminated
was half like sinking and half like height
or huge structures of wind and glacier.

I came to the iron edge, the narrows
of the air, the shroud of fields and stone,
to the stellar emptiness of the final steps
and the dizzying spiral highway:
yet broad sea, oh death! not wave by wave you come
but like a gallop of nighttime clarity
or the absolute numbers of night.

You never came poking in pockets, nor could
you visit except in red robes,
in an auroral carpet enclosing silence,
in lofty and buried legacies of tears.

I could not in each creature love a tree
with its own small autumn on its back (the death of a
    thousand leaves),
all the false deaths and resurrections
with no earth, no depths:
I wanted to swim in the broadest lives,
in the openest river mouths,
and as men kept denying me little by little,
blocking path and door so I would not touch
with my streaming hands their wound of emptiness,
then I went street after street and river after river,
city after city and bed after bed,
and my brackish mask crossed through waste places,
and in the last low hovels, no light, no fire,
no bread, no stone, no silence, alone,
I roamed round dying of my own death.

V

No eras tú, muerte grave, ave de plumas férreas,
lo que el pobre heredero de las habitaciones
llevaba entre alimentos apresurados, bajo la piel vacía:
era algo, un pobre pétalo de cuerda exterminada:
un átomo del pecho que no vino al combate
o el áspero rocío que no cayó en la frente.
Era lo que no pudo renacer, un pedazo
de la pequeña muerte sin paz ni territorio:
un hueso, una campana que morían en él.
Yo levanté las vendas del yodo, hundí las manos
en los pobres dolores que mataban la muerte,
y no encontré en la herida sino una racha fría
que entraba por los vagos intersticios del alma.

V

Solemn death it was not you, iron-plumed bird,
that the poor successor to those dwellings
carried among gulps of food, under his empty skin:
something it was, a spent petal of worn-out rope,
a shred of heart that fell short of struggle
or the harsh dew that never reached his face.
It was what could not be reborn, a bit
of petty death with no peace or place:
a bone, a bell, that were dying within him.
I lifted the iodine bandages, plunged my hands
into meager griefs that were killing off death,
and all I found in the wound was a cold gust
that passed through loose gaps in the soul.

VI

Entonces en la escala de la tierra he subido
entre la atroz maraña de las selvas perdidas
hasta ti, Macchu Picchu.
Alta ciudad de piedras escalares,
por fin morada del que lo terrestre
no escondió en las dormidas vestiduras.
En ti, como dos líneas paralelas,
la cuna del relámpago y del hombre
se mecían en un viento de espinas.

Madre de piedra, espuma de los cóndores.

Alto arrecife de la aurora humana.

Pala perdida en la primera arena.

Ésta fue la morada, éste es el sitio:
aquí los anchos granos del maíz ascendieron
y bajaron de nuevo como granizo rojo.

Aquí la hebra dorada salió de la vicuña
a vestir los amores, los túmulos, las madres,
el rey, las oraciones, los guerreros.

Aquí los pies del hombre descansaron de noche
junto a los pies del águila, en las altas guaridas
carniceras, y en la aurora
pisaron con los pies del trueno la niebla enrarecida,
y tocaron las tierras y las piedras
hasta reconocerlas en la noche o la muerte.

Miro las vestiduras y las manos,
el vestigio del agua en la oquedad sonora,
la pared suavizada por el tacto de un rostro
que miró con mis ojos las lámparas terrestres,
que aceitó con mis manos las desaparecidas
maderas: porque todo, ropaje, piel, vasijas,
palabras, vino, panes,
se fue, cayó a la tierra.

VI

Then on the ladder of the earth I climbed
through the lost jungle's tortured thicket
up to you, Macchu Picchu.
High city of laddered stones,
at last the dwelling of what earth
never covered in vestments of sleep.
In you like two lines parallel,
the cradles of lightning and man
rocked in a wind of thorns.

Mother of stone, spume of condors.

High reef of the human dawn.

Spade lost in the primal sand.

This was the dwelling, this is the place:
here the broad grains of maize rose up
and fell again like red hail.

Here gold thread came off the vicuña
to clothe lovers, tombs, and mothers,
king and prayers and warriors.

Here men's feet rested at night
next to the eagles' feet, in the ravenous
high nests, and at dawn
they stepped with the thunder's feet onto thinning mists
and touched the soil and the stones
till they knew them come night or death.

I look at clothes and hands,
the trace of water in an echoing tub,
the wall brushed smooth by the touch of a face
that looked with my eyes at the lights of earth,
that oiled with my hands the vanished
beams: because everything, clothing, skin, jars,
words, wine, bread,
is gone, fallen to earth.

Y el aire entró con dedos
de azahar sobre todos los dormidos:
mil años de aire, meses, semanas de aire,
de viento azul, de cordillera férrea,
que fueron como suaves huracanes de pasos
lustrando el solitario recinto de la piedra.

And the air came in with the touch
of lemon blossom over everyone sleeping:
a thousand years of air, months, weeks of air,
of blue wind and iron cordillera,
that were like gentle hurricane footsteps
polishing the lonely boundary of stone.

VII

Muertos de un solo abismo, sombras de una hondonada,
la profunda, es así como al tamaño
de vuestra magnitud
vino la verdadera, la más abrasadora
muerte y desde las rocas taladradas,
desde los capiteles escarlata,
desde los acueductos escalares
os desplomasteis como en un otoño
en una sola muerte.
Hoy el aire vacío ya no llora,
ya no conoce vuestros pies de arcilla,
yo olvidó vuestros cántaros que filtraban el cielo
cuando lo derramaban los cuchillos del rayo,
y el árbol poderoso fue comido
por la niebla, y cortado por la racha.

Él sostuvo una mano que cayó de repente
desde la altura hasta el final del tiempo.
Ya no sois, manos de araña, débiles
hebras, tela enmarañada:
cuanto fuisteis cayó: costumbres, sílabas
raídas, máscaras de luz deslumbradora.

Pero una permanencia de piedra y de palabra:
la ciudad como un vaso, se levantó en las manos
de todos, vivos, muertos, callados, sostenidos,
de tanta muerte, un muro, de tanta vida un golpe
de pétalos de piedra: la rosa permanente, la morada:
este arrecife andino de colonias glaciales.

Cuando la mano de color de arcilla
se convirtió en arcilla, y cuando los pequeños párpados se cerraron
llenos de ásperos muros, poblados de castillos,
y cuando todo el hombre se enredó en su agujero,
quedó la exactitud enarbolada:
el alto sitio de la aurora humana:
la más alta vasija que contuvo el silencio:
una vida de piedra después de tantas vidas.

VII

You dead of a single abyss, shadows of one ravine,
the deepest, thus on a scale
with your greatness there came
the true, the most consuming
death and from the drilled-out rocks,
from the red-topped columns,
from the laddered aqueducts
you plummeted as in autumn
to one sole death.
Today the empty air does not weep,
is not familiar with your clayey feet,
forgets your pitchers that filtered the sky
when knives of lightning spilled it out,
and eaten by mist the mighty
tree was cut down by gusts.

It held up a hand that fell suddenly
down from the height to the end of time.
You're no more now, spidery hands, frail
fibers, entangled web—
whatever you were fell away: customs, frayed
syllables, masks of dazzling light.

Yet a permanence of stone and word,
the city like a bowl, rose up in the hands
of all, living, dead, silenced, sustained,
a wall out of so much death, out of so much life a shock
of stone petals: the permanent rose, the dwelling place:
the glacial outposts on this Andean reef.

When the clay-colored hand
turned to clay and the eyes' small lids fell shut,
filled with rugged walls, crowded with castles,
and when man lay all tangled in his hole,
there remained an upraised exactitude:
the high site of the human dawn:
the highest vessel that held silence in:
a life of stone after so many lives.

VIII

Sube conmigo, amor americano.

Besa conmigo las piedras secretas.
La plata torrencial del Urubamba
hace volar el polen a su copa amarilla.
Vuela el vacío de la enredadera,
la planta pétrea, la guirnalda dura
sobre el silencio del cajón serrano.
Ven, minúscula vida, entre las alas
de la tierra, mientras—cristal y frío, aire golpeado
apartando esmeraldas combatidas,
oh agua salvaje, bajas de la nieve.

Amor, amor, hasta la noche abrupta,
desde el sonoro pedernal andino,
hacia la aurora de rodillas rojas,
contempla el hijo ciego de la nieve.

Oh, Wilkamayu de sonoros hilos,
cuando rompes tus truenos lineales
en blanca espuma, como herida nieve,
cuando tu vendaval acantilado
canta y castiga despertando al cielo,
qué idioma traes a la oreja apenas
desarraigada de tu espuma andina?

Quién apresó el relámpago del frío
y lo dejó en la altura encadenado,
repartido en sus lágrimas glaciales,
sacudido en sus rápidas espadas,
golpeando sus estambres aguerridos,
conducido en su cama de guerrero,
sobresaltado en su final de roca?

VIII

Climb up with me, American love.

Kiss the secret stones with me.
The torrential silver of the Urubamba
sends pollen flying to its yellow cup.
The empty vine goes flying,
the stony plant, the stiff garland
over the silent mountain gorge.
Come, minuscule life, between the wings
of the earth, while—crystal and cold, a buffeted air
dividing the clash of emeralds—
oh wild water you come down from the snow.

Love, love, until the sudden night,
from the Andes' ringing flintstone,
to the red knees of dawn,
study the blind child of the snow.

Oh Wilkamayu of resonant threads,
when you shatter your bands of thunder
into white spume, like wounded snow,
when your steep gale
sings and slashes arousing the sky,
what language do you bring to the ear
barely uprooted from your Andean foam?

Who seized the lightning of the cold
and left it chained on the heights,
split into its chilling tears,
shaken in its rapid swords,
beating its war-worn stamens,
borne on its warrior bed,
stormed in its rock-bound end?

Qué dicen tus destellos acosados?
Tu secreto relámpago rebelde
antes viajó poblado de palabras?
Quién va rompiendo sílabas heladas,
idiomas negros, estandartes de oro,
bocas profundas, gritos sometidos,
en tus delgadas aguas arteriales?

Quién va cortando párpados florales
que vienen a mirar desde la tierra?
Quién precipita los racimos muertos
que bajan en tus manos de cascada
a desgranar su noche desgranada
en el carbón de la geología?

Quién despeña la rama de los vínculos?
Quién otra vez sepulta los adioses?

Amor, amor, no toques la frontera,
ni adores la cabeza sumergida:
deja que el tiempo cumpla su estatura
en su salón de manantiales rotos,
y, entre al agua veloz y las murallas,
recoge el aire del desfiladero,
las paralelas láminas del viento,
el canal ciego de las cordilleras,
el áspero saludo del rocío,
y sube, flor a flor, por la espesura,
pisando la serpiente despeñada.

En la escarpada zona, piedra y bosque,
polvo de estrellas verdes, selva clara,
Mantur estalla como un lago vivo
o como un nuevo piso del silencio.

What do your tormented flashings say?
Your secret insurgent lightning—did it
once travel thronging with words?
Who goes on crushing frozen syllables,
black languages, banners of gold,
bottomless mouths, throttled shouts,
in your slender arterial waters?

Who goes clipping floral eyelids
that come to gaze from the earth?
Who hurls the dead stalks down
that drop in your cascading hands
to thresh their threshed-out night
in geologic coal?

Who flings down the linking branch?
Who yet again buries farewells?

Love, love, do not touch the brink
or worship the sunken head:
let time extend full span
in its hall of broken wellsprings,
and between ramparts and rapid water
gather the air in the pass,
the wind's parallel plating,
the blind channel of the cordillera,
the bitter greeting of the dew,
and climb through the denseness flower by flower,
trampling the serpent flung to earth.

In this cliff-hung region, stone and forest,
dust of green stars, jungle clarity,
Mantur breaks out like a living lake
or a new ledge of silence.

Ven a mi propio ser, al alba mía,
hasta las soledades coronadas.

El reino muerto vive todavía.

Y en el Reloj la sombra sanguinaria
del cóndor cruza como una nave negra.

Come to my very being, to my own dawn,
up to the crowning solitude.

The dead realm lives on still.

And across the Sundial like a black ship
the ravening shadow of the condor cruises.

IX

Águila sideral, viña de bruma.
Bastión perdido, cimitarra ciega.
Cinturón estrellado, pan solemne.
Escala torrencial, párpado inmenso.
Túnica triangular, polen de piedra.
Lámpara de granito, pan de piedra.
Serpiente mineral, rosa de piedra.
Nave enterrada, manantial de piedra.
Caballo de la luna, luz de piedra.
Escuadra equinoccial, vapor de piedra.
Geometría final, libro de piedra.
Témpano entre las ráfagas labrado.
Madrépora del tiempo sumergido.
Muralla por los dedos suavizada.
Techumbre por las plumas combatida.
Ramos de espejo, bases de tormenta.
Tronos volcados por la enredadera.
Régimen de la garra encarnizada.
Vendaval sostenido en la vertiente.
Inmóvil catarata de turquesa.
Campana patriarcal de los dormidos.
Argolla de las nieves dominadas.
Hierro acostado sobre sus estatuas.
Inaccesible temporal cerrado.
Manos de puma, roca sanguinaria.
Torre sombrera, discusión de nieve.
Noche elevada en dedos y raíces.
Ventana de las nieblas, paloma endurecida.
Planta nocturna, estatua de los truenos.
Cordillera esencial, techo marino.
Arquitectura de águilas perdidas.
Cuerda del cielo, abeja de la altura.
Nivel sangriento, estrella construída.
Burbuja mineral, luna de cuarzo.
Serpiente andina, frente de amaranto.

Sidereal eagle, vineyard of mist.
Bulwark lost, blind scimitar.
Starred belt, sacred bread.
Torrential ladder, giant eyelid.
Triangled tunic, pollen of stone.
Granite lamp, bread of stone.
Mineral serpent, rose of stone.
Buried ship, wellspring of stone.
Lunar horse, light of stone.
Equinox square, vapor of stone.
Final geometry, book of stone.
Iceberg carved by the squalls.
Coral of sunken time.
Rampart smoothed by fingers.
Roof struck by feathers.
Branching of mirrors, ground of tempests.
Thrones overturned by twining weeds.
Rule of the ravenous claw.
Gale sustained on the slope.
Immobile turquoise cataract.
Sleepers' patriarchal bell.
Collar of subjected snows.
Iron lying on its statues.
Inaccessible storm sealed off.
Puma hands, bloodthirsty rock.
Shading tower, dispute of snow.
Night raised in fingers and roots.
Window on the mist, hardened dove.
Nocturnal plant, statue of thunder.
Root of the cordillera, roof of the sea.
Architecture of lost eagles.
Cord of the sky, bee of the heights.
Bloodstained level, constructed star.
Mineral bubble, moon of quartz.
Andean serpent, brow of amaranth.

Cúpula del silencio, patria pura.
Novia del mar, árbol de catedrales.
Ramo de sal, cerezo de alas negras.
Dentadura nevada, trueno frío.
Luna arañada, piedra amenazante.
Cabellera del frío, acción del aire.
Volcán de manos, catarata oscura.
Ola de plata, dirección del tiempo.

Dome of silence, purebred homeland.
Bride of the sea, cathedral tree.
Salt branch, blackwinged cherry tree.
Snowswept teeth, cold thunder.
Scraped moon, menacing stone.
Crest of the cold, pull of the air.
Volcano of hands, dark cataract.
Silver wave, direction of time.

Piedra en la piedra, el hombre, dónde estuvo?
Aire en el aire, el hombre, dónde estuvo?
Tiempo en el tiempo, el hombre, dónde estuvo?
Fuiste también el pedacito roto
de hombre inconcluso, de águila vacía
que por las calles de hoy, que por las huellas,
que por las hojas del otoño muerto
va machacando el alma hasta la tumba?
La pobre mano, el pie, la pobre vida . . .
Los días de la luz deshilachada
en ti, como la lluvia
sobre las banderillas de la fiesta,
dieron pétalo a pétalo de su alimento oscuro
en la boca vacía?
                    Hambre, coral del hombre,
hambre, planta secreta, raíz de los leñadores,
hambre, subió tu raya de arrecife
hasta estas altas torres desprendidas?

Yo te interrogo, sal de los caminos,
muéstrame la cuchara, déjame, arquitectura,
roer con un palito los estambres de piedra,
subir todos los escalones del aire hasta el vacío,
rascar la entraña hasta tocar el hombre.

Macchu Picchu, pusiste
piedra en la piedra, y en la base, harapo?
Carbón sobre carbón, y en el fondo la lágrima?
Fuego en el oro, y en él, temblando el rojo
goterón de la sangre?
Devuélveme el esclavo que enterraste!
Sacude de las tierras el pan duro
del miserable, muéstrame los vestidos

X

Stone upon stone, and man, where was he?
Air upon air, and man, where was he?
Time upon time, and man, where was he?
Were you too then the broken bit
of half-spent humankind, an empty eagle, that
through the streets today, through footsteps,
through the dead autumn's leaves,
keeps crushing its soul until the grave?
The meager hand, the foot, the meager life . . .
Did the days of unraveled light
in you, like rain
on pennants at a festival,
give off their dark food petal by petal
into your empty mouth?
                 Hunger, coral of humankind,
hunger, hidden plant, root of the woodcutter,
hunger, did your reef-edge climb
to these high and ruinous towers?

I question you, salt of the roads,
show me the trowel; architecture, let me
grind stone stamens with a stick,
climb every step of air up to the void,
scrape in the womb till I touch man.

Macchu Picchu, did you set
stone upon stone on a base of rags?
Coal over coal and at bottom, tears?
Fire on the gold and within it, trembling, the red
splash of blood?
Give me back the slave you buried!
Shake from the earth the hard bread
of the poor, show me the servant's

231

del siervo y su ventana.
Dime cómo durmió cuando vivía.
Dime si fue su sueño
ronco, entreabierto, como un hoyo negro
hecho por la fatiga sobre el muro.
El muro, el muro! Si sobre su sueño
gravitó cada piso de piedra, y si cayó bajo ella
como bajo una luna, con el sueño!

Antigua América, novia sumergida,
también tus dedos,
al salir de la selva hacia el alto vacío de los dioses,
bajo los estandartes nupciales de la luz y el decoro,
mezclándose al trueno de los tambores y de las lanzas,
también, también tus dedos,
los que la rosa abstracta y la línea del frío, los
que el pecho sangriento del nuevo cereal trasladaron
hasta la tela de materia radiante, hasta las duras cavidades,
también, también, América enterrada, guardaste en lo más bajo,
en el amargo intestino, como un águila, el hambre?

clothes and his window.
Tell me how he slept while he lived.
Tell me if his sleep
was snoring, gaping like a black hole
that weariness dug in the wall.
The wall, the wall! If every course of stone
weighed down his sleep, and if he fell underneath
as under a moon, with his sleep!

Ancient America, sunken bride,
your fingers too,
leaving the jungle for the empty height of the gods,
under bridal banners of light and reverence,
blending with thunder from the drums and lances,
yours, your fingers too,
those that the abstract rose and the rim of cold, the
bloodstained body of the new grain bore up
to a web of radiant matter, to the hardened hollows,
you too, buried America, did you keep in the deepest part
of your bitter gut, like an eagle, hunger?

A través del confuso esplendor,
a través de la noche de piedra, déjame hundir la mano
y deja que en mi palpite, como un ave mil años
   prisionera,
el viejo corazón del olvidado!
Déjame olvidar hoy esta dicha, que es más ancha que el mar,
porque el hombre es más ancho que el mar y que sus islas,
y hay que caer en él como en un pozo para salir del fondo
con un ramo de agua secreta y de verdades sumergidas.
Déjame olvidar, ancha piedra, la proporción poderosa,
la trascendente medida, las piedras del panal,
y de la escuadra déjame hoy resbalar
la mano sobre la hipotenusa de áspera sangre y cilicio.
Cuando, como una herradura de élitros rojos, el cóndor furibundo
me golpea las sienes en el orden del vuelo
y el huracán de plumas carniceras barre el polvo sombrío
de las escalinatas diagonales, no veo a la bestia veloz,
no veo el ciego ciclo de sus garras,
veo el antiguo ser, servidor, el dormido
en los campos, veo un cuerpo, mil cuerpos, un hombre,
   mil mujeres,
bajo la racha negra, negros de lluvia y noche,
con la piedra pesada de la estatua:
Juan Cortapiedras, hijo de Wiracocha,
Juan Comefrío, hijo de estrella verde,
Juan Piesdescalzos, nieto de la turquesa,
sube a nacer conmigo, hermano.

Through the dazing splendor,
through the night of stone, let me plunge my hand
and let there beat in me, like a bird a thousand years
   imprisoned,
the old forgotten human heart!
Let me forget today this joy that is broader than the sea,
because man is broader than sea and islands
and we must fall in him as in a well to rise from the bottom
with a branch of secret water and sunken truths.
Let me forget, broad stone, the sovereign symmetry,
transcendent measure, honeycombed stones,
and from the square edge let me this day slide
my hand down the hypotenuse of haircloth and bitter blood.
When, like a horseshoe of red-cased wings, the furious condor
hammers my temples in the order of flight
and the hurricane's blood-dipped feathers sweep the dark dust
on diagonal stairways, I see not the swift beast,
not the blind cycling of its claws,
I see the ancient human, a human slave, sleeping
in the fields, I see one body, a thousand bodies, a man, a
   thousand women
under black gusts, blackened by rain and night,
with the stonework's massive carving:
Jack Stonebreaker, son of Wiracocha,
Jack Coldbiter, son of the green star,
Jack Barefoot, grandson of the turquoise,
rise to be born with me, brother.

XII

Sube a nacer conmigo, hermano.

Dame la mano desde la profunda
zona de tu dolor diseminado.
No volverás del fondo de las rocas.
No volverás del tiempo subterráneo.
No volverá tu voz endurecida.
No volverán tus ojos taladrados.
Mírame desde el fondo de la tierra,
labrador, tejedor, pastor callado:
domador de guanacos tutelares:
albañil del andamio desafiado:
aguador de las lágrimas andinas:
joyero de los dedos machacados:
agricultor temblando en la semilla:
alfarero en tu greda derramado:
traed a la copa de esta nueva vida
vuestros viejos dolores enterrados.
Mostradme vuestra sangre y vuestro surco,
decidme: aquí fui castigado,
porque la joya no brilló o la tierra
no entregó a tiempo la piedra o el grano:
señaladme la piedra en que caísteis
y la madera en que os crucificaron,
encendedme los viejos pedernales,
las viejas lámparas, los látigos pegados
a través de los siglos en las llagas
y las hachas de brillo ensangrentado.
Yo vengo a hablar por vuestra boca muerta.
A través de la tierra juntad todos
los silenciosos labios derramados
y desde el fondo habladme toda esta larga noche
como si yo estuviera con vosotros anclado,

XII

Rise to be born with me, brother.

Give me your hand out of the deep
region seeded by all your grief.
You won't come back from bottom rock.
You won't come back from time under ground.
No coming back with your hardened voice.
No coming back with your drilled-out eyes.
Look at me from the bottom of earth,
plowman, weaver, voiceless shepherd:
trainer of guardian llamas:
mason on a dangerous scaffold:
water-bearer of Andean tears:
goldsmith with fingers bruised:
farmer trembling over the seed:
potter spilled on your clay:
bring all your age-old buried
griefs to the cup of this new life.
Show me your blood and your furrow,
say to me: here I was punished
when a gem didn't shine or the earth
give forth its stone or grain on time:
mark me the stone you stumbled on
and the wood they crucified you on,
strike light for me from your old flints,
the ancient lamps, the whiplash stuck
within your wounds through centuries,
and the axes' brightness stained with blood.
I come to speak through your dead mouth.
All through the earth join all
the silent wasted lips
and speak from the depths to me all this long night
as if I were anchored here with you,

contadme todo, cadena a cadena,
eslabón a eslabón, y paso a paso,
afilad los cuchillos que guardasteis,
ponedlos en mi pecho y en mi mano,
como un río de rayos amarillos,
como un río de tigres enterrados,
y dejadme llorar, horas, días, años,
edades ciegas, siglos estelares.

Dadme el silencio, el agua, la esperanza.

Dadme la lucha, el hierro, los volcanes.

Apegadme los cuerpos como imanes.

Acudid a mis venas y a mi boca.

Hablad por mis palabras y mi sangre.

tell me everything, chain by chain,
link by link, and step by step,
file the knives you kept by you,
drive them into my chest and my hand
like a river of riving yellow light,
like a river where buried jaguars lie,
and let me weep, hours, days, years,
blind ages, stellar centuries.

Give me silence, water, hope.

Give me struggle, iron, volcanoes.

Fasten your bodies to me like magnets.

Hasten to my veins to my mouth.

Speak through my words and my blood.

NOTES

NOTES

Original publication data on all works by or about Neruda, including English translations, will be cited only in the first occurrence in the notes. These data may also be found in the Bibliography. In quoting and translating Neruda's work, the text I follow is: Pablo Neruda, *Obras completas*, 4th ed., 3 vols. (Buenos Aires: Losada, 1973). This edition will be cited as OC; citations from the books it includes will give page references from OC.

For my translations of numerous passages and two full poems by Neruda, I do not provide the Spanish in the text or notes, since I am using this poetry more for descriptive or narrative purposes than as instances of verse translation. All translations are mine unless otherwise specified. In quoting verse, I occasionally use three ellipsis points rather than a line of them to indicate that a line or more of verse has been omitted.

Introduction

1. For selected criticism on Neruda, see my bibliography and those by Alfonso Escudero and Hernán Loyola in OC. Besides some good articles, three books in English have been devoted to Neruda, by Frank Riess, René de Costa, and Salvatore Bizzarro. A translation of Emir Rodríguez Monegal's book is forthcoming from the University of Chicago Press.

2. George Steiner, *After Babel: Aspects of Language and Translation* (London: Oxford Univ. Press, 1975), pp. 273–74 (also has a fine bibliography). I should mention here Vladimir Nabokov's translation (with commentary) of Pushkin's *Eugene Onegin* (Princeton: Princeton Univ. Press, 1964; rev. ed., 1975)—an exhaustive but inimitable production.

3. The poem was first published in Spanish in the *Revista Nacional de Cultura* (Caracas, Venezuela), no. 57 (July–Aug. 1946), 77–78, and no. 58 (Sept.–Oct. 1946), 103–12; OC, I, 331–44.

Chapter One

1. George Steiner, "Introduction," *The Penguin Book of Modern Verse Translation* (Baltimore: Penguin, 1966), p. 25.

2. Neruda, *Canto general* (Mexico City: [Talleres Gráficos de la Nación], 1950). I retain Neruda's spelling of *Macchu Picchu*, instead of the more accepted Machu Picchu.

3. For Williams's Neruda translation, see p. 22 and note 40 below. For Williams's translation of Paz's "Himno entre ruinas," see Octavio Paz, *Early Poems: 1935–1955* (New York: New Directions, 1973), pp. 94–99. See also John Felstiner, "Through a Spanish Looking Glass: Williams's Poetry in Translation," *Américas* (Wash., D.C.), 29, nos. 11–12 (Nov.–Dec. 1977), 5–8.

4. Neruda, *The Heights of Macchu Picchu*, trans. Nathaniel Tarn (London: Jonathan Cape, 1966; New York: Farrar, Straus and Giroux, 1967).

5. Robert Lowell, *For the Union Dead* (New York: Farrar, Straus and Giroux, 1964).

6. Canto XII. Further excerpts from *Alturas de Macchu Picchu* will be identified in the text by canto number.

7. (Santiago: Nascimento, 1924).

8. Neruda, *Residencia en la tierra, 1925–1931* (Santiago: Nascimento, 1933). *Residencia en la tierra, 1925–1931; Residencia en la tierra, 1931–1935*, 2 vols. (Madrid: Cruz y Raya, 1935).

9. Neruda, "Explico algunas cosas" ("I Explain Some Things"), in *España en el corazón* (Santiago: Ercilla, 1937); OC, I, 273.

10. Neruda speaks of his "endless bond" in "La copa de sangre" (1938), OC, III, 651. His first poem about Chile was "Almagro" (1938), retitled "Descubridores de Chile" in *Canto general*, OC, I, 363.

11. Neruda, *Confieso que he vivido: Memorias* (Buenos Aires: Losada, 1974), p. 211. Most of these memoirs appeared in an earlier version as "Las vidas del poeta," in *O Cruzeiro Internacional* (Río de Janeiro) in ten successive numbers, January 16 through June 1, 1962. Some of Neruda's additions for the 1974 edition are italicized. The book is in English as *Memoirs*, trans. Hardie St. Martin (New York: Farrar, Straus and Giroux, 1977).

12. *Canto general de Chile: Fragmentos* [Mexico City, 1943]. Neruda wrote an expanded version, which became Bk. VII of *Canto general*. *América, no invoco tu nombre en vano* appeared in *América* (Mexico City), no. 19 (July 1943). This poem became Bk. VI of *Canto general*.

13. *Confieso*, p. 230. In the earlier version (see note 11, above), "my own hands" was "I myself."

14. For a deluxe edition with fine photographs, see *Alturas de Macchu Picchu*, photographs by Graziano Gasparini (Buenos Aires: Losada, 1972). For criticism of *Alturas de Macchu Picchu*, see Chapter V, note 2.

15. A 1947 recording was made in Santiago by Iberoamérica, Archivo de la Palabra. The second recording is by Odeon; I believe it was done in 1955. A Caedmon recording of the poem, probably from 1966, is also available: CDL 51215. Neruda, "Algo sobre mi poesía y mi vida" ("A Word about My Poetry and My Life"), *Aurora* (Santiago), no. 1 (July 1954), 13, speaks of "a new stage."

16. G. Dundas Craig, *The Modernist Trend in Spanish-American Poetry*

(Berkeley: Univ. of California Press, 1934), pp. 226–35, 330–33. For a list of translations and anthologies, see the bibliography in OC. For a fairly detailed account of Neruda's reception in the U.S. and England, see Esperanza Figueroa, "Pablo Neruda en Inglés," *Revista Iberoamericana* (Pittsburgh), 39, nos. 82–83 (Jan.–June 1973), 301–47.

17. Lloyd Mallan, Mary and C. V. Wicker, and J. L. Grucci, trans., *Three Spanish American Poets: Pellicer, Neruda, Andrade* (Albuquerque: Sage Books [Swallow and Critchlow], 1942).

18. Dudley Fitts, ed., *Anthology of Contemporary Latin American Poetry* (Norfolk, Conn.: New Directions, 1942).

19. *Ibid.*, p. 619.

20. H. R. Hays, ed., *Twelve Spanish American Poets* (New Haven: Yale Univ. Press, 1943; rpt. Boston: Beacon, 1972).

21. *Residence on Earth and Other Poems*, trans. Angel Flores (Norfolk, Conn.: New Directions, 1946).

22. Julio Cortázar, "Lettre ouverte," preface to Pablo Neruda, *Résidence sur la terre*, trans. Guy Suarès (Paris: Gallimard, 1972), p. 12. Cortázar, "Neruda entre nosotros," *Plural* (Mexico City), March 1974, 39.

23. Cantos I–III, *France Libre* (London), 11, no. 63 (Jan. 15, 1946), 207–8; cantos IV–XI, *Confluences* (Paris), no. 9 (Feb. 1946). The entire translation appeared in *Hauteurs de Macchu-Picchu*, trans. Roger Caillois (Paris: Pierre Seghers, 1961).

24. *Revista Nacional de Cultura* (Caracas), no. 57 (July–Aug. 1946), 77–85 (Cantos I–VII), and no. 58 (Sept.–Oct. 1946), 103–12 (Cantos VIII–XII). *Expresión* (Buenos Aires), no. 1 (Dec. 1946).

25. *Alturas de Macchu Picchu* (Santiago: Librería Neira, 1947).

26. See G. S. Fraser, *News from South America* (London: Harvill, 1949), pp. 173–75. *Adam* (London), 16, nos. 180–81 (March–April 1948). Translations by G. R. Coulthard, commentary by Coulthard and Fraser.

27. H. R. Hays, "Heights of Macchu Picchu," *The Tiger's Eye* (Oct. 20, 1948), 112–21.

28. "East Coker," I.

29. Neruda, "Heights of Macchu Picchu," in *Let the Rail Splitter Awake and Other Poems* (New York: Masses and Mainstream, 1950). Previous translations of Neruda appeared in the Nov. 1949, Jan. 1950, and April 1950 issues of *Masses and Mainstream*.

30. Angel Flores, "Summits of Macchu Picchu," in Whit Burnett, ed., *The World's Best* (New York: Dial, 1950), pp. 355–67.

31. George Kubler, "Machu Picchu," *Perspecta: The Yale Architectural Journal*, 6 (1960), 53.

32. OC, I, 812. Apart from a passing reference to Stalin in "Nuevo canto de amor a Stalingrado" (1943), OC, I, 296, see the poem *Let the Rail Splitter Awake* (1948), OC, I, 581–82; "Catástrofe en Sewell" (1949), OC, I, 570; and "En su muerte" (1954), OC, I, 807–13, a poem on Stalin's death.

33. Neruda, "Discurso pronunciado en el Congreso de la Paz en

México" (1949), in Neruda, *Poesía política*, ed. Margarita Aguirre (Santiago: Austral, 1953), II, 213–25; rpt. as "Our Duty Toward Life," trans. Joseph M. Bernstein, in Neruda, *Let the Rail Splitter Awake and Other Poems*, pp. 9–18.

34. See *Let the Rail Splitter Awake*, OC, I, 574. With this brief phrase from Whitman, as with a few other brief phrases in the book, I do not indicate the line break in my quotation.

35. Committee on Un-American Activities, *Guide to Subversive Organizations and Publications*, rev. ed. (Wash., D.C.: House of Representatives, 1961), pp. 167, 228.

36. See OC, I, 577, 427.

37. E. Rodríguez Monegal, *El viajero inmóvil: Introducción a Pablo Neruda* (Buenos Aires: Losada, 1966), p. 86. Jiménez's essay was reprinted in his *Españoles de tres mundos* (Buenos Aires: Losada, 1942), and after Jiménez won the Nobel Prize in 1956, it appeared again in Madrid, Mexico, and Paris (see bibliographical data in OC, III, 1128).

38. Kenneth Rexroth, trans., *Thirty Spanish Poems of Love and Exile* (San Francisco: City Lights, 1955). Christopher Logue, *The Man Who Told His Love* (Northwood, Middlesex, Eng.: Scorpion, 1958). Here and in succeeding references to *Veinte poemas de amor y una canción desesperada*, I abbreviate the title. Logue later published his adaptations in Neruda, *Songs*, trans. Christopher Logue (London: Hutchinson, 1959). George Steiner reprints two of these in *The Penguin Book of Modern Verse Translation*, pp. 287–88.

39. Neruda, "Oda a la pereza," *Odas elementales* (Buenos Aires: Losada, 1954). For Williams's translation of Loyalist poetry see M. J. Bernadete and Rolfe Humphries, eds., *And Spain Sings* (New York: Vanguard, 1937).

40. *New World Writing*, no. 14 (New York: Mentor, 1958), p. 99.

41. See Steven Gould Axelrod, *Robert Lowell: Life and Art* (Princeton: Princeton Univ. Press, 1978), pp. 82–99.

42. See *The Fifties*, no. 1 (1958) and no. 3 (1959). For *The Sixties*, no. 7 (Winter 1964) Bly wrote five Neruda translations and an essay on the poet.

43. Neruda, *Twenty Poems*, trans. James Wright and Robert Bly (Madison, Minn.: The Sixties Press, 1967).

44. *Selected Poems of Pablo Neruda*, trans. Ben Belitt (New York: Grove, 1961).

45. *Ibid.*, p. 127.

46. My analogy derives from *Don Quixote*, Bk. II, Ch. 62.

47. *The Elementary Odes of Pablo Neruda*, trans. Carlos Lozano (New York: Cypress, 1961). Neruda, *Residence on Earth*, trans. Clayton Eshleman (San Francisco: Amber House, 1962).

48. For these and other collections in and out of print, see my bibliography.

49. Octavio Paz, *Traducción: literatura y literalidad* (Barcelona: Tusquets, 1971); rpt. as "Teoría y práctica de la traducción," in Paz, *El signo y el garabato* (Mexico City: Joaquín Mortiz, 1973).

50. Willard Ropes Trask, in *Translation*, 6 (Winter, 1978–79), 263–65, says he translates verse only into prose. But his prose versions have the qualities of verse. A good literal prose version of *Alturas de Macchu Picchu* by Tom Raworth appears in E. Caracciolo-Trejo, ed., *The Penguin Book of Latin American Verse* (Baltimore: Penguin, 1971), pp. 128–50.

51. Rita Guibert, *Seven Voices*, trans. Frances Partridge (1972; rpt. New York: Random House, Vintage Books, 1973), pp. 35–36. This is the most extensive interview with Neruda available. I have altered it very slightly in one spot, but have not seen the original Spanish.

52. These translations were published in small magazines: Baudelaire, 1967; Rilke, 1926; Joyce, 1933; Blake, 1935; Whitman, 1935—see OC, bibliography. The first four are reprinted in OC, III, 763–81.

53. William Shakespeare, *Romeo y Julieta*, trans. Pablo Neruda (Buenos Aires: Losada, 1964).

54. Quoted in Hernán Loyola, "Neruda traduce a Shakespeare," *Aurora* (Santiago), 2, no. 5 (Jan.–March 1965), 150.

55. Guibert, p. 36.

56. César Vallejo, "La nueva poesía norteamericana" (1929), in *Aula Vallejo*, 5–7, ed. Juan Larrea (Córdoba, Arg.: Univ. Nacional, 1967), pp. 67–70.

57. Neruda, "La palabra," in *Plenos poderes* (Buenos Aires: Losada, 1962); OC, II, 974.

58. Neruda, "Viaje por las costas del mundo" (1943), OC, II, 563.

59. Ugné Karvelis, "Une Journée à Isla Negra," *Europe* (Paris), nos. 537–38 (Jan.–Feb. 1974), 49.

60. Walt Whitman, "Pasto de llamas," trans. Pablo Neruda, in *El aviso de escarmentados del año que acaba y escarmiento de avisados para el que empieza de 1935* (Madrid: Cruz y Raya, 1935), pp. 61–64; rpt. *Repertorio Americano*, no. 922 (Sept. 20, 1941), 265.

61. Luis Rosales, "Prólogo," in Pablo Neruda, *Poesía*, 2 vols. (Madrid: Noguer, 1974), I, 40.

62. "Entrada a la madera" ("Entrance into Wood"), "Apogeo del apio" ("Apogee of Celery"), "Estatuto del vino" ("Ordinance of Wine"), OC, I, 229, 230, 232.

63. Neruda, *Résidence sur la terre*, trans. Guy Suarès, p. 105.

64. G. R. Coulthard, in *Adam*.

65. *The Heights of Macchu Picchu*, trans. Nathaniel Tarn. Further references to this translation, since they are identified by canto in my text, will not be cited.

66. T. S. Eliot, *Four Quartets*: "Burnt Norton," II.

67. George Steiner, *After Babel*, p. 408. See also Walter Benjamin, "The Task of the Translator" (1923), trans. James Hynd and E. M. Valk, *Delos*, 2 (1968), 76–99, and Steiner's discussion of this essay, pp. 63–65. The essay, trans. Harry Zohn, also appears in Walter Benjamin, *Illuminations*, ed. Hannah Arendt (New York: Schocken, 1969), pp. 69–82.

68. Paul Valéry, in one of the finest meditations on verse translations, says that in translating Virgil's *Eclogues*, he proceeded "from the finished poem . . . back to its nascent state," and that the work of trans-

lation "causes us in some way to try walking in the tracks left by the author . . . to work back to the virtual moment of [the poem's] formation. . . . From that vividly imagined state one must make one's way down toward its resolution in a work in a different tongue." "Variations on the *Eclogues*" (1953), in Paul Valéry, *The Art of Poetry*, trans. Denise Folliot (London: Routledge and Kegan Paul, 1958), pp. 304-5. See also Steiner, pp. 346-47.

Chapter Two

1. "Provincia de la infancia," in *Anillos* (Santiago: Nascimento, 1926); OC, I, 142.
2. "La copa de sangre," OC, III, 650.
3. *Confieso*, pp. 11-12.
4. "Infancia y poesía" ("Childhood and Poetry," 1954), in *Obras completas*, ed. Hernán Loyola, 2 vols., 3rd ed. (Buenos Aires: Losada, 1967), I, 26.
5. *Ibid.*, p. 30.
6. *Ibid.*, p. 34.
7. *Ibid.*
8. "Nacimiento" ("Birth"), in vol. I of *Memorial de Isla Negra*, 5 vols. (Buenos Aires: Losada, 1964); OC, II, 1022. The poet was her first child, born nine months after she married: Hernán Loyola, "Itinerario de Pablo Neruda," *Anales de la Universidad de Chile*, 129, nos. 157-60 (Jan.– Dec. 1971), 9-10. This article contains valuable biographical detail. An earlier version appeared as the introduction to Neruda, *Antología esencial*, ed. Hernán Loyola (Buenos Aires: Losada, 1971), pp. 7-37.
9. "La tierra austral," in *Memorial de Isla Negra*, I; OC, II, 1029.
10. OC, III, 776. Neruda was translating Blake's *Visions of the Daughters of Albion*. See also Ch. V, p. 185.
11. "Luna," quoted in Hernán Loyola, *Ser y morir en Pablo Neruda, 1918-1945* (Santiago: Editora Santiago, 1967), pp. 22-23.
12. "Nacimiento," OC, II, 1022.
13. "Infancia y poesía," pp. 28, 35. Here and elsewhere, when a paragraph of the text includes more than one quotation from a single source, I cite them in order in a single note.
14. "La frontera (1904)," *Canto general*; OC, I, 693.
15. See Louis C. Faron, "Symbolic Values and the Integration of Society Among the Mapuche of Chile," in John Middleton, ed., *Myth and Cosmos* (New York: Natural History Press, 1971), pp. 167-83.
16. "El padre" ("The Father"), in *Memorial de Isla Negra*, I; OC, II, 1025-27.
17. *Confieso*, pp. 16, 22. Juvencio Valle remembers Neruda, as a schoolboy, being given tea with extra milk by his stepmother, "because he was very thin and needed it!": Delia Domínguez and Jorge Marchant Lazcano, "El mundo de la infancia de Pablo Neruda," *Paula* (Santiago), July 17, 1979, p. 42.
18. "Infancia y poesía," p. 28.

19. "La mamadre" ("The Stepmother"), in *Memorial de Isla Negra*, I; OC, II, 1024.

20. *Donde nace la lluvia*, Vol. I in *Memorial de Isla Negra*.

21. "El padre," OC, II, 1025.

22. *Confieso*, p. 30.

23. In "Algo sobre mi poesía y mi vida," p. 15, Neruda says "I needed a name so my father would not see my poems in magazines. He blamed my bad marks in math on my verses." Neruda had been moved by a story by the Czech writer Jan Neruda, who "wrote a lot about the humble people in Prague's poor districts." The name Pablo is after Paul Verlaine and possibly Paul Valéry; also, in Neruda's first serious love affair, he imagined himself as Paolo, after Dante's Paolo and Francesca: Neruda, "Album Terusa 1923," ed. Hernán Loyola, *Anales de la Universidad de Chile*, 129, nos. 157–60 (Jan.–Dec. 1971), 49.

24. See Loyola, "Itinerario," p. 11; Loyola, *Ser y morir*, p. 25; Aguirre, p. 33.

25. "La copa de sangre," OC, III, 650; "Infancia y poesía," p. 33.

26. "La copa de sangre," OC, III, 651; "Infancia y poesía," p. 33.

27. "Infancia y poesía," p. 32.

28. *Ibid.*, p. 34.

29. "Viaje por las costas del mundo," OC, II, 563.

30. "Infancia y poesía," p. 30.

31. "Viaje por las costas del mundo," OC, II, 563.

32. Alfredo Cardona Peña, *Pablo Neruda y otros ensayos* (Mexico City: Andrea, 1955), p. 25.

33. *Confieso*, p. 24.

34. "Album Terusa 1923," p. 49.

35. "Playa del sur," in *Crepusculario* ("Twilight Book") (Santiago: Claridad, 1923); OC, I, 69.

36. For an example of a later and perfectly concerted treatment of the ocean by Neruda, see the footnote on p. 85.

37. "La canción de la fiesta," *Claridad* (Santiago), no. 38 (Oct. 15, 1921); OC, III, 607. Diego Muñoz, in Domínguez and Lazcano, "El mundo de la infancia de Pablo Neruda," p. 101, remarks that Neruda attracted particular attention as the first provincial poet to win this prize.

38. OC, II, 1030; *Confieso*, p. 27; OC, III, 651.

39. "Inicial" ("Initial"), OC, I, 37.

40. Margarita Aguirre, *Las vidas de Pablo Neruda* (Santiago: Zig-Zag, 1967), p. 139. Many of these early verses show the influence of Latin-American modernists such as Julio Herrera y Reissig and Carlos Sabat Ercasty, though Neruda's personal force comes through in them more strongly.

41. *El hondero entusiasta, 1923–1924* (Santiago: Letras, 1933); OC, I, 155. Literally, the title means "The Enthusiastic Slinger."

42. "Algunas reflexiones improvisadas sobre mis trabajos" ("Some Improvised Reflections on My Works"), OC, III, 709.

43. *El hondero entusiasta*, poem 7; OC, I, 161.
44. *Ibid.*, poem 2; OC, I, 155.
45. G. Dundas Craig, *The Modernist Trend in Spanish-American Poetry*, p. 332.
46. "Album Terusa 1923," p. 51.
47. *Ibid.*
48. "Con los brazos abiertos," in Raúl Silva Castro, *Pablo Neruda* (Santiago: Universitaria, 1964), p. 236.
49. "Amor," OC, I, 50.
50. From *Crepusculario*: "Me peina el viento los cabellos" ("The Wind Combs My Hair"), "Campesina" ("Peasant Girl"); OC, I, 60, 66.
51. Poems 9 and 11; OC, I, 164, 165.
52. Poem 7; OC, I, 162.
53. Poem 8; OC, I, 162.
54. The term "lover's breviary" comes from Jaime Concha, "Sexo y pobreza" ("Sex and Poverty"), *Revista Iberoamericana* (Pittsburgh), 39, nos. 82–83 (Jan.–June 1973), 137.
55. Poem 1; OC, I, 83. The twenty poems are variously addressed to two women, one from Temuco, one from Santiago (Emir Rodríguez Monegal, *El viajero inmóvil*, p. 49), but for my analysis the distinction does not apply.
56. Poems, 5, 3; OC, I, 85, 84.
57. Neruda, *Twenty Love Poems and a Song of Despair*, trans. W. S. Merwin (London: Jonathan Cape, 1968), p. 9.
58. Neruda, *The Early Poems*, trans. David Ossman and Carlos B. Hagen (New York: New Rivers, 1969), p. 53.
59. Poems 1, 16; OC, I, 83, 95.
60. Poem 13; OC, I, 91.
61. Julio Cortázar, "Neruda entre nosotros," pp. 38–39.
62. Poem 8; OC, I, 88.
63. OC, I, 182.
64. OC, I, 180.

Chapter Three

1. Neruda's bibliography shows the publication date to be August 1926 (OC, III, 945), but I believe this to be wrong. His biographer shows the poem published in July 1925 (Aguirre, *Las vidas de Pablo Neruda*, p. 13). Neruda himself, in a 1930 letter reproduced in Aguirre, p. 181, cites 1925 as the date of "Galope muerto," and in Cardona Peña, *Pablo Neruda*, p. 28, he is quoted indirectly as attributing the poem to 1925.
2. *Residencia en la tierra: 1925–1931* (Santiago: Nascimento, 1933). See Neruda's letters in Aguirre, pp. 178–86.
3. (Santiago), no. 132 (July 1925). The numbers of *Claridad* for this year are missing from the Biblioteca Nacional in Santiago, so I am unable to verify the poem's appearance.
4. Rafael Alberti, "De mon amitié avec Pablo Neruda," *Europe*, nos. 419–20 (March–April 1964), 71–72.
5. No. 81 (March 1930), 332–33.

6. Charles K. Colhoun, *Criterion*, Oct. 1930, 203.

7. Aguirre, p. 180.

8. Cardona Peña, p. 28.

9. The English versions are in *Residence on Earth*, trans. Donald D. Walsh (New York: New Directions, 1973), p. 3 and *Residence on Earth and Other Poems*, trans. Angel Flores, p. 9. The poem has never, to my knowledge, been anthologized in English and seldom in Spanish. Some of the many studies of *Residencia en la tierra* may be found in Amado Alonso, *Poesía y estilo de Pablo Neruda*, 3rd ed. (Buenos Aires: Sudamericana, 1966); Emir Rodríguez Monegal, *El viajero inmóvil*; Jaime Concha, *Neruda 1904–1936* (Santiago: Universitaria, 1972), and "Interpretación de *Residencia en la tierra*," *Mapocho* (Santiago), 1, no. 2 (July 1963), 5–39; Alfredo Lozada, *El monismo agónico de Pablo Neruda* (Mexico City: B. Costa-Amic, 1971); Jean Franco, *An Introduction to Spanish-American Literature* (Cambridge: Cambridge Univ. Press, 1969), pp. 282–86; *Review*, 72 (Spring 1974); Gordon Brotherston, *Latin American Poetry: Origins and Presence* (Cambridge, Eng.: Cambridge Univ. Press, 1975), pp. 104–21. The first essay on Neruda to appear in the United States was in Spanish, and contains acute comments on his poetry through 1935: Concha Meléndez, "Pablo Neruda en su extremo imperio," *Revista Hispánica Moderna* (New York), 3, no. 1 (Oct. 1936), 1–31.

10. Cortázar, "Lettre ouverte," p. 12.

11. Neruda wrote mainly for the student magazine *Juventud*. See the bibliography in OC, III, 997–1004.

12. Hernán Loyola, "Itinerario de Pablo Neruda," p. 11.

13. Rubén Azócar, "Testimonio," *Aurora* (Santiago), July–Dec. 1964, 215. Diego Muñoz also notes Neruda's anxiety "at having cheated his parents' plans" (Delia Domínguez and Jorge Marchant Lazcano, "El mundo de la infancia de Pablo Neruda," p. 101).

14. See Frank Bonilla and Myron Glazer, *Student Politics in Chile* (New York: Basic Books, 1970), pp. 8–59; Julio César Jobet, *Luis Emilio Recabarren* (Santiago: Prensa latinoamericana, 1955), pp. 68–70, 141–43; Frederico G. Gil, *The Political System of Chile* (Boston: Houghton-Mifflin, 1966), pp. 51–61.

15. *Confieso*, p. 72.

16. Aguirre, p. 218. The masthead of *Claridad* proclaimed it a "Journal of Sociology, Criticism and Actualities": Aguirre, p. 132.

17. See Brotherston, p. 4; Jorge Carrera Andrade, *Reflections on Spanish-American Poetry* (Albany: State Univ. of New York Press, 1973), pp. 49–50; Guillermo de Torre, *Historia de las literaturas de vanguardia* (Madrid: Guadarrama, 1965). There is no sign and little likelihood that Neruda had read García Lorca by 1925.

18. Unpublished talk (1954), in Aguirre, p. 119.

19. Neruda, "Algunas reflexiones," OC, III, 712; *Confieso*, p. 388. *Tentativa del hombre infinito* (Santiago: Nascimento, 1926). For detailed discussions of *Tentativa del hombre infinito*, see René de Costa, "Pablo Neruda's *Tentativa del hombre infinito*: Notes for a Reappraisal," *Modern Philology*, 73 (1975–76), 136–47, and Jaime Alazraki, "El surrealismo de

Tentativa del hombre infinito de Pablo Neruda," *Hispanic Review*, 40 (Winter 1972), 31-39.

20. César Vallejo, *Trilce* (Lima, 1922). Neruda knew the second edition (Madrid: Iberoamericana, 1931), with a preface by José Bergamín that mentions Neruda somewhat disparagingly in contrast with Vallejo. See also Jean Franco, *César Vallejo: The Dialectics of Poetry and Silence* (Cambridge, Eng.: Cambridge Univ. Press, 1976), pp. 138-39.

21. César Vallejo, "Apuntes para un estudio," *Obras completas* (Lima: Mosca Azul, 1973), II, 161.

22. The text is taken from OC, I, 169-70, and differs from the 1930 text in minor points of punctuation and in stanza 4, l. 4, which originally read *dominios* instead of *caminos*.

23. *Libro de las preguntas* (Buenos Aires: Losada, 1974), p. 85.

24. *King Lear*, IV, i, 36; Sonnet 60.

25. Alonso, pp. 132-33.

26. Alonso, pp. 132-33, 200. See also Leo Spitzer, "La enumeración caótica en la poesía moderna," in *Lingüística e historia literaria*, 2nd ed. (Madrid: Gredos, 1961), pp. 274-300. In this version of the essay, first published separately in 1945 (Buenos Aires: Facultad de Filosofía y Letras) but not in the English edition of his book, Spitzer discusses the ancient stylistic procedure of enumeration in reference to Neruda's *Residencia en la tierra*, calling Neruda's vision of things disarticulated and pessimistic. But he appears to have used only Alonso's book as his source. Alonso also regrets Neruda's "abundant use, grammatically indecorous, of the gerund, which, more than within the strict norms of Spanish, moves in [Neruda's] lines with the exotic freedom of the English present participle" (p. 117).

27. Silva Castro, *Pablo Neruda*, p. 64.

28. Aguirre, pp. 178-79.

29. *Ibid.*, p. 181.

30. The talk, read over Montevideo radio in March 1939, was published in its rudimentary version as "Quevedo adentro" ("Quevedo Within") in Neruda, *Neruda entre nosotros* (Montevideo: Ediciones A.I.A.P.E., 1939). The quotations are taken from "Viaje al corazón de Quevedo" ("Journey to the Heart of Quevedo"), in Neruda, *Viajes* (Santiago: Nascimento, 1955), p. 34. In 1935 Neruda edited some Quevedo sonnets, including "Cerrar podrá": "Quevedo (Cartas y sonetos de la muerte)," *Cruz y Raya*, no. 33 (Dec. 1935). He says (*Viajes*, p. 201) that he first read Quevedo's lyrics in 1935, but as early as 1929 he remembers "returning" to Quevedo (*Confieso*, p. 133).

31. Aguirre, p. 179; OC, I, 227.

32. My translation of *mezclando todos los limbos sus colas* as "all the planets splicing their tails" may be all wrong. *Limbo*, besides its theological sense, can mean either the hem of a garment or the border of a planet. My guess makes as much sense as anything else, I hope.

33. Neruda, *Résidence sur la terre*, trans. Guy Suarès, p. 15.

34. Cf. Neruda, *Residence on Earth*, trans. Donald D. Walsh, p. 3.

35. Alonso, p. 228.

36. *Ibid.*, p. 198.

37. The term has a long history in philosophy and criticism. I have in mind Coleridge's use of it: "On Poesy or Art" (1818) in *Miscellanies*, ed. T. Ashe (London, 1885), pp. 42–49.

38. Cortázar, "Neruda entre nosotros," p. 39.

39. Federico García Lorca, "Presentación de Pablo Neruda," in *Obras completas*, 14th ed. (Madrid: Aguilar, 1968), pp. 148, 147.

40. Cortázar, "Lettre ouverte," p. 12.

41. Aguirre, p. 147. For a biography, see Fernando Alegría, *Recabarren* (Santiago: Antares, 1938).

42. See R. B. Cunninghame Graham, *The Horses of the Conquest* (London: Heinemann, 1930), pp. 22–23, and Miguel León-Portilla, *Pre-Columbian Literatures of Mexico* (Norman: Univ. of Oklahoma Press, 1969), p. 149. For *Canto general*, see "Cortés" and "Las agonías," OC, I, 348, 358.

43. *The Notebooks of Samuel Taylor Coleridge*, ed. Kathleen Coburn (New York: Bollingen Foundation, 1957), I: 1794–1804, 495 f54, 1589 f56.

44. *Shakespearean Criticism*, ed. Thomas Middleton Raysor (1930; 2d ed. London: J. M. Dent, 1960), I, 198. Although Coleridge did not use the term "organic form" consistently (see Reeve Parker, *Coleridge's Meditative Art* [Ithaca: Cornell Univ. Press, 1975], p. 248), it seems quite apposite in this case.

45. Wordsworth: II, 626; Keats: "Ode on a Grecian Urn"; Whitman: l. 107; Hopkins: "The Windhover" and *Poems and Prose of Gerard Manley Hopkins*, ed. W. H. Gardner (Baltimore: Penguin, 1953), pp. 114, 115; Eliot: "East Coker," V and "Burnt Norton," II; Williams: "Paterson: The Falls," in *Selected Poems* (New York: New Directions, 1968), pp. 112–13, and *Paterson* (New York: New Directions, 1963), p. 163; Melville: *Moby Dick*, Ch. 133; Faulkner, *Absalom, Absalom!* (New York: Modern Library, 1951), pp. 8, 175.

46. "La barcarola," OC, III, 180; Aguirre, p. 179.

47. Aguirre, pp. 179, 181.

48. García Lorca, p. 148.

49. He used André Gide's translation of Rilke, which had just come out: *Claridad*, no. 135 (Oct.–Nov. 1926); OC, III, 763–65.

50. Broom, admiral, coffins: "Sólo la muerte"; plant: "Trabajo frío"; "Vuelve el otoño"; OC, I, 209, 202, 246.

51. OC, I, 194–95.

52. *Confieso*, pp. 132, 121.

53. OC, I, 199–200.

54. *Confieso*, p. 133.

55. Aguirre, p. 187.

56. "Melancolía en la familia" ("Melancholy in the Family"), "Maternidad" ("Maternity"), "Enfermedades en mi casa" ("Illnesses in My House"), OC, I, 219, 221, 222. The child was born macrocephalic, according to Juan Larrea, *Del Surrealismo a Machupicchu* (Mexico City: Joaquín Mortiz, 1967), p. 104. Robert Pring-Mill says: "Soon after the war

began, Neruda finally left Maruca [his wife] for Delia del Carril" ("Introduction," in *Pablo Neruda: A Basic Anthology* [Oxford: Dolphin, 1975], p. xxvii). See also Ch. IV, note 22, below.

57. It is not always possible to date the poems of *Residencia en la tierra* exactly. But some did appear first in magazines, and others refer to periods of Neruda's life; also, he arranged the poems more or less chronologically.

58. OC, I, 227.

59. OC, I, 215–16.

60. "Unidad," "Sabor," OC, I, 173, 174.

61. "Sonata y destrucciones," OC, I, 186.

62. Neruda, *Residence on Earth*, trans. Donald D. Walsh, p. 53.

63. "Significa sombras," OC, I, 203.

64. García Lorca, p. 147.

65. "No hay olvido (sonata)" ("There Is No Oblivion (Sonata)"), OC, I, 247.

66. Neruda, *Selected Poems*, ed. Nathaniel Tarn (New York: Delacorte, 1972), p. 121; *Selected Poems of Pablo Neruda*, trans. Ben Belitt, p. 97.

67. García Lorca, p. 148.

68. I do not know just when he wrote the *cantos materiales*, which were first published in April 1935 as his "latest testimonies" (Margarita Aguirre, *Las vidas de Pablo Neruda*, p. 197). He probably did not compose them in Chile or Argentina before May 1934, nor is it likely that he composed them shortly after his daughter's birth in October 1934. They probably date from mid-1934 or early 1935.

69. Mistral, *Recados: Contando a Chile* (Santiago: Edit. del Pacífico, 1957), p. 166.

70. Neruda, "Infancia y poesía," p. 30.

71. OC, I, 229–30.

72. Neruda, *Selected Poems*, ed. Tarn, p. 113; Neruda, *Residence*, trans. Walsh, p. 155.

73. *Confieso*, p. 44.

74. In "Los nacimientos" ("The Births"), from *El gran océano* ("The Great Ocean"), Bk. XIV of *Canto general*, Neruda addresses the ocean as *madre materia* (OC, I, 656).

75. Jaime Concha, in "Alain Sicard: La pensée poétique de Pablo Neruda," *Literatura Chilena en el Exilio*, 12 (Oct. 1979), 2–6, also stresses the "dialectic" and the "dynamism" within several images from "Entrada a la madera," and he calls the poem a "live gallop," compared to "Galope muerto."

Chapter Four

1. "Viaje al corazón de Quevedo," in *Viajes*, p. 541.

2. Neruda, "Amistades y enemistades literarias" (1940), OC, III, 648.

3. Federico García Lorca, "Presentación de Pablo Neruda."

4. Neruda, *Tres cantos materiales: Homenaje a Pablo Neruda de los poetas españoles* (Madrid: Plutarco, 1935). See Aguirre, p. 197.

5. Neruda, *Primeros poemas de amor* (Madrid: Héroe, 1936); see Aguirre, p. 15.

6. "Poesías de Villamediana presentadas por Pablo Neruda," *Cruz y Raya*, no. 28 (July 1935). "Quevedo (Cartas y sonetos de la muerte)," *Cruz y Raya*, no. 33 (Dec. 1935). Villamediana was not well known at the time Neruda edited him, and Quevedo was only recently being revived: see Robert Pring-Mill, "Introduction," in *Pablo Neruda*, p. xxiv. Neruda was also reading the Golden Age poets Luis de Góngora and Pedro de Espinosa at the time: *Confieso*, pp. 163, 165.

7. James Joyce, "Música de cámara," trans. Pablo Neruda, *Poesía* (Buenos Aires), nos. 6–7 (Oct.–Nov. 1933); OC, III, 766–67. For an analysis of these translations, see Dario Puccini, "Dos notas sobre Pablo Neruda," *Anales de la Universidad de Chile*, 129, nos. 157–60 (Jan.–Dec. 1971), 134–38.

8. William Blake, *Visiones de las hijas de Albion* and *El viajero mental*, trans. Pablo Neruda, *Cruz y Raya*, no. 20 (Nov. 1934); OC, III, 767–81.

9. Walt Whitman, "Pasto de llamas," 2, 3, 30; see Ch. I, note 60.

10. *Caballo Verde para la Poesía* ("Green Horse for Poetry") (Madrid), Oct. 1935, Nov. 1935, Dec. 1935, Jan 1936.

11. *Confieso*, p. 164.

12. Juan Ramón Jiménez, *Españoles de tres mundos* (Buenos Aires: Losada, 1942), quoted in Emir Rodríguez Monegal, *El viajero inmóvil*, p. 86.

13. "Sobre una poesía sin pureza," OC, III, 636.

14. Walt Whitman, *Song of Myself*, 30.

15. "Sobre una poesía sin pureza," OC, III, 637.

16. *Ibid.*

17. "Conducta y poesía," *Caballo Verde para la Poesía*, 1, no. 3; OC, III, 638–39.

18. Neruda in at least two places (Cardona Peña, *Pablo Neruda y otros ensayos*, p. 31, and *Confieso*, p. 165) says that five numbers were printed, but the OC bibliography lists only four.

19. *Confieso*, p. 165.

20. Neruda, "Las vidas del poeta," *O Cruzeiro Internacional* (Río de Janeiro), April 16, 1962, 34.

21. Cardona Peña, p. 32.

22. See Robert Pring-Mill, "Introduction," in *Pablo Neruda*, pp. xxvii–xxviii, and Rodríguez Monegal, p. 93. Salvatore Bizzarro, *Pablo Neruda: All Poets the Poet* (Metuchen, N.J.: The Scarecrow Press, 1979) includes his May 1975 interview with Delia del Carril, then in her nineties. Bizzarro says that she was a member of the Communist Party when Neruda met her in 1934; also that she started living with Neruda in 1934, which seems doubtful to me (pp. 138–39). Delia del Carril says they were married before García Lorca's death in July 1936 (p. 141).

23. Neruda, "Federico García Lorca" (Feb. 1937), OC, III, 640; *Confieso*, pp. 166–67.

24. *Confieso*, p. 153.

25. Federico García Lorca and Pablo Neruda, "Discurso al alimón sobre Rubén Darío" (late 1933), OC, III, 629–31.

26. Reproduced in Neruda, OC, I, facing p. 1000. García Lorca was close to the Spanish surrealist painters and had already in 1927 exhibited his drawings: C. B. Morris, *Surrealism and Spain, 1920–1936* (Cambridge, Eng.: Cambridge Univ. Press, 1972), p. 15.

27. García Lorca, "Presentación de Pablo Neruda," pp. 147–48.

28. "Oda a Federico García Lorca," *Residencia en la tierra*, II (1935); OC, I, 236–39.

29. *Confieso*, p. 166. Neruda says the date was July 19, 1936, but in some notes to his *Viajes* (1955), p. 202, he prints Claude Couffon's account of García Lorca's last days, which says that he left Madrid for Granada on July 16.

30. Neruda, "Federico García Lorca" (Feb. 1937), OC, III, 640, 642, 644.

31. Katherine Bail Hoskins, *Today the Struggle: Literature and Politics in England During the Spanish Civil War* (Austin: Univ. of Texas Press, 1969), p. 17. Replying to a poll asking authors to take sides in the war, T. S. Eliot wrote: "While I am naturally sympathetic, I still feel that it is best that at least a few men of letters should remain isolated, and take no part in these collective activities" (Hoskins, p. 20). But in his magazine *Criterion* (London), 16, no. 62 (Oct. 1936), 68, he criticized the Left in Spain and said that whichever side won, it would be merely a secular victory and thus avoid the "real issue," which was spiritual.

32. See Leslie Fiedler, "A Second Life: The English Translations of Neruda" (mimeographed lecture), presented at the "Symposium on Pablo Neruda" (Univ. of Illinois at Urbana-Champaign, May 3, 1972).

33. OC, III, 637.

34. The first version of the poem was titled "Es así" ("It's Like This"), and published under Neruda's name in *El Mono Azul* (Madrid), 2, no 22 (July 1, 1937), 1. My translation is based on OC, I, 271–73. The first version differs as follows: line 23 reads *la luz dura de junio jugaba con tu pelo*, "the hard light of June played with your hair"; line 51 begins *y por la calle*, "and in the street"; between lines 52 and 53 in OC there occur three additional lines, *Asesinos de pueblos pobres, asesinos de niños, / asesinos de casas pobres y cercados, / asesinos de madres ya vestidas de luto*, "Assassins of poor towns, assassins of children, / assassins of poor and besieged homes, / assassins of mothers already dressed in mourning"; line 71 reads *del corazón, canallas*, "of your heart, rabble"; in line 72, an inverted question mark occurs before *Preguntaréis*, which suggests that *Preguntaréis por qué su poesía* means "Will you ask why his poetry," not "You will ask: why does your poetry," as Donald Walsh has it (*Residence on Earth*, p. 261); line 75 reads *de los grandes ríos de su patria natal*, "about the great rivers of his native homeland."

35. *Confieso*, p. 180.

36. García Lorca, "Presentación," p. 147.

37. Part of Neruda's March 1939 prefatory note to *Las furias y las penas* (Santiago: Nascimento, 1939); OC, I, 260.

38. Aguirre, p. 201; "Canto a las madres de los milicianos muertos," *El Mono Azul*, 1, no. 5 (Sept. 24, 1936), 3; OC, I, 273–74.

39. Neruda, "Viaje al corazón de Quevedo," p. 544.

40. "Canto sobre unas ruinas" (Nov. 1936), OC, I, 284–85.

41. For views of the change in Neruda, see Amado Alonso, *Poesía y estilo de Pablo Neruda*, ch. 8, and Raúl Silva Castro, *Pablo Neruda*, pp. 190–213. In Feb. 1943 Neruda in an interview called Silva Castro a "known Fascist": Andrés Requena, "Neruda: Poeta de la humanidad," *Norte* (New York), April 1943, 8. See also Hernán Loyola, *Ser y morir en Pablo Neruda: 1918–1945*, pp. 163–69; Rodríguez Monegal, pp. 228–35; Jaime Concha, "El descubrimiento del pueblo en la poesía de Neruda," *Aurora* (Santiago), nos. 3–4 (July–Dec. 1964), 128–38, rpt. in *Hispanic Studies* (Univ. of So. Carolina), no. 1 (1974), 85–95.

42. *Confieso*, p. 190, and Cardona Peña, p. 32.

43. "Reunión bajo las nuevas banderas" (1940), OC, I, 266–67.

44. 1949: speech given at the Congress for Peace in Madrid, Sept. 1949, in Neruda, *Poesía política*, ed. Margarita Aguirre (Santiago: Austral, 1953), II, rpt. as "Our Duty Toward Life," in *Let the Rail Splitter Awake*, pp. 12–13. 1950: Cardona Peña, p. 32.

45. (Santiago: Ercilla, 1937). He arrived in Santiago on Oct. 10 (Aguirre, p. 16) and the book was published on Nov. 13 (OC, III, 950).

46. "Cómo era España," OC, I, 277.

47. (Ejército del Este, Spain: Ediciones Literarias del Comisariado, 1938.)

48. Nov. 1941 letter by Altolaguirre, OC, III, 908–9. He says Neruda's book was printed in Monserrat monastery.

49. Aguirre, p. 44.

50. *Ibid.*, p. 43. "Almagro" (OC, I, 363) was published first in July 1940, later in *Canto general de Chile* [Mexico City, n.p., 1943], n.pag. An expanded version of this collection forms Bk. VII of *Canto general*.

51. Jean Descola, *The Conquistadors* (New York: Viking, 1957), p. 301, says that 10,000 Indians died on the way, but Jaime Eyzaguirre, *Historia de Chile: Génesis de la nacionalidad* (Santiago: Zig-Zag, 1964), p. 47, says that only 1500 went in the first place, which is probably closer to the truth. William H. Prescott's *History of the Conquest of Peru* (1847) does not give any figures.

52. OC, I, 363.

53. "La copa de sangre," OC, III, 651.

54. See Aguirre, p. 16, and OC, III, 950, 932, 944.

55. See OC, III, 1011. Chilean patriots of the Independence period had published a newspaper called *La Aurora de Chile* (1812–13).

56. According to Clayton Eshleman, "Translator's Foreword," in César Vallejo, *Poemas humanos: Human Poems* (New York: Grove, 1968), p. xii.

57. Aguirre, p. 16; Jean Franco, *César Vallejo*, p. 284.

58. "César Vallejo ha muerto," OC, III, 645.

59. See Gordon Brotherston, *Latin American Poetry*, pp. 134–36; Eshleman, "Translator's Foreword," p. xv; Franco, *César Vallejo*, p. 252.

60. "Oda de invierno al río Mapocho," OC, I, 552–53. The poem was published simultaneously in Santiago, Mexico City, and Barcelona (OC, III, 957).

61. "Algo sobre mi poesía y mi vida," pp. 12–13,

62. Neruda, "España no ha muerto," in *Neruda entre nosotros* (Montevideo: Ediciones A.I.A.P.E., 1939), p. 41. In his talk "Quevedo adentro," Neruda in 1939 called Quevedo's sonnet "Cerrar podrá mis ojos" a "voice of hope over the ruins" (p. 57). See also Rodríguez Monegal, p. 100.

63. See *Confieso*, p. 192; Hernán Loyola, "Itinerario de Pablo Neruda," p. 15; Aguirre, pp. 15–16, 204–6, 208. An excellent discussion of this period can be found in Franco, *César Vallejo*, pp. 223–33.

64. "Himno y regreso (1939)," OC, I, 529–30. The poem eventually formed part of *Canto general de Chile*.

65. "Océano," "Atacama," "Botánica," OC, I, 534–35, 537–38, 544–45.

66. "La copa de sangre," OC, III, 651. About the translation of names of plants indigenous to Chile, Neruda once remarked: "At times I receive endless lists of words whose meaning the Bulgarian, Chinese, or Italian translator wants to know. What does 'copihue' mean? What does 'loica' mean?" ("Algo sobre mi poesía," p. 15).

67. "Himno y regreso," OC, I, 529.

68. OC, III, 958.

69. Maurice Halperin, "Pablo Neruda in Mexico," *Books Abroad*, 15, no. 12 (1941), 168.

70. "Quiero volver al sur (1941)," OC, I, 530–31. This poem, along with "Tocopilla," was first published in *Letras de México*, no. 4 (April 15, 1941).

71. "Melancolía cerca de Orizaba (1942)" ("Melancholy Near Orizaba [1942]"), OC, I, 533.

72. "Oratorio menor en la muerte de Silvestre Revueltas," OC, I, 632–33. See Wilberto Cantón, "Pablo Neruda en México (1940–1943)" (1950), *Anales de la Universidad de Chile*, 129, nos. 157–60 (Jan.–Dec. 1971), 264. The event is recorded in *El Nacional* (Mexico City), Oct. 7, 1940.

73. *Confieso*, p. 215.

74. "Un canto para Bolívar" ("A Song for Bolivar"), OC, I, 302–3. The event occurred on July 24, 1941: OC, III, 951; Cantón, p. 265.

75. This incident took place on Dec. 29, 1941: Cantón, pp. 265–66.

76. "Canto a Stalingrado," read on Sept. 30, 1942, in the Mexican Electricians Union auditorium (see OC, III, 952), OC, I, 292–94.

77. Hugh Thomas, *The Spanish Civil War* (New York: Harper and Row, 1961; rpt. 1963), pp. 362, 455; Roy A. Medvedev, *Let History Judge: The Origins and Consequences of Stalinism* (New York: Knopf, 1972), pp. 188, 216, 231.

78. Andrés Requena, "Neruda: Poeta de la humanidad," pp. 7–8.

79. *Confieso*, p. 211.

80. *Canto general de Chile* [Mexico; n.p., 1943], n. pag.
81. See the interview "Pablo Neruda" in *L'Express* (Paris), no. 1053 (Sept. 13–19, 1971), 106–23; also *Confieso*, p. 213. Chile's military junta reportedly had the mural destroyed in 1975, but this report may not be true. See *Chile vencerá* (New York), 2, no. 1 (Feb.–Mar. 1976), 3.
82. Neruda, Introduction to "Los frescos de Xavier Guerrero en Chillán," *Ars* (Mexico City), 1, no. 5 (May 1943), 60. The muralists went to Chillán as a gesture of support after the 1939 earthquake there.
83. Juan Ramón Jiménez, "Carta a Pablo Neruda," *Repertorio Americano*, no. 39 (Jan. 17, 1942), 12.
84. The poems first appeared in *América* (Mexico City), no. 19 (July 1943); rpt. Bk. VI, *Canto general*.
85. "Los dictadores," OC, I, 521–22.
86. "Un río" may not have appeared in the Mexican publication of *América, no invoco tu nombre en vano* (*América*, no. 19, July 1943). My text comes from Luis Nieto, ed., *Pablo Neruda: Miliciano corazón de América* (Cuzco, Peru: Talleres Gráficos La Económica, 1943), pp. 42–43. The poem also appeared in collections of 1945 and 1948, according to the bibliography in OC (III, 960), but was left out of *Canto general* (1950) and all editions of *Obras completas*, including the OC appendices of poems not published in book form. The Spanish is as follows:

> Yo quiero ir por el Papaloápan
> como tantas veces por el terroso espejo,
> tocando con las uñas el agua poderosa:
> quiero ir hacia las mátrices; hacia la contextura
> de sus originales ramajes de cristal:
> ir, mojarme la frente, hundir en la secreta
> confusión del rocío
> la piel la sed el sueño.
> El sábalo saliendo del agua
> como un violín de plata,
> y en la orilla las flores atmosféricas,
> y las alas inmóviles
> en un calor de espacio defendido
> por espadas azules.

87. "América," "América, no invoco tu nombre en vano," OC, I, 525–26, 527.
88. On this theme, see John Felstiner, "Arauco Redivivus in Pablo Neruda," *Review* (New York), 25–26 (1980), 110–16. See also note 128 below.
89. "Algo sobre mi poesía," p. 12.
90. For a vivid account of this popular history, see Fernando Alegría, *Lautaro, joven libertador de Arauco* (Santiago: Zig-Zag, 1943), pp. 89–93.
91. "Pablo Neruda" (interview), *L'Express*; *Confieso*, p. 23. In "Infancia y poesía" (1954), *Obras completas*, 3rd ed., pp. 33–34, Neruda mentions a newspaper editor from Temuco "who had a great influence on

me: Orlando Masson." Masson defended the Indians against injustice and "wrote and printed the first book of poetry between the Bío Bío and the Magellan Straits . . . *Flores de Arauco.* I read those verses with great emotion."

92. Jean Franco, *César Vallejo*, p. 2; *Confieso*, p. 93.

93. Simon Collier, *Ideas and Politics of Chilean Independence: 1808–1833* (Cambridge, Eng., Cambridge Univ. Press, 1967), pp. 27–28, 212–17.

94. *OC*, III, 650.

95. "Oratorio menor en la muerte de Silvestre Revueltas," *OC*, I, 632.

96. *Confieso*, p. 222. Apparently only one or two issues of the magazine came out. The two paragraphs Neruda wrote on this episode are not in the first version of his memoirs (1962), but were added in revision (1972–73).

97. "Viaje por las costas del mundo," *OC*, II, 561–62. About the demise of Araucania, Neruda remarked in "Infancia y poesía," p. 34: "Temuco was the heart's end of Araucania."

98. Neruda reports in his memoirs (*Confieso*, p. 189) on the sympathy for Nazism, especially in the south of Chile.

99. See *OC*, III, 959. On Aug. 27, 1943, he read "En los muros de México" ("On the Walls of Mexico"), *OC*, I, 705–8. See also the editorial in *El Nacional* (Mexico City), Aug. 30, 1943; rpt. "Adiós a Pablo Neruda," *Repertorio Americano*, no. 964 (Oct. 13, 1943), 275.

100. "Palabras de Pablo Neruda" (Sept. 11, 1943), *Repertorio Americano*, no. 964 (Oct. 13, 1943), 274–75.

101. He read "Viaje al corazón de Quevedo," "Viaje alrededor de mi poesía" (unpublished), and also "Viaje por las costas del mundo" ("Journey to the Shores of the World"), from which the quotations are taken; *OC*, II, 556–79. See Andrés Holguín, "Tres conferencias de Pablo Neruda," *Revista de las Indias* (Bogotá), no. 56 (Aug. 1943), 267–70.

102. Verses quoted in "Viaje por las costas del mundo," *OC*, II, 576.

103. "Las lámparas deben continuar encendidas" ("The Lamps Must Stay Lit") (Oct. 21, 1943), *OC*, III, 651–52.

104. *Ibid.*, p. 652.

105. There are highways and train routes between Lima and Cuzco, but they are long. Possibly Neruda flew over the Andes, since air service began sometime during the war.

106. The material in this paragraph is taken from a rare pamphlet, cited previously: Luis Nieto, ed., *Pablo Neruda: Miliciano corazón de América*, pp. 11, 53, 56. A small anthology of Neruda's poems, printed during this visit to Peru, says Neruda was "born to sing to the People," and calls him "simple as the wheat that grows on the Andean slopes": *Cantos de Pablo Neruda* (Lima, Peru: Ediciones Hora del Hombre, 1943), prefatory note.

107. Miriam Beltrán, *Cuzco: Window on Peru* (New York: Knopf, 1970) has valuable information on Cuzco and Macchu Picchu. See also Philip Ainsworth Means, *Ancient Civilizations of the Andes* (New York: Scribner's, 1931), p. 254. Neruda may have known this book.

108. Hiram Bingham, *Lost City of the Incas* (1948; rpt. New York: Atheneum, 1963), p. 152. Larrea, *Del Surrealismo a Machupicchu*, pp. 198, 202–6, posits a post-Conquest date (1534) for the founding of Macchu Picchu.

109. This description of Inca civilization is based on Lewis Hanke, ed., *History of Latin American Civilization: Sources and Interpretations*, vol. I, *The Colonial Experience*, 2nd ed. (Boston: Little, Brown, 1973), pp. 53–84, and Luis Martín, *The Kingdom of the Sun: A Short History of Peru* (New York: Scribner's, 1974), pp. 3–20.

110. "Pablo Neruda habla," *El Siglo* (Santiago), Dec. 5, 1943, 12.

111. George Kubler, "Machu Picchu," *Perspecta: The Yale Architectural Journal*, 6 (1960), 49–50. The most recent and thorough survey on Macchu Picchu reports that the leading Peruvian archaeologists are still divided as to when the city was built and what function it served: Simone Waisbard, *Macchu Picchu, Cité Perdue des Incas* (1974); trans. *The Mysteries of Macchu Picchu* (New York: Avon, 1979).

112. Bingham's discovery (pp. 190–99) that most of the skeletal remains found at Macchu Picchu were female led him and others to speculate that the city was used by the Chosen Women or Virgins of the Sun, whose lives were devoted to weaving and other services for the Sun and the Inca priesthood. But that cannot be ascertained.

113. J. Uriel García, *El nuevo indio: Ensayos indianistas sobre la sierra surperuana*, 2nd ed. (Cuzco: Rozas, 1937), pp. 59–60.

114. Kubler, p. 54.

115. Neruda spoke at a ceremony for Uriel García in Dec. 1939: OC, III, 1013. The interview "Pablo Neruda habla," in *El Siglo*, mentions that Neruda went to Macchu Picchu with Uriel García. See José Uriel García, "Machu Picchu," *Cuadernos americanos*, 20, no. 4 (July–Aug. 1961), 161–251. Uriel García was a friend of Martín Chambi, whose 1934 photograph of Macchu Picchu appears in this book. See also Roderic A. Camp, "Martín Chambi, Photographer of the Andes," *Latin American Research Review*, 13, 2 (1978), 223–28, and Edward Ranney, "Martín Chambi, Poet of Light," *Earthwatch News*, 1, 1 (1979), 3–6.

116. On Mariátegui and cultural nationalism in general, see Martín, pp. 242–45; E. Bradford Burns, *Latin America: A Concise Interpretative History* (New York: Prentice-Hall, 1972), pp. 168–71; Jean Franco, *The Modern Culture of Latin America: Society and the Artist* (New York: Praeger, 1967), Ch. 3.

117. Andrés Requena, "Neruda: Poeta de la humanidad," p. 8, and Neruda, "Las lámparas," OC, III, 654.

118. OC, I, 348.

119. *Confieso*, p. 230.

120. *Ibid.*, p. 229. Though Neruda gave up his consular post voluntarily, he felt in 1943, as he had in Spain in 1936, that diplomatic service constrained his political activity.

121. "Algo sobre mi poesía," p. 13.

122. "Pablo Neruda habla," *El Siglo*, Dec. 5, 1943, p. 12.

123. *Confieso*, p. 230.

124. *Ibid.*, p. 232. See Gil, *The Political System of Chile*, p. 5.
125. *Ibid.*
126. Neruda, "Viaje al norte de Chile" ("Journey to the North of Chile") (1946), OC, II, 580.
127. *Confieso*, pp. 203–4. Neruda's impressionistic additions to the memoirs, made in 1972–73, appear in italics in both the Spanish and the English editions.
128. See note 88 above. After references in Bk. I of *Canto general* ("At the base of nameless America / Arauco lay among dizzying waters," OC, I, 329), and in Bk. IV, *The Liberators* ("from that rain fermented / in the volcanoes' cup / the lofty breasts sprang out," OC, I, 381), the most significant references are: (1) A 1962 talk where Neruda says that Ercilla's epic created "the vibrant natural catalogue of our patrimony. Birds, plants, waters, customs, ceremonies, language, arrows, aromas, snow, and tides that are ours, all were named at last in *La Araucana*, and by means of the word began to live." He adds that "despite *La Araucana's* painful pride, our Indians are still illiterate, landless, and barefoot" (OC, III, 689). (2) A 1963 essay, which says of the *chahual*, "this ancestral plant was worshiped by the Araucanians: now ancient Arauco is gone." But the huge plant is growing now: "Seeing its flowers surge up again over centuries of obscure deaths, layers and layers of forgotten blood, I believe that the earth's past is blossoming against what we now are" (OC, III, 64). (3) Some unpublished remarks Neruda made in Dec. 1971 in Stockholm, where he had gone to receive the Nobel Prize. Neruda said that in his mind he returns "to Araucania's lilac gardens . . . to mourning Indians the Conquest left behind" (Swedish Consulate, San Francisco, private communication, Dec. 1971). (4) His polemical verses against the Vietnam war, *Incitación al Nixonicidio y alabanza de la revolución chilena* (Santiago: Quimantú, 1973), which end by interweaving his own verses with some stirring ones of Ercilla's.
129. "Saludo al norte," *El Siglo*, Feb. 27, 1945, reproduced in 1945 in what Aguirre, p. 215, calls "an extremely popular edition" (see OC, III, 1018), and in OC, III, 655–59. Robert Pring-Mill, "Introduction," p. xxxvii, has a good paragraph on this poem.
130. Alberto Ganderats, "Neruda a lo humano y a lo poético" (interview), *El Mercurio* (Santiago), Apr. 20, 1969, p. 7.
131. See Rodríguez Monegal, p. 115, and Neruda's talk to Chile's P.E.N. club and others, *El Siglo*, June 24, 1945.
132. On Prestes, see José Maria Bello, *A History of Modern Brazil, 1889–1964* (Stanford, Calif.: Stanford Univ. Press, 1966), p. 253, and *Confieso*, pp. 418–21.
133. "Dura elegía" ("Hard Elegy"), OC, I, 307–9, read on June 18, 1943; see also Cantón, p. 266.
134. See "Brasil visto por Neruda," *Vea* (Santiago), Aug. 29, 1945. The event took place on July 15, 1945.
135. Neruda's poem appears as "Dicho en Pacaembú (Brasil, 1945)" in OC, I, 454–56. When he first read the poem Neruda called it "Caballero de la esperanza" ("Horseman of Hope").
136. *Confieso*, p. 420. A reading of Neruda's that I witnessed in San-

tiago in 1968 drew a large and very enthusiastic crowd of working people and families.

137. Neruda, "Algo sobre mi poesía," p. 13.

138. Report of Neruda's speech of Nov. 20, 1945, *El Mercurio*, Nov. 21, 1945.

139. Roger Caillois, "La Cité et le poème," *Europe* (Paris), nos. 537–38 (Jan.–Feb. 1974), 57.

Chapter Five

1. "Algo sobre mi poesía y mi vida," p. 13.

2. Studies of *Alturas de Macchu Picchu* may be found in Hernán Loyola, *Ser y morir*; Frank Riess, *The Word and the Stone*; Emir Rodríguez Monegal, *El viajero inmóvil*; Jaime Concha, "El descubrimiento del pueblo en la poesía de Neruda"; Mario Rodríguez Fernández, "El tema de la muerte en *Alturas de Macchu Picchu* de Pablo Neruda," *Anales de la Universidad de Chile*, 131 (July–Sept. 1964), 23–50; Hugo Montes, "Acerca de *Alturas de Macchu Picchu*," *Mapocho* (Santiago), 2, no. 6 (1964), 120–34; Leonidas Morales T., "Estructura mítica de *Alturas de Macchu Picchu*," *Estudios Filológicos* (Univ. Austral, Valdivia, Chile), 1 (1964), 167–83; Juan Loveluck, "*Alturas de Macchu Picchu*: Cantos I–V," *Revista Iberoamericana* (Pittsburgh), 39, nos. 82–83 (Jan.–June 1973), 175–88; Cedomil Goić, "*Alturas de Macchu Picchu*: la torre y el abismo," *Anales de la Universidad de Chile*, 129, nos. 157–60 (Jan.–Dec. 1971), 153–65; Robert Pring-Mill, Preface to *The Heights of Macchu Picchu*, trans. Nathaniel Tarn, pp. vii–xix. See also the excellent bibliography on recent studies of Neruda: Enrico Mario Santí, "Fuentes para el conocimiento de Pablo Neruda, 1967–1974," in *Simposio Pablo Neruda*, ed. Isaac Jack Lévy and Juan Loveluck (Columbia, So. Carolina: Las Américas, 1975), pp. 355–82. My discussion here uses the text of *Alturas de Macchu Picchu* from OC. That text differs from other versions in the spacing of verse paragraphs and from the first magazine version in punctuation and in the omission of one line (see pp. 174, 197). In Canto VIII, I follow earlier editions in spacing separately the third line from the end. The poem's full texts are printed in this book so that a line ending with a period at the base of a page marks a stanza break (Canto IX has no stanzas).

3. *Letters of Rainer Maria Rilke: 1910–1926*, trans. Jane Bannard Greene and M. D. Herter Norton (New York: Norton, 1969), pp. 279, 318–19. A more recent example of affinity between a poet-translator and a poet may be found in Clayton Eshleman's introduction to César Vallejo, *The Complete Posthumous Poetry*, trans. Clayton Eshleman and José Rubia Barcia (Berkeley: Univ. of California Press, 1979).

4. See Hugh Kenner, "Beckett Translating Beckett: Comment C'est," *Delos*, 5 (1970), 194–211.

5. Waldeen's translation in *Let the Rail Splitter Awake and Other Poems*, trans. Joseph M. Bernstein et al.; Angel Flores's translation, "Summits of Macchu Picchu," in *The World's Best*, ed. Whit Burnett; Nathaniel Tarn, *The Heights of Macchu Picchu*.

6. Tarn says "I came / lavish, at autumn's coronation, with the leaves'

/ proffer of currency," which seems to lose the sense of *despedir* (*The Heights of Macchu Picchu*, p. 3).

7. OC, I, 87.

8. *Confieso*, pp. 204, 229.

9. "Burnt Norton," V; "The Dry Salvages," V.

10. See Neruda's 1933 lyric, "Unidad": "There is something dense, unified, deeply seated, / repeating its number, its identical sign"—*su señal idéntica*; OC, I, 173.

11. "Algo sobre mi poesía," p. 13.

12. For translations, see the bibliography in OC, III, 1067-1106.

13. Angel Flores, "Summits of Macchu Picchu; H. R. Hays, in *Twelve Spanish American Poets*; Nathaniel Tarn, *The Heights of Macchu Picchu*; and Ben Belitt, in *Selected Poems of Pablo Neruda*.

14. I am indebted to Flores's translation for the construction of the last line.

15. Belitt, *Selected Poems of Pablo Neruda*, p. 123.

16. Quoted in Jaime Alazraki, "Para una poética de la poesía póstuma de Pablo Neruda," in *Simposio Pablo Neruda*, ed. Isaac Jack Lévy and Juan Loveluck, p. 63.

17. "Burnt Norton," III.

18. *Ibid.*; "East Coker," III.

19. "Burnt Norton," V.

20. Gordon Brotherston, *Latin American Poetry*, pp. 51-53.

21. "East Coker," I; "Little Gidding," I.

22. See Frank Riess, *The Word and the Stone*, pp. 8-10, 135-42.

23. The commas appeared in the version published in the *Revista Nacional de Cultura* (Caracas), no. 57 (July-Aug. 1946), 77-78, and no. 58 (Sept.-Oct. 1946), 103-12. In the Caedmon recording only, Neruda's voice runs on from *sostenidos* to *de tanta muerte*. A later edition of the poem, *Alturas de Macchu Picchu* (Santiago: Nascimento, 1954), has colons after *palabra* and also *sostenidos*. Evidently there is no definitive punctuation.

24. See Bingham, *Lost City of the Incas*, p. 124, on the name Wilkamayu, and Burr Cartwright Brundage, *Lords of Cuzco: A History and Description of the Inca People in Their Final Days* (Norman: Univ. of Oklahoma Press, 1967), p. 160.

25. See G.H.S. Bushnell, *Peru* (New York: Praeger, 1957), p. 30. Brundage, in *Lords of Cuzco*, p. 169, makes a pertinent observation: "a deserted and silent town . . . was described by the Incas in the term *chinnic llacta*, 'a city which keeps silent forever.'"

26. OC, I, 316.

27. Larrea, *Del surrealismo a Machupicchu*, pp. 141-59. Larrea was a friend and editor of Vallejo's. See Neruda's angry "Oda a Juan Tarrea," OC, II, 342-47. Brotherston, pp. 51-53, criticizes Neruda's neglect of contemporary Indian life and his using Spanish heritage and imagery while also lamenting the Conquest.

28. "East Coker," V.

29. OC, III, 776. He was translating Blake's *Visions of the Daughters of*

Albion, in 1935. In Lima, just before seeing Macchu Picchu, Neruda called Peru "the womb of America" (*matriz de América*; OC, III, 651), and later described Macchu Picchu as the "omphalos of a deserted world" (*Confieso*, p. 230).

30. William Carlos Williams, *In the American Grain* (New York: Boni, 1925), p. 214.

31. *Four Quartets*, "Little Gidding," V.

32. Whitman, *Song of Myself*, 24. For revealing studies and documents on Whitman's reception in Latin America, see Fernando Alegría, *Walt Whitman en Hispanoamérica* (Mexico City: [Talleres Gráficos "Galeza"], 1954), and Gay Wilson Allen, ed., *Walt Whitman Abroad* (Syracuse, N.Y.: Syracuse Univ. Press, 1955).

33. *Song of Myself*, 33.

34. Discussions with the Chilean poet Enrique Lihn and others have almost, but not quite, convinced me that "drive" is too doubtful a choice.

35. See Bushnell, p. 48, and Brundage, *Lords of Cuzco*, p. 333.

36. The poem was received by Asia News Service (Berkeley, Calif.) from Prensa Latina, a Cuban news service. It was based on Neruda's poem "Las satrapías" (1948), OC, I, 472.

37. *New York Times*, Sept. 26, 1973.

38. Andrew Graham-Yooll, "Cigar-talk" (review of Neruda's *Memoirs*), *London Magazine*, 19, no. 4 (July 1979), 94–96, also says that Jacobo Timerman's Buenos Aires daily, *La Opinión*, ran the altered poem.

BIBLIOGRAPHY

WORKS OF NERUDA CITED IN THE NOTES

Books and Collections

Anillos. Santiago: Nascimento, 1926.
Antología esencial. Ed. Hernán Loyola. Buenos Aires: Losada, 1971.
Canto general. Mexico City: [Talleres Gráficos de la Nación], 1950.
Canto general de Chile: Fragmentos. Mexico City: n.p., 1943.
Confieso que he vivido: Memorias. Buenos Aires: Losada, 1974.
España en el corazón. Santiago: Ercilla, 1937.
España en el corazón. Ejército del Este, Spain: Ediciones Literarias del Comisariado, 1938.
Las furias y las penas. Santiago: Nascimento, 1939.
El hondero entusiasta, 1923–1924. Santiago: Letras, 1933.
Libro de las preguntas. Buenos Aires: Losada, 1974.
Memorial de Isla Negra. 5 vols. Buenos Aires: Losada, 1964.
Obras completas. 3rd ed., 2 vols. Buenos Aires: Losada, 1967.
Obras completas [OC]. 4th ed., 3 vols. Buenos Aires: Losada, 1973.
Odas elementales. Buenos Aires: Losada, 1954.
Pablo Neruda: Miliciano corazón de América. Ed. Luis Nieto. Cuzco, Peru: Talleres Gráficos La Económica, 1943.
Plenos poderes. Buenos Aires: Losada, 1962.
Poesía política. Ed. Margarita Aguirre. 2 vols. Santiago: Austral, 1953.
Residencia en la tierra, 1925–1931. Santiago: Nascimento, 1933. *Residencia en la tierra, 1925–1931* and *Residencia en la tierra, 1931–1935.* 2 vols. Madrid: Cruz y Raya, 1935.
Tentativo del hombre infinito. Santiago: Nascimento, 1926.
Tres cantos materiales: Homenaje a Pablo Neruda de los poetas españoles. Madrid: Plutarco, 1935.
Veinte poemas de amor y una canción desesperada. Santiago: Nascimento, 1924.
Viajes. Santiago: Nascimento, 1955.

Selected essays, articles, and interviews not reprinted in
Obras completas, *4th ed.*

"Album Terusa 1923." Ed. Hernán Loyola. *Anales de la Universidad de Chile,* 129, nos. 157–60 (Jan.–Dec. 1971), 45–55.

"Algo sobre mi poesía y mi vida." *Aurora* (Santiago), 1 (July 1954), 10–21.

"Brasil visto por Neruda." *Vea* (Santiago), Aug. 29, 1945.

"Discurso pronunciado en el Congreso de la Paz en México" (1949). In Neruda, *Poesía política*. Rpt. as "Our Duty toward Life." In Neruda, *Let the Rail Splitter Awake and Other Poems*, 9–18.

"España no ha muerto." In *Neruda entre nosotros*. Montevideo: Ediciones A.I.A.P.E., 1939, 37–51.

"Infancia y poesía" (1954). In *Obras completas*. Ed. Hernán Loyola. 3rd ed., 2 vols. Buenos Aires: Losada, 1967, I, 25–38.

Introduction to "Los frescos de Xavier Guerrero en Chillán." *Ars* (Mexico City), I, no. 5 (May 1943), 60.

"Neruda a lo humano y a lo poético" (interview). Alberto Ganderats. *El Mercurio* (Santiago), Apr. 20, 1969, 7.

"Neruda: Poeta de la humanidad" (interview). Andrés Requena. *Norte* (New York), April 1943, 5–8.

"Pablo Neruda" (interview). *L'Express* (Paris), no. 1053 (Sept. 13–19, 1971), 106–23.

"Pablo Neruda" (interview). In Rita Guibert, *Seven Voices*. Trans. Frances Partridge. New York: Alfred A. Knopf, 1972; rpt. Vintage Books, 1973, 3–74.

"Pablo Neruda habla" (interview). *El Siglo* (Santiago), Dec. 5, 1943, 12.

"Pablo Neruda in Mexico" (interview). Maurice Halperin. *Books Abroad*, 15, no. 12 (1941), 164–68.

"Palabras de Pablo Neruda" (Sept. 11, 1943). *Repertorio Americano*, no. 964 (Oct. 13, 1943), 274–75.

"Quevedo adentro." In *Neruda entre nosotros*. Montevideo: Ediciones A.I.A.P.E., 1939, 53–58.

"Las vidas del poeta." *O Cruzeiro Internacional* (Río de Janeiro), January 16–June 1, 1962.

ENGLISH TRANSLATIONS OF NERUDA

Adam (London), 16, (March–April 1948).

Anthology of Contemporary Latin American Poetry. Ed. Dudley Fitts. Norfolk, Conn.: New Directions, 1942.

Bestiary/Bestiario. Trans. Elsa Neuberger. Illus. Antonio Frasconi. New York: Harcourt, Brace and World, 1965.

The Captain's Verses. Trans. Donald D. Walsh. New York: New Directions, 1972.

The Early Poems. Trans. David Ossman and Carlos B. Hagen. New York: New Rivers, 1969.

The Elementary Odes of Pablo Neruda. Trans. Carlos Lozano. New York: Cypress, 1961.

Extravagaria. Trans. Alastair Reid. New York: Farrar, Straus and Giroux, 1974.

Five Decades: A Selection (Poems: 1925–1970). Trans. Ben Belitt. New York: Grove, 1974.

Fully Empowered. Trans. Alastair Reid. New York: Farrar, Straus and Giroux, 1975.
The Heights of Macchu Picchu. Trans. Nathaniel Tarn. London: Jonathan Cape, 1966; New York: Farrar, Straus and Giroux. 1967.
Incitement to Nixonicide and Praise for the Chilean Revolution. Trans. Steve Kowit. Houston, Texas: Quixote, 1979.
Isla Negra Notebook. Trans. Alastair Reid. New York: Farrar, Straus and Giroux, forthcoming.
Let the Rail Splitter Awake and Other Poems. Trans. Joseph M. Bernstein, "Waldeen," et al. New York: Masses and Mainstream, 1950.
The Man Who Told His Love. Trans. Christopher Logue. Northwood, Middlesex, Eng.: Scorpion, 1958.
Memoirs. Trans. Hardie St. Martin. New York: Farrar, Straus and Giroux, 1977.
The Modernist Trend in Spanish-American Poetry. Ed. G. Dundas Craig. Berkeley: Univ. of California Press, 1934.
Neruda and Vallejo: Selected Poems. Ed. Robert Bly. Boston: Beacon, 1971.
A New Decade (Poems: 1958–1967). Trans. Ben Belitt and Alastair Reid. New York: Grove, 1969.
New Poems: 1968–1970. Trans. Ben Belitt. New York: Grove, 1972.
The Penguin Book of Latin American Verse. Ed. E. Caracciolo-Trejo. Baltimore: Penguin, 1971.
Residence on Earth. Trans. Clayton Eshleman. San Francisco: Amber House, 1962.
Residence on Earth. Trans. Donald D. Walsh. New York: New Directions, 1973.
Residence on Earth and Other Poems. Trans. Angel Flores. Norfolk, Conn.: New Directions, 1946.
Selected Poems. Trans. Anthony Kerrigan, W. S. Merwin, Alastair Reid, and Nathaniel Tarn. New York: Delacorte, 1972.
Selected Poems of Pablo Neruda. Trans. Ben Belitt. New York: Grove, 1961.
Selected Translations, 1948–1968. Trans. W. S. Merwin. New York: Atheneum, 1975.
Song of Protest. Trans. Miguel Algarín. New York: Morrow, 1976.
Songs. Trans. Christopher Logue. London: Hutchinson, 1959.
Splendor and Death of Joaquín Murieta. Trans. Ben Belitt. New York: Farrar, Straus and Giroux, 1972.
"Summits of Macchu Picchu." Trans. Angel Flores. In *The World's Best.* Ed. Whit Burnett. New York: Dial, 1950.
Thirty Spanish Poems of Love and Exile. Trans. Kenneth Rexroth. San Francisco: City Lights, 1955.
Three Spanish American Poets: Pellicer, Neruda, Andrade. Trans. Lloyd Mallan, Mary and C. V. Wicker, and J. L. Grucci. Albuquerque: Sage Books [Swallow and Critchlow], 1942.
Toward the Splendid City: Nobel Lecture. New York: Farrar, Straus and Giroux, 1974.
Twelve Spanish American Poets. Ed. H. R. Hays. New Haven: Yale University Press, 1943; rpt. Boston: Beacon, 1972.

Twenty Love Poems and a Song of Despair. Trans. W. S. Merwin. London: Jonathan Cape, 1969; New York: Penguin, 1976.
Twenty Poems. Trans. Robert Bly and James Wright. Madison, Minn.: The Sixties Press, 1967.
We Are Many. Trans. Alastair Reid. New York: Grossman, 1968.

SELECTED WORKS ABOUT NERUDA

"Adiós a Pablo Neruda." *El Nacional* (Mexico City), Aug. 30, 1943; rpt. *Repertorio Americano,* no. 964 (Oct. 13, 1943), 275.
Aguirre, Margarita. *Las vidas de Pablo Neruda.* Santiago: Zig-Zag, 1967.
Alazraki, Jaime. "El surrealismo de *Tentativa del hombre infinito* de Pablo Neruda." *Hispanic Review,* 40 (Winter 1972), 31–39.
———. "Para una poética de la poesía póstuma de Pablo Neruda." In *Simposio Pablo Neruda.* Ed. Isaac Jack Lévy and Juan Loveluck. Columbia, So. Carolina: Las Américas, 1975, 43–73.
———. *Poética y poesía de Pablo Neruda.* New York: Las Américas, 1965.
Alberti, Rafael. "De mon amitié avec Pablo Neruda." *Europe* (Paris), nos. 419–20 (March–April 1964), 71–75.
Alegría, Fernando. "Prólogo." In Pablo Neruda. *Canto general.* Caracas: Ayacucho, 1976.
———. *Walt Whitman en Hispanoamérica.* Mexico City: [Talleres Gráficos "Galeza"], 1954.
Alonso, Amado. *Poesía y estilo de Pablo Neruda.* 3rd ed. Buenos Aires: Sudamérica, 1966.
Azócar, Rubén. "Testimonio." *Aurora* (Santiago), July–Dec. 1964, 215.
Belitt, Ben. *Adam's Dream: A Preface to Translation.* New York: Grove, 1978.
Bizzarro, Salvatore. *Pablo Neruda: All Poets the Poet.* Metuchen, N.J.: Scarecrow, 1979.
Brotherston, Gordon. *Latin American Poetry: Origins and Presence.* Cambridge, Eng.: Cambridge Univ. Press, 1975.
Caillois, Roger. "La Cité et le poème." *Europe* (Paris), nos. 537–38 (Jan.–Feb. 1974), 57–61.
Cantón, Wilberto. "Pablo Neruda en México (1940–1943)" (1950). *Anales de la Universidad de Chile,* 129, nos. 157–60 (Jan.–Dec. 1971), 263–69.
Cardona Peña, Alfredo. *Pablo Neruda y otros ensayos.* Mexico City: Andrea, 1955.
Colhoun, Charles K. Review of March 1930 *Revista de Occidente. Criterion,* Oct. 1930, 203.
Concha, Jaime. "El descubrimiento del pueblo en la poesía de Neruda." *Aurora* (Santiago), nos. 3–4 (July–Dec. 1964), 128–38; rpt. in *Hispanic Studies,* no. 1 (1974), 85–95.
———. "Interpretación de *Residencia en la tierra.*" *Mapocho,* July 1963, 5–39.
———. *Neruda 1904–1936.* Santiago: Universitaria, 1972.
———. "Sexo y pobreza." *Revista Iberoamericana,* 39, nos. 82–83 (Jan.–June 1973), 135–58.

Cortázar, Julio. "Lettre Ouverte." In Pablo Neruda. *Résidence sur la terre*. Trans. Guy Suarès. Paris: Gallimard, 1972, 5–12.

————. "Neruda entre nosotros." *Plural* (Mexico City), March 1974, 38–41.

Costa, René de. "Pablo Neruda's *Tentativa del hombre infinito*: Notes for a Reappraisal." *Modern Philology*, 73 (1975–76), 136–47.

————. *The Poetry of Pablo Neruda*. Cambridge, Mass.: Harvard Univ. Press, 1979.

Domínguez, Delia and Jorge Marchant Lazcano. "El mundo de la infancia de Pablo Neruda." *Paula* (Santiago), July 17, 1979, 37–45, 101.

Eshleman, Clayton. "Neruda: an elemental response." *TriQuarterly*, 15 (Spring 1969), 228–37.

Felstiner, John. "Arauco Redivivus in Pablo Neruda." *Review*, 25–26 (1980), 110–16.

————. "La danza inmóvil, el vendaval sostenido: *Four Quartets* de T. S. Eliot y *Alturas de Macchu Picchu*." *Anales de la Universidad de Chile*, 129, nos. 157–60 (Jan.–Dec. 1971), 176–96.

————. "A Feminist Reading of Neruda." *Parnassus*, 3, no. 2 (Spring–Summer 1975), 90–112.

————. "In Translation." *American Poetry Review*, 5, no. 2 (1976), 39–43.

————. "Neruda in Translation." *Yale Review*, 61, no. 2 (Winter 1972), 226–51.

————. "Pablo Neruda, 1904–1973." *New Republic*, Oct. 13, 1973, 27.

————. "Pablo Neruda: Nobel Prize at Isla Negra." *New Republic*, Dec. 25, 1971, 29–30.

————. Review of René de Costa. *The Poetry of Pablo Neruda*. *New Republic*, June 16, 1979, 36–38.

————. "Translating Pablo Neruda's 'Galope muerto.'" *PMLA*, 93 (1978), 185–95.

Fiedler, Leslie. "A Second Life: The English Translations of Neruda" (mimeographed lecture). "Symposium on Pablo Neruda," University of Illinois at Urbana-Champaign. May 3, 1972.

Figueroa, Esperanza. "Pablo Neruda en Inglés." *Revista Iberoamericana*, 39, nos. 82–83 (Jan.–June 1973), 301–47.

Flores, Angel, ed. *Aproximaciones a Pablo Neruda*. Barcelona: Libres de Sineira, 1974.

Franco, Jean. "Introduction." In Pablo Neruda. *Selected Poems*. Ed. Nathaniel Tarn. Harmondsworth, Middlesex, Eng.: Penguin, 1966.

————. "Orfeo en utopía: el poeta y la colectividad en el *Canto general*." In *Simposio Pablo Neruda*. Ed. Isaac Jack Lévy and Juan Loveluck. Columbia, So. Carolina: Las Américas, 1975, 269–89.

Fraser, G. S. *News from South America*. London: Harvill, 1949.

García Lorca, Federico. "Presentación de Pablo Neruda." *Obras completas*. 14th ed. Madrid: Aguilar, 1968, 147–48.

Goić, Cedomil. "*Alturas de Macchu Picchu*: la torre y el abismo." *Anales de la Universidad de Chile*, 129, nos. 157–60 (Jan.–Dec. 1971), 153–65.

Holguín, Andrés. "Tres conferencias de Pablo Neruda." *Revista de las Indias* (Bogotá), no. 56 (Aug. 1943), 267–70.

Jiménez, Juan Ramón. "Carta a Pablo Neruda." *Repertorio Americano,* no. 39 (Jan. 17, 1942), 12.

Larrea, Juan. *Del Surrealismo a Machupicchu.* Mexico City: Joaquín Mortiz, 1967.

Loveluck, Juan. "*Alturas de Macchu Picchu:* Cantos I–V." *Revista Iberoamericana,* 39, nos. 82–83 (Jan.–June 1973), 175–88.

Lowenfels, Walter, ed. *For Neruda, For Chile: An International Anthology.* Boston: Beacon, 1975.

Loyola, Hernán. "Itinerario de Pablo Neruda." *Anales de la Universidad de Chile,* 129, nos. 157–60 (Jan.–Dec. 1972), 9–28.

————. "Neruda traduce a Shakespeare." *Aurora* (Santiago), 2, no. 5 (Jan.–March 1965), 150.

————. *Ser y morir en Pablo Neruda, 1918–1945.* Santiago: Editora Santiago, 1967.

Lozada, Alfredo. *El monismo agónico de Pablo Neruda.* Mexico City: B. Costa-Amic, 1971.

Marcenac, Jean. *Pablo Neruda.* 3rd ed. Paris: Seghers, 1971.

Mistral, Gabriela. *Recados: Contando a Chile.* Santiago: Editorial del Pacífico, 1957.

Montes, Hugo. "Acerca de *Alturas de Macchu Picchu*." *Mapocho,* 2, no. 6 (1964), 120–34.

Morales T., Leonidas. "Estructura mítica de *Alturas de Macchu Picchu*." *Estudios Filológicos,* 1 (1964), 167–83.

Paseyro, Ricardo. "The Dead Word of Pablo Neruda." *TriQuarterly,* 15 (Spring 1969), 203–27.

Pring-Mill, Robert. "Introduction." In *Pablo Neruda: A Basic Anthology.* Oxford: Dolphin, 1975, xv–lxxix.

————. Preface. In Pablo Neruda. *The Heights of Macchu Picchu.* Trans. Nathaniel Tarn. New York: Farrar, Straus and Giroux, 1967, vii–xix.

Puccini, Dario. "Dos notas sobre Pablo Neruda." *Anales de la Universidad de Chile,* 129, nos. 157–60 (Jan.–Dec. 1971), 134–38.

Reid, Alastair. "A Visit to Neruda." *Encounter,* 25, no. 3 (Sept. 1965), 67–70.

Riess, Frank. *The Word and the Stone: Language and Imagery in Neruda's "Canto general."* London: Oxford Univ. Press, 1972.

Rodman, Selden. *South America of the Poets.* Carbondale, Illinois: Southern Illinois Univ. Press, 1970.

Rodríguez Fernández, Mario. "El tema de la muerte en *Alturas de Macchu Picchu*." *Anales de la Universidad de Chile,* no. 131 (July–Sept. 1964), 23–50.

Rodríguez Monegal, Emir. *El viajero inmóvil: Introducción a Pablo Neruda.* Buenos Aires: Losada, 1966.

Rosales, Luis. "Prólogo." In Pablo Neruda. *Poesía.* 2 vols. Madrid: Noguer, 1974, I, 11–83.

Rosenthal, M. L. "Voyage into Neruda." *Review,* 72 (Spring 1974), 30–32.

Santí, Enrico Mario. "*Canto general*: The Politics of the Book." *Symposium,* 32, no. 3 (Fall 1978), 254–75.

————. "Fuentes para el conocimiento de Pablo Neruda, 1967–1974." In *Simposio Pablo Neruda*. Ed. Isaac Jack Lévy and Juan Loveluck. Columbia, So. Carolina: Las Américas, 1975, 355–82.

Silva Castro, Raúl. *Pablo Neruda*. Santiago: Universitaria, 1964.

Spitzer, Leo. "La enumeración caótica en la poesía moderna." In *Lingüística e historia literaria*. 2nd ed. Madrid: Gredos, 1961, 247–300.

Yurkievich, Saul. "Mito e historia: Dos generadores del *Canto general*." *Revista Iberoamericana*, 39, nos. 82–83 (Jan.–June 1973), 111–35.

ACKNOWLEDGMENTS FOR THE USE OF

COPYRIGHTED MATERIALS

Selections from the Spanish LAS UVAS Y EL VIENTO by Pablo Neruda, Copyright 1954 by Pablo Neruda. From CREPUSCULARIO by Pablo Neruda, Santiago de Chile, 1923. From VEINTE POEMAS DE AMOR by Pablo Neruda, Santiago de Chile, 1924. From MEMORIAL DE ISLA NEGRA by Pablo Neruda, © Editorial Losada, S.A. Buenos Aires, 1964. From CANTO GENERAL by Pablo Neruda, © Editorial Losada, S.A. Buenos Aires, 1955. From OBRAS COMPLETAS by Pablo Neruda, © Editorial Losada, S.A. Buenos Aires, 1957. Translated by John Felstiner. English language translation Copyright © 1980 by Farrar, Straus and Giroux, Inc. Reprinted with the permission of Farrar, Straus and Giroux, Inc., and Souvenir Press Ltd., London.

"Galope muerto" and "Entrada a la madera" in English translation by John Felstiner, and in Spanish; "Walking Around" and "Explico algunas cosas" in English translation by John Felstiner: published by permission of New Directions, publishers of Pablo Neruda, RESIDENCE ON EARTH, translated by Donald D. Walsh. © Editorial Losada, S.A. Buenos Aires, 1958, 1961, 1962. Copyright © 1973 by Pablo Neruda and Donald D. Walsh. All Rights Reserved.

Selection from "Ode to Laziness," Pablo Neruda's "Oda a la pereza" as translated by William Carlos Williams, from NEW WORLD WRITING # 14 (1958). All Rights Reserved. Reprinted by permission of New Directions, agents.

English translation by John Felstiner and Spanish text of *Alturas de Macchu Picchu* from OBRAS COMPLETAS by Pablo Neruda, © Editorial Losada, S.A. Buenos Aires, 1973, published by permission of Editorial Losada, the Estate of Pablo Neruda, and Jonathan Cape, Ltd.

Selection from Pablo Neruda, SELECTED POEMS OF PABLO NERUDA, translated by Ben Belitt, © 1961 by Grove Press. Reprinted with the permission of Grove Press.

Photographs by Edward Ranney courtesy of the photographer. Photograph by Martín Chambi courtesy of Edward Ranney and the Chambi family. Photograph of Neruda and García Lorca reprinted with the permission of Matilde Neruda. Three drawings by Federico García Lorca published by permission of New Directions, agents for the Estate of Federico García Lorca.

INDEX